SEMEIA 40

TEXT AND TEXTUALITY

Editor of this Issue:
Charles E. Winquist

©1987
by the Society of Biblical Literature

SEMEIA 40

Copyright © 1987 by the Society of Biblical Literature

All rights reserved. No part of this work may be reproduced or transmitted in any form or by any means, electronic or mechanical, including photocopying and recording, or by means of any information storage or retrieval system, except as may be expressly permitted by the 1976 Copyright Act or in writing from the publisher. Requests for permission should be addressed in writing to the Rights and Permissions Office, Society of Biblical Literature, 825 Houston Mill Road, Atlanta, GA 30329, USA.

ISSN 0095-571X
ISBN 978-1-58983-587-0

Printed in the United States of America
on acid-free paper

CONTENTS

Contributors to this Issue v

Preface 1

Theological Text
    Robert P. Scharlemann 5

Shades of Difference
    Mark C. Taylor 21

From Textuality to Scripture: The End of Theology as Writing
    Carl Raschke 39

The Question of the Book: Religion as Texture
    David L. Miller 53

Failing Speech: Post-Holocaust
Writing and the Discourse of Postmodernism
    Susan E. Shapiro 65

Finitude, Death, and Reverence for Life
    Carol P. Christ 93

Living Earth and Living Christ: Thoughts on Carol P. Christ's
Finitude, Death, and Reverence for Life
    John Dominic Crossan 109

From Scripture to Textuality
    Kent Harold Richards 119

Text and Contextuality in Reference to Islam
    Richard C. Martin 125

Romancing the Tome: Rabbinic Hermeneutics and the Theory of
Literature
    William Scott Green 147

CONTRIBUTORS TO THIS ISSUE

Carol P. Christ
 Departments of Religious Studies and Women's Studies
 San Jose State University
 San Jose, CA 95192

John Dominic Crossan
 Department of Religious Studies
 DePaul University
 Chicago, Illinois 60604

William Scott Green
 Department of Religious and Classical Studies
 University of Rochester
 Rochester, New York 14627

Richard Martin
 Department of Religious Studies
 Arizona State University
 Tempe, Arizona 85287

David Miller
 Department of Religion
 Syracuse University
 Syracuse, New York 13210

Carl Raschke
 Department of Religious Studies
 University of Denver
 Denver, Colorado 80208

Kent Richards
 Iliff School of Theology
 2201 S. University Boulevard
 Denver, Colorado 80210

Robert Scharlemann
 Department of Religious Studies
 University of Virginia
 Charlottesville, Virginia 22903

Susan Shapiro
  Department of Religion
  Syracuse University
  Syracuse, New York 13210

Mark Taylor
  Department of Religion
  Williams College
  Williamstown, Massachusetts 01267

PREFACE

Proclamations of the death of God, the loss of the self, the closure of the book, the end of theology and the end of history have become familiar, albeit enigmatic, formulations associated with the emergence of postmodernist critical reflection. A common element in the work of theoretical spokespersons of postmodernity has been the denial of epistemic privilege to language as a mirror of reality. Theories of discourse have proliferated that have reflexively questioned their own status and materiality.

What is a text? What is a book? What is scripture? These questions have resonance in all discursive disciplines and immediate implications for the hermeneutical and exegetical work of textual critics in Rabbinic, Quranic and Biblical studies. This issue of *Semeia* was conceived as an opportunity to conjoin theoretical reflections on the meanings of text and textuality with responses from textual critics who regularly work with sacred textual traditions in western culture. The theoretical articles challenge the assumptions of modernist theories of interpretation and liberal romanticist hermeneutics from diverse perspectives of feminist criticism, deconstructionist theories of discourse and post-Holocaust studies. They are also a critique of each other as are the critical responses from the textual critics. There is, however, a common assault on logocentrism. By raising the question of the text, the meaning of the author gives way to the meaning of the text. It is not assumed that there is concurrence as to what is meant by "text". Is *Dasein* a text? Is the earth a text? Is silence a text? Does a text differ from a book?

The limits of representation and the otherness of language are themes that have expression in all of the theoretical articles. The valorization of insights varies but a central problematic is formed that pushes the critic beyond an original naivete of reading.

Robert Scharlemann opens this issue of *Semeia* with a specific focus on the theological text. He notes that in Barth's dialectical theology authentic testimony is the category of the theological and the emphasis is on a critique of theological listening. The shift to the text in postmodernism is an acknowledgment that one writes because one does not speak. An authentic text is a direct writing. In text production we enact the "I" and create the world.

In theological text production instantiation and ideation mark a text that is not a text at all. Scharlemann claims that the writing of God instantiates a negativity that in its turn is a negation of the negative. Its ostensive connection to the "I" is to the one God is not. Is reading analogous to the performance of music, or is it the making of a new text? The theological writing of "God" is an otherness within writing itself and it is because of this affirmation that textual interpretation must be understood as a self-surpassing.

The articles of Mark Taylor and Carl Raschke further complicate and elucidate the problematic of book, the problem of otherness and the significance of scripture (Raschke). Taylor reads the Hegelian preoccupation with otherness from the perspective of Nietzsche and sees in Hegel the closure of the book and the beginning of writing. While the book seeks closure, the text of writing remains open. The otherness of the "outside" of a text affirmed "inside" the text is understood by Taylor as the "almost nothing" of difference. This difference is never mastered and for Taylor in contrast to Scharlemann the writing of God is better understood as the writing of the death of God.

Raschke associates textuality with phenomenality but for him it is the self-surpassing character of language that allows an understanding of scripture. It is in scripture that the infinite is recovered out of the finite and the problem of the text appears with the loss of the significance of scripture. Words become scripture when they reveal what cannot be inscribed as part of discourse. This means that for Raschke (and it is here that we understand the reference to Luther in his essay) faith is the ground of a transcendental semantics that is not a metaphysics of presence.

The figurations and valorizations of textuality differ across the three opening articles and it is a sensitivity to pictures of language in language that characterizes David Miller's article. He suggests that words, like people, have an unconscious and imaginal history. In the connection of power and knowledge it makes a political difference whether we imagine a text as a pot that contains a knowledge of reality or as a tapestry. The contrasting images of text production as potting or weaving are examined as they contribute to the contrasting notions of religion as a context of belief and action or as a texture of life. It makes a difference for understanding textual interpretation whether the text is an open weave or a container. The limits of representation are imaged as a penal colony of texts and this is a problem for writing and reading.

The political urgency of thinking the problematic of textuality is also an important theme for Carol Christ and Susan Shapiro. Christ argues that the "nuclear mentality" is built on a denial of finitude. She shows that there are clues to survival in the feminist challenge to classical dualism. The finite and sensual body of the earth is a text to be read and that work is understood to be a radical deconstruction and reconstruction of inherited traditions.

When Shapiro examines postmodernist writing she compares it with post-Holocaust writing and sees in both a preoccupation with the limits of representational discourse. She asks whether these two modes of discourse can be read as one. Two aporias of representation, the failure of speech and expiration of breath in telling the event of the Holocaust and the general limits of referential discourse, are construed by Edmond Jabes as one and the same. Against this judgment, Shapiro contrasts the poetics of expiration in the works of Nellie Sachs and Paul Celan. This difference, is, of course, important for the development of Holocaust studies and gives particular focus to the question of the historical uniqueness of the Holocaust. It challenges theories of discourse that cannot valence historical events within the limits of referential discourse. And, in relationship to the central concern of this issue of *Semeia* exploring the concepts of text and textuality, it opens the possibility that the Holocaust alters the very conditions of writing.

It is at the point of questioning and understanding the very conditions of writing that we can affirm a convergence of insights in the theoretical essays. There is a valorization of the otherness of language in assessing the conditions for text production. This is a challenge, sometimes political and historical, and sometimes theological and epistemological, to the interpreters and critics of texts because it fashions a notion of textuality that is amenable to neither literalism nor positivism as an interpretive strategy.

Four textual critics agreed to be respondents in this volume. William Scott Green works in Rabbinic studies; Richard Martin in Quranic studies, Kent Richards with the Hebrew Bible, and John Dominic Crossan with the New Testament. They were free to respond to the general questions of the volume or to particular essays. They have augumented the general essays with practical criticism and further theoretical reflection.

I acknowledge and thank the Graduate School of California State University, Chico, for a development grant for manuscript preparation and Joan M. Amatucci for copy editing this issue of *Semeia*.

Charles E. Winquist
Syracuse University

THEOLOGICAL TEXT

Robert P. Scharlemann
University of Virginia

ABSTRACT

The essay undertakes to answer the question of what a theological text is first by defining a text as one in which the meaning instantiates the world meant (and one which is therefore the extreme opposite of a text in which the meaning is one that could never be instantiated) and then by pursuing the possibility of treating human existence (Dasein) as the writing that turns nature into creature, i.e., shows the meaning of coming to be and passing away, and literary art as the work that turns works ("facture") into scripture, i.e., shows the meaning of Dasein as creature. In this framework, theological text, as the writing of God, is what no actual text is; hence, a theological text is the nontext of any text. What such a "nontext" is may be intimated by the writing and saying of the Tetragram: a writing that is both written and crossed out (if the saying of "Adonai" is thought of as crossing out the writing of "Jahweh").

The hallmark of dialectical theology, of the "theology of the Word" which reigned more or less without serious challenge during the period extending from 1920 to the mid-1960s, was the manner in which the Word of God was distinguished from any written text, even that of the Old and New Testaments. It is true that Karl Barth's commentary on Paul's letter to the Romans was a *written* work, seeking to enable twentieth-century readers to understand Paul's letter again as a living testimony to the matter of divine judgment and grace of which Paul's words spoke; and it is also true that many among the educated contemporaries were, thanks to Barth's writing, able to do just that. Even so, Barth's emphasis was neither upon the sacredness of scripture nor upon its written character. That he interpreted Paul instead of Lao-tse, or someone else, he ascribed to his vocation as a Protestant minister, not to any special quality of the books of the Old and New Testaments. The categories of the sacred and of the written did not express the nature of the theological. Instead, the Word of God was understood as that No to our Yes and, in turn, that Yes within the No which could be *heard* as the voice speaking through the writing that becomes vocal in preaching. The Pauline expression *fides ex auditu*—faith that comes from hearing—characterized as a whole dialectical theology's understanding of the theological mode of existence that is always between the times. In Barth's case, there is an irony in his having left, with almost unparalleled completeness, a written record of just about everything he said or did as a theologian.

From this point of view, dialectical theology might be said to have provided a critique of theological listening in the midst of the speaking and hearing that make up the setting of kerygma. The task of preaching is to let the word of God—both the word "God" and the speaking that is of God—happen in the proclamation itself. That this concern was due in part to the peculiarity of Protestant theology's being oriented toward preaching does not alter its general importance. Even Karl Rahner could entitle his theological anthropology "Hearers of the Word." Announcing and listening were, in this theology, the fundamental acts through which human and theological existence were constituted. Bultmann's difference with Heidegger did not have to do with whether the concept of authentic existence was the concept implied in the term "faith"; it had to do, rather, with Bultmann's contention that this mode of existence could not be achieved by reflection or resolution but only by a gift and an acceptance—the gift given through proclamation and accepted through listening. In this, there was an echo of Kierkegaard's distinction between infinite resignation and faith. Infinite resignation, the resolve to give up everything for the sake of nothing, is the culmination of ethical achievement and lies within the power of human decision as such; faith, or the getting back of what has been given up, is by contrast, not an ethical possibility but a theological gift. Hence, the self that is lost, whether in despair or in infinite resignation, cannot be regained through its own further resolve but only through its acceptance of the gift of its self from what is quite other than itself and all its possibilities. How does that gift occur? Dialectical theology answered: Through the proclamation of words that are in actuality—that is, *when* preached and heard—the Word of God, the No to human existence which is also a Yes to it. In this framework, texts are the writing which is to be given living power through being made audible in preaching, and faith is "ob-oedience," the real hearkening beyond the sounds of the human voice and the textual words to the No and Yes of the one who is not-I, not-this, and not nothing either. The text of preaching is like the score of a musical composition: it contains the notes of a performance, in which the performing instrument is the witnessing voice of the preacher and for which there is no guarantee that the Word of God will itself be heard when the performance is given. Not the category of "sacred writing," then, but that of "authentic testimony," is the category of the theological: the witness, in speaking most on his or her own, with no other support than the power of the testimony itself, may happen to speak most apart from himself, and that happening is the living Word of God. If the writings of the Old and New Testaments can be understood to be the Word of God, then this is due not to their being sacred but to the possibility that in them are inscribed notes for a performance of authentic witness.

This was the nature of dialectical theology's critique of speaking and hearing. It did not take up specific questions of writing and reading. It did not ask what the writing of God might be, as writing; it did not give a parallel critique of the acts of writing and reading. What is the writing of "God," of "God is," of "God is God," and of "God is God as not God"? These are questions raised by more recent preoccupation with language as writing, as exemplified by the French literary philosophers.[1] What is a text, this product of writing that is open to reading, and what is a theological text? What is the writing of "God" and the writing of God? Since exilic times, what was written as Jahweh in Hebrew was pronounced as Adonai. The "One Who Is" of writing became the "My Lord" of saying. Does this way of pronouncing the written name reflect the common phenomenon of taboo, which makes worshipers fear to pronounce the divine name because doing so summons the power of the divine essence and thus violates it? Or does it perhaps represent something different—an intersection between writing and saying, in which the being that can be written ("The One Who Is") is actualized only through a speaking that, at once, overwrites the writing and binds the reader-speaker ("My Lord")?

I. Text

"Text" can be defined by a double contrast: first, a text is a written work, in contrast to an oral performance; second, a text is a writing upon which commentaries can be written but which is not itself a commentary upon another text. To spell out these points, let me begin with Ricoeur's notion of text as discourse fixed in writing.

In "Qu'est ce qu'un texte?" Ricoeur delineates the concept of text by reference to discourse. A text is, he says, any discourse that is fixed in writing, "tout discours fixé par l'écriture" (181); this fixation is constitutive of the text itself. Yet he goes on to show that, contrary to initial appearances, this does not mean that writing is only a fixing of the oral; for writing changes our relation to the things enunciated in the discourse (a genuine text is not the writing down of an anterior spoken word but a direct writing—one writes because one does *not* speak),[2] to the author (reading a book is to consider its author as already dead), and to the world of reference that embraces author and us (the ostensive world of spoken language is obliterated and replaced by the quasi-world of texts or literature), and it also changes both the author (so that it is less the author who speaks than the text itself) and the interlocutor (the one to whom the discourse is addressed is not a particular person but anyone who can read). Fixation in writing, then, removes a discourse from the particularity of actual conversation: the meaning of the author is replaced by the meaning of the text, the world which is common to speaker and hearer in conversation is replaced (or intersected) by the world projected through the text itself, and the hearer of a particular time and place gives way to a hearer who is any reader of the text.

Consistent with this, Ricoeur views an interpretation as a "reading" of a text. That is to say, reading a text is tantamount to a new writing, a writing in one's own words of what is written in the words of the text. This stands in contrast to the view that interpretation is not a new text but an aid to get back to the text, so that (as Gadamer puts it) a successful interpretation is one that does away with itself because it gets the reader back into the original text. When reading a text is understood in the former way—as a new writing—one of the functions of a text is to create ever new texts; when it is understood in the latter way, it is not the function of a text to create new texts but to call for its own rereading. The difference between these two views has to do with whether one thinks of a text as similar in status to the notes of a musical composition. To play a Bach fugue is to give an interpretation of it; but it is an interpretation through performance, not through a new set of notes or a new composition. If reading a text is comparable to a performance of this sort, then reading is not the writing of a new text but the rewriting of the written text.

It seems to me that this consideration introduces another constituent element of a text. A text is not just any fixation of discourse in writing. Rather, a text is that written discourse upon which other texts can be written, as interpretations, and to which other texts are referred, but which, in turn, is not referred to any anterior text. (All texts are writings; but not all writings are texts.) This is the conception of text which was at work in traditional Protestant interpretations of the Bible and which is also reflected in Schleiermacher's remark that Jesus' own utterances in the New Testament, insofar as there are any such, are neither religious nor dogmatic language but at most "texts" for such language. To be a text means, in this way, to be original, not referrable for its meaning (its sense or reference) to a previous text. A text not referrable to an antecedent text is a writing in which there is a convergence between the meaning and the reality. As such, a text plays the same role toward interpretation as do poetic utterances for the later Heidegger. In *Sein und Zeit*, Heidegger treated language as the embodiment of Dasein's self-understanding, so that one could read behind the language to the understanding it expressed; in his later meditations on poetry, it is no longer a matter of interpreting the language to get at the self-understanding embodied in it but a matter of being continually provoked to thinking by the power of being that is given in the poetic words themselves, not as expressions of Dasein's self-understanding but as self-announcements of being. Following this line of thought, we can say that "text" means that kind of writing which can be interpreted by other writing or speaking but which in its own turn is not the interpretation of previous writing or speaking but the very presentation of the reality it means. It is a writing in which being and meaning coincide and which, therefore, cannot be reworded but only rewritten or resaid, that is, appropriated in its originality.

II. Instantiation and Abstraction

A text in this sense is a discourse whose function is like that of ostensives or instantiators in sentences. Thinking moves in the medium of language between *instantiation* and *abstraction*. We can distinguish two moments in the whole movement. The first moment is one in which we combine ostensives with common names ("'This' [i.e., what the word points out] is a tree"); the second is one in which we combine a common name with a definition ("a tree is a woody perennial plant . . ."). The matter with which thinking as such is involved is the being that joins the perceived particular with its name and that name with its abstractly thought genus. To understand *this as* a tree and *a tree as* a plant is to think the being that is manifest at a certain place and time and that is expressed in the copula by which particular and universal are connected. Particular objects are, thus, in one direction, subsumed under generic notions and, in another direction, individualized through ostensives. More concrete than ostensives are instantiators (such as "I"), or words whose meaning cannot be thought without producing the one to which the word refers; and more abstract than generic notions is a notion like "thing," which applies to any and every object of thought. The terms designating abstract notions can be referred to the terms for common names, and these can be referred further to the ostensives or instantiators. But these last cannot, in turn, be referred to other terms; with them the linguistic line begins.[3] Similarly, "text" can be defined as a written discourse from which other discourse starts and to which it refers but which, in turn, cannot be referred to other discourse.

All language moves, then, between the two extremes of instantiation and ideation: at the one end is the language in which meaning and reality converge (as is the case with texts and with instantiators like "I" and ostensives like "this" and "here" and "now"); at the other end, the language in which the meaning is separated from any and all reality (as is the case with Kant's Ideas of pure theoretical reason). To say that reality and meaning converge in a word or a text is to say that as soon as one understands the meaning of the words one also knows that there is a nonlinguistic reference for them and what that reference is; to say that meaning and reality are separated is to say that as soon as one understands the meaning of the words one also knows that there cannot be any nonlinguistic reference for them. Kant treated the self ("I"), the intelligible world (the non-empirical world), and God as Ideas—that is, as meanings needed to complete knowledge theoretically but not capable of constituting any objects of knowledge. But in recognizing a practical employment of reason, he also indicated the way in which these Ideas can become instantiators; for in the act of freedom, when one responds to the moral imperative for no other reason than that one can do so, a person enacts the "I" and creates the world that, theoretically, remain only Ideas. Hence, the same three Ideas which, theoretically, are purely ideational, since they carry meanings that can refer only to other meanings but not to real objects, are, practically, instantiators.

The Kantian distinction between pure theoretical and pure practical reason, however, contains an unexplicated distinction between an Idea that can be connected to *any* reality (and hence to no determinate reality in contrast to another one) and an Idea that can *not* be connected to reality at all. The predicate of "thing," for example, is purely an idea in the sense that it can be applied to anything whatsoever, even to itself, and hence cannot define anything in particular. It cannot be used to distinguish one thing from another thing. It is purely abstract, then, because of its indiscriminate applicability. (Existence is not a predicate, as Kant put it.) The predicate of "nothing," by contrast, is purely an idea for just the opposite reason—it cannot be applied to anything at all, not even to the word that names it and the meaning that the word bears. Both of them are purely abstract Ideas. The Ideas of self and God ("I" and "God") can be read as abstract for a similar reason: just as "thing" and "nothing" are pure Ideas because the one can be predicated of all things indiscriminately (and therefore of no thing determinatively) and the other cannot be predicated of anything at all (not even of itself), so "I" and "God") are pure Ideas because the one enacts any subject at all (anyone who thinks or says "I" is the self meant by the word) and the other enacts the negative of any subject ("God" is the one who "I" and any or all other things are not). The "intelligible world," as a world in which subjects and predicates are perfectly identical, is a world beyond being, because in such a world there is no "is," "was," or "will be" any more. In the intelligible world we have not "A is A" but just "A"; but being can appear only when there is both a difference and an identity between subject and predicate. These same Ideas, however, can also be read as instantiators. Then each of them has a necessary connection to a particular reality at the time when they are thought. The convergence of meaning and reality can be accomplished either through instantiating or through ostensive words; the detachment of meaning from reality can be accomplished either through universalization or negation. When meaning is detached from reality, its reference is never a reality but always another meaning; when it converges with reality, its reference is never another meaning but always a reality.

That the Ideas of God and self can in one respect appear to be incapable of referring to any reality and, in a second respect, appear to refer necessarily to some reality indicates the dialectic they contain. The Idea of God is an idea of what cannot be merely a meaning but must also be a reality—that, in effect, is the core of Anselm's ontological proof of God. At the same time, the Idea of God can never be exhibited in an object of experience—that is the heart of Kant's critique of the proof. But, as dialectical theology has ever since seen, these two sides belong together. The Idea of God is the idea of one who can never be merely an idea (and must therefore be connected with some reality), and at the same time it is the idea of one who can never be identified with a reality (and cannot therefore be connected with any reality—God is not "a being," as Tillich put it). Metaphysics separated these two sides from each other and created the classical contradiction between theism and atheism, the one asserting the necessity of the reality of God, the other denying the possibility, both on the basis of the same idea and the same mode of thinking. That idea and mode of thinking are that God is God and cannot be not-God. The post-metaphysical idea, to which I think both dialectical theology and the deconstructive transcendence of nihilism bear witness, is that God is God both as God and as not-God. The writing of this God is, accordingly, a text that, in a sense to be defined further, is not a text at all.

We can understand "text" here to include everything from the writing of names to the writing of whole discourses, even though, technically (if a text is discourse fixed in writing), the minimal unit of a text is not a name but at least a noun-verb sentence if not a proposition in the form of judgment. "A" alone is a name, not discourse; "A is" is a sentence, the minimal unit of narrative or *mythos;* and "A is x" is a judgment, the minimal unit of discourse or *logos*. "Socrates talks" and "Jesus said" are narrative; "Socrates is the one talking" and "Jesus is the one who said" are discursive. This is to say that, strictly defined, the minimal text for the idea of God is not the name "God" but at least the narrative "God is" or the judgment "God is God," as the minimal text for the idea of self is not "I" but "I am" or "I am I." The latter judgment says that the being of the self lies in the connection between the subjectivity of "I" and the here and now of saying; the former—"God is God"—says that the being of God lies in the non-identification of God with any subject (not-I) and with any here and now. In the present essay, I shall be using text in a less strict sense to include names and narratives as well as discourse.

If we examine the *logoi* mentioned, we can see what range is covered between their instantiation and their pure ideation. The basic judgment of existence (Dasein in the existential sense of that term) is "I am this-one-here" or "I am here-now"; I become this one here when thinking the meaning of "I." The instantiative "I" is connected with an ostensive "this-one." The proposition "I am I" can be read metaphysically as expressing a timeless identity of the self; or it can be read as expressing the identity of "I" with this-one-here. In this latter, nonmetaphysical sense, the connection between universal and individual is not that of a genus and a particular but of the "is" and "as" of being: I am I as this one here. "God is God" (which can be read: "*God* [i.e., no one and no thing else] is God" and "God is *God* [i.e., not this-one-here or anywhere else]") has a similar set of connections. To think the meaning of "God" is to instantiate the negative and to connect it with an ostensive; in understanding the meaning of the name, I become the one who God is not and who is not God, my here-and-now is shown as the time and place at which God is not; God is present as the one absent in my presence. The mode of existence of God is that of the negative which appears upon the "I" and the "this" but also upon the meaning of "nothing"; for to understand the meaning of "God" is to know that God is not only not-I and not-anything but also not-nothing either. The Idea of God is instantiated as the negative and the negation of that negative in turn.[4]

If a text has the double characteristic of being discourse fixed in writing and of being a writing in which meaning and reality converge, then "God is God" as the fundamental theological text is a writing in which the meaning of God as the negation of the negative of nothing is also a reality. We easily notice the difference between hearing someone say "I am . . ." and reading the words "I am. . . ." If we heard a Descartes say to us, "I am a thinking being," we would initially identify the "I" with Descartes. But if we read the text in which he wrote, "I am a thinking being," the "I" is no longer that of Descartes's person but it is the subject instantiated in the very one who thinks the meaning of those written words. Writing thus removes the autobiographical reference and makes the meaning universal.[5] In a similar manner, the text "God is God," disassociated from the time and place of someone's saying it, is no longer a negation of some particular person and thing but is the negative instantiated in the very one who understands the words of that text and *at the time* of the understanding. But there are some intermediate steps between text and theological text, involving Dasein as the text that writes "creature" upon the coming to be and passing away that are nature and death, and literary art as the textuality that writes "scripture" upon the world of making. In what sense can Dasein be said to be a text at all? To answer this, we need to consider what it means to be a writing.

III. Nature:Creature::Facture:Scripture

Writing is a form of language; it is neither a thing nor a thought alone, neither real nor mental alone, but a thought-thing or thing-thought, a medium of thought and thing which is equally original with both. (Their equal originality is shown by the fact that each of the three can be traced back infinitely within its own sphere—words to other words to still other words, things to other things to still other things, ideas to other ideas to still other ideas—but for each of them the absolute beginning is the threefold unity of thought-word-thing, represented in words by instantiating words, in ideas by ideas of what cannot be merely an idea [i.e., dialectical ideas], and in things by things that have meaning [i.e., symbols].) But it differs from oral language in its being fixed—it occupies space and it does not disappear unless it is erased. Thus, an arrow used to indicate the direction of a path in a forest is a writing, even if it is the same arrow that is used with a bow and shot at a target, because the arrow indicating direction is a thing we can "read," we do not merely ascertain that it is an arrow or that it is shot with a bow. Dasein, or self-conscious existence, is a writing in the same way: when it is the sign used to fix the meaning of coming-to-be and passing-away, or when it is that natural thing which fixes the meaning of the whole of nature in its *Sein zum Tode*. In this way, Dasein is the entity which one can read as the writing of nature—the writing that is written both by and about nature. It is a writing because, unlike spoken language, it occupies space and does not disappear until it is erased by the *mors* that is its end; even then it is not really erased but overwritten. Dasein is, in short, the text that turns nature into creature. That is to say, we can "read" any human being in the same way that we can read a pointing arrow along a forest path or read the words written on a sheet of paper.

Whether these writings are also texts—that is, writings in which meaning and reality converge so that the reality appears when the writing is read and is there only with words of that writing and not with other words—depends upon whether they can be put into other words. I can interpret the arrow in the forest by saying "This is the direction to go if you want to follow the path marked out." The arrow is not a text; for I could use those other words to say the same thing more explicitly. Is Dasein a text? Can it be put into lexical words that make more explicit what it says in nonlexical words? The answer to that question is less clear. But it seems to me that Dasein, unlike such an arrow-sign, is indeed a text, upon which other writings can be written, as commentaries and interpretations, and to which other writings can be referred, but which in its own turn is not referrable to another writing. This seems to be the answer given when one asks, for example, for the text which writes the meaning of nature upon starvation in Ethiopia today. The text of that disaster is the human face itself, not the newspaper accounts and perhaps not even a poem of lamentation. Could even such a poem write the reality of *mors* in *natura* more originally than Dasein has already written it with the figure of its own body? Indeed, can *any* poem write the creaturehood of nature as originally as the real Dasein? But I leave that as a open question.

Dasein turns nature into creature by writing, with its own figure, the meaning of coming-to-be and passing-away. But Dasein, which is such a writing in nature, is also capable of writing on its own, of producing scripture. There is a "facture"—the possibility of a making, whether of tools or of pure art—within the creatureliness of nature. Scripture is to that facture that creature is to nature: the inscription of articulated meaning. This marks a second step toward theological text: text as the scripture in facture, the writing in making. Again, a preliminary question is what writing is.

If writing is considered to be analogous to the score of a musical composition, then each reading of that writing has the nature of a performance. To read a written poem is comparable to performing a musical composition; in the one case the instrument is the human voice, in the other case it is another kind of instrument; but in both cases the relation between writing and reading is that of a score and its performance. But if writing is considered as analogous to, say, the sculpting of a sculpture, then the reading of a text cannot be accomplished by performing the written words but only by making a new text. In this case, previous writing provides the material for a work in the same way that stone might provide the material for a piece of sculpture. The textuality of writing refers to this capacity of written works to provide the material for new writings. Gadamer and Derrida can be taken as representatives of each of these two theories. Hence, Derrida's deconstruction is on the order of a dissolution of texts with a view to creating new texts; Gadamer's hermeneutics is on the order of a commentary on texts with view to making possible an intelligible reading of them.

Views of the nature of reading differ accordingly. If writing is viewed as a score for performance, then reading it amounts to writing it on one's own—performing it—and commentaries serve the purpose of showing how to read the originals, that is, how to perform the writing. But if writing provides material for new writing, then reading it amounts to writing something new by using the materials of the old text, and a commentary is not intended to lead back to the original text but to incorporate it as material of a new text, in the way that a work of art reshapes the material it uses.

At issue in these two theories is not the question which of them is the more correct. Each of them has validity, and they complement each other. The notion that reading is performance is clearly true when we have to do with such instantiating words as "I" or "God" and with such texts as "I am I" and "God is God." Their meaning is so closely bound to those words and texts that it cannot be put into other words or texts; it can only be understood and actualized anew by reading and writing again. But most texts are not of that sort. Furthermore, reading in the sense of a new writing depends on reading as the performance of texts; otherwise it lacks any rooting in reality. And, conversely, reading as performance depends upon reading as new writing; otherwise, there could be no appropriation of the meaning of the text by the reader. Language as a given is the condition of language as a work; and language as a work is the realization of language as a given. We could not speak if there were no language given us to learn; but there could be no language if we did not continually remake what is given.

What we are seeking here, however, is to see what scripture contributes to the sphere of facture. If, through the writing that Dasein is, nature can be understood as creature, what happens to art through textual art?[6] From the *Dies irae:* "Mors stupebit et natura, / Cum resurget creatura / Iudicanti reponsura. // Liber scriptus proferetur / In quo totum continetur / Unde mundus iudicetur." Nature and death—coming-to-be and passing-away—are silenced by the rising of creature in response to the *iudicans*. In the silence, a "written book" is brought forth, from whose contents the whole world can be judged. What is this *liber scriptus?* Perhaps one can say that just as nature endowed with meaning is creature, so art endowed with meaning is writing. Dasein, as the preliterary writing of nature turns nature into creature—so that nature speaks of something other than coming to be and passing away. Similarly, literary art turns all making into a writing—it lets all art be read not merely as work but as a writing. This might be illustrated by some remarks of Niels Bohr about Shakespeare's *Hamlet* that Werner Heisenberg reported in his autobiography (66–67). The two physicists were visiting castle of Kronborg, to which the legend of Hamlet is connected. Bohr then noted what difference it made to the castle once it was associated with Hamlet; for then, suddenly, "the walls and ramparts speak a different language. . . . No one can prove that Hamlet really lived, to say nothing of whether he lived here. But we all know what questions Shakespeare bound to this figure. . . , and so the figure had to find some place on the earth, and it found that in Kronborg. But when we know this, Kronborg is a different castle [from what it is just as an edifice of stone]." This is the way in which writing turns a work into a text one can read. So too, it is possible to say in words what a painting says on canvas and what a musical composition says through instruments. For the literary art that makes writings out of other writings is the art which writes the meaning of unmaking and making. In that sense the *liber scriptus* brings to light the hidden possibility. Or, viewed differently, if Dasein is the book in which the meaning of nature and death can be read, then literary art is the book in which the meaning of Dasein itself can be read. "Nature" is the world as a mute reality (a coming-to-be and passing-away that carries no meaning); "creature" is that world read through the text of Dasein, a writing that articulates a meaning in nature. "Facture" (to coin the word) is what Dasein has made (from tools to art works to science); "scripture" is a making that has articulated meaning for its very material, namely, written words—unlike statues, buildings, paintings, whose meaning can be put into words but is not explicit in the very material of the works.

IV. Theological Text

If Daesin is the text that overwrites facture with "scripture," what, shall we say, is a theological text? To answer this, we can follow two different clues.

The first clue is the practice in post-Exilic Judaism of reading the name "Jahweh" (or "The One Who Is," which puts into a name the text "I am who I am") as "Adonai" (or "My Lord," which recognizes the "I" as outside my own personal being, i.e., it acknowledges the ecstatic reality of the meaning of "I"). The text of "I am" is therewith crossed out by the vocative speech of "My lord." This is one way in which spoken language not only intersects but, as it were, crosses out the written language. But it crosses it out, rather than erases it, which is to say, it allows the text to be a text even while making a nontext appear upon it. The cancellation can work in the other direction as well. In such a case, "Adonai" represents what originally can only be a spoken address, never a writing or a text. One can *say* "Adonai" to another and thereby establish a living relation, in which the other is made actual not only as a "you" but also as the "I" outside one's own person. Hence, to write "Jahweh" where one says "Adonai" is to write across the spoken address and to make not-an-address appear upon the address. The writing of "I am I" and the saying of "My Lord" thus cross each other out without erasing each other. In John's Gospel, Thomas the Twin, who is the Doubter, is the one to put the two together in the avowal made in the face of the Resurrected, who, whatever the physiographical characteristics, was at least, for the disciples, the living image of death vanquished: "ὁ κυριός μου καὶ ὁ θεός μου, My lord and my God." Just the one who says both Yes and No and neither Yes nor No—that is, the Doubter par excellence—is the one who can let his testimony be a text that is crossed out by an address or an address that is crossed out by a text, both in one; and just this confession is the response to and text of what appears beyond the disappearance that is death.

This represents one way in which writing can be both written and crossed out in order to show the meaning of negating the negation. Heidegger tried something similar when, to express the be-ing of being as the negating of (the negation of) nonbeing, he would write the word "being" and then place an X across it.[7] Likewise, it is clear that what Tillich calls "the symbol of the cross," i.e., the symbol which symbolizes the symbolic character of all religious symbols, plays the role in his theology of simultaneously denying the identity between a symbol and what it symbolizes and of affirming the identity through this denial. It is, as it were, the symbol that crosses out, or "breaks" or refracts, primary symbols and, by crossing them out, shows the meaning and reality in them. Following this clue, we can think of a theological text as the text "God is God" whose meaning appears when it is crossed out, in the way in which Adonai and Jahweh cross each other out or the symbol of the cross and other religious symbols cross each other out. This kind of surtext differs from a surname added to a given name (because it is not added to but also written over the given); but it also differs from the kind of replacement of name that Juliet suggest to Romeo: "Thou art theyself though not a Montague. . . . Romeo, doff thy name, And for that name, which is no part of thee, Take all myself" (*Romeo and Juliet*, II,ii).

A second clue is offered by the formula of the nonmetaphysical thinking of being: "A is A as not A." This is the "being . . . as not" which I take to be the more precise formulation of the "being like" which appears in parables that begin "The Kingdom of Heaven is like. . ." Such a parable shows the Kingdom of Heaven as a kingdom that is not a kingdom. It does so, first, by the way in which "Kingdom of Heaven" instantiates the negative upon any kingdom. When we hear the name "The Kingdom of Heaven," what is shown to our understanding is what any real kingdom is *not*—the "otherness" of any kingdom. That is to say: as an instantiating word, "Kingdom of Heaven" shows otherness with reference to any kingdom whatsoever. The rest of the parable serves, then, to describe how this otherness appears in meaning and reality—in the tale of a person who finds a treasure in a field and sells everything to buy that field, or in the tale of a vineyard owner who pays all his workers the same wage, regardless of how long they have worked. Neither of these things is either a kingdom or the Kingdom of Heaven. But it is *as* these nonheavenly nonkingdoms that the Kingdom of Heaven concretely appears; the Kingdom of Heaven is the Kingdom of Heaven as these events which as such are not the Kingdom of Heaven but worldly occurrences. Such parables are intended, first, to instantiate otherness concretely, that is, to show the "not" of some concrete reality, and, second, to show how the otherness appears when it is not being what it is.

Following this clue, we can identify a theological text in a similar way. As a writing, the writing of God is, in any case, not any actual writing; everything written is written by someone or something other than God, and no writing is a writing of God. To write of the writing of God is, therefore, to refer to an otherness within writing itself. Similarly, as a text, "God is God" (written by God) is, in any case, no actual text. It cannot be found written down anywhere; it is nowhere given as a text to be read, interpreted, commented, or destrued and reconstrued. "Text of God" is, in this sense, the other text of every text, or the otherness that can appear upon any text. This Text of God can be further described—in the way that the Kingdom of Heaven is further described—by some ordinary text, or by the image of the *liber scriptus* that is brought out to tell the final story of all events, which are not the Text of God but *as* which the Text of God can appear. Here too the apophantic thought is that the Text of God *is* itself *as* what it is not. Adonai makes of Jahweh a nontext; but as this nontext Jahweh is the text it is. "The Writing of God" writes, similarly, a "not" across any text; but then the text, which is a text but not the Text of God ("God is God," written by God), can be the text *as* which the Text of God is what it is.

It is by following such clues that, it seems to me, one can think the meaning and being of a theological text—not as a sacred text, nor as the one text that is in all texts, but as a text which, the other of any text, is what it is by being, at times, what it is not.

NOTES

[1] Derrida, Levinas, and Foucault all have their roots in Husserl's and Heidegger's phenomenology. There is, therefore, a double movement toward the concern with textuality: from phenomenology, and from theology. Accompanying the change is also the question of the meaning of time and how it affects textuality. I have not gone into that question at all in the present essay. Derrida and Levinas, for example, have both indicated that even Heidegger's understanding of future, or *Zukunft*, which is the pre-eminent mode of time for human existence, presupposes a background of the now and the present (or is, somehow, still "metaphysical"); and Lacan, typically for this French school of thought, thinks of this primary mode as a future perfect time (not "I shall do tomorrow" but "I shall have done tomorrow"). This, as Ijsseling puts it, "Is the mode of *non-presence* which is presented, feared, or desired as being present" (Samuel Ijsseling, "Hermeneutics and Textuality: Questions Concerning Phenomenology," in *Studies in Phenomenology and the Human Sciences*, edited by John Sallis [Atlantic Highlands, N.J.: Humanities Press, 1979], p. 8). "Presence is either that for which one hopes, or that which one fears will occur, while behaving as if it is already there; or like that which is lost for good with only a trace left behind and which one tries continuously to restore or find again. The latter occurs by means of signs and symbols. These do not refer to something

that is present but to other signs and symbols, as words in a dictionary refer to other words. What is meant is only what is not present, and the world we live in is a framework of meanings. Reality is of the order of discourse or of the order of speaking and writing and of listening and reading" (ibid.).

[2] One needs to make some distinctions about why one does not speak but writes. John Stuart Mill, for example, clearly wrote his *On Liberty* because he thought this was the only way in which there would be time for him to make his thoughts available. Such a case is different from one in which one writes because one cannot really speak the same thing or because one does not want one's authorship to be known.

[3] This I take to be Benveniste's basic objection to de Saussure's theory of sign: In one sense, it may be true that the connection between the English word "tree" and the object tree is arbitrary (other languages have different words for the same object); but, in another sense, it is not arbitrary (because if I am a speaker of English the word "tree" does make me think of that object and not of some other object.) Furthermore, in actual understanding, we do have to depend upon there being some words whose meaning is immediately understood if we are to give other meanings to other words. At *some* point—even if it is a movable point—intelligibility of language depends upon that convergence of sign, sense, and thing.

[4] This provides a different way of describing the subject matter of theology from the one used in the analogy of being. Aquinas, for example, says that the subject matter of theology, unlike that of other sciences, is not given as such but is given only in its effects (the world). Hence, theology needs to read back from the world as effect to the one who is its cause. If, however, we take into account the instantiating capacity of language, then we can say that the subject matter of theology is given in the very word "God" and in the negative that it shows upon anything and anyone.

[5] One can be a self, or I, just through thinking the meaning of the word "I"; but one cannot exist as a self for others in the world without the presence of the very word "I."

[6] Art in general, Kant wrote, "Is distinguished from nature as making *(facere)* from acting or operating *(agere)*, and the product or result of the former from the product or result of the latter as work *(opus)* from effects *(effectus)*" (*Critique of Judgment*, 173).

[7] Note that this can be written but not said.

WORKS CONSULTED

Heisenberg, Werner
    1973   *Der Teil und das Ganze: Gespräche im Umkreis der Atomphysik*. Munich: Deutscher Taschenbuchverlag.

Ricoeur, Paul
    1970   "Qu'est ce qu'un texte? Expliquer et comprendre." Pp. 181–200 in *Hermeneutik und Dialektik, Aufsätze II: Hans-Géorg Gadamer zum 70. Geburtstag*. Eds. Rudiger Bubner, Konrad Cramer, and Reiner Wiehl. Tübingen: J.C.B. Mohr (Paul Siebeck).

SHADES OF DIFFERENCE

Mark C. Taylor
Williams College

ABSTRACT

In current discussions among literary critics, the notion of the text is repeatedly defined in relation to the idea of the book. While the text is always incomplete and never simply the work of a purposeful author, the book is supposed to be the completed product of an intentional agent. To achieve the closure toward which the book is directed, the author must reconcile differences within a systematic totality that is structured as a teleological narrative. Meaning is a function of spatial and temporal placement within a coherent plot.

Writers like Georges Bataille, Maurice Blanchot, Emmanuel Levinas, and Jacques Derrida argue the extended notion of the book underlying most Western philosphy and theology comes to completion in Hegel's systematic philosophy. From this point of view, *The Encyclopedia of the Philosophical Sciences* represents the most exhaustive effort to write a book that is both totally comprehensive and completely comprehensible. It is not, however, clear whether this project is possible on Hegel's own terms. When the *Phenomenology* is approached through Nietzsche's account of interpretation and Peirce's theory of the sign, it becomes possible to appreciate the force of Derrida's rereading of Hegel as the last philosopher of the book and the first thinker of writing.

The following analysis focuses on Hegel's consideration of the criteria of judgment employed by the various forms of consciousness that unfold before the gaze of the speculative philosopher. By arguing that observed consciousness gives itself the criterion by which it judges itself, Hegel inadvertently suggests that the object of consciousness is, in effect, a sign. Rather than representations of things or ideas, signs might be signs of other signs. The interplay of signs implies the rhetorical character of all human thought and language. If rhetoric never gives way to knowledge *sensu strictissimo*, the completion of the book is either impossible or forever delayed. The impossibility or deferral of the book opens the time and space of writing in which difference is never mastered and otherness never reduced to the same. As the inscription of radical alterity, textual writing and writerly texts mark the end of philosophy and expose a new opening for the religious imagination.

{*epigraphein*}

What would happen if one were to publish all of Hegel's prefaces together in a separate volume, like James's in *The Art of the Novel* {or Kierkegaard's *Prefaces*}? what if Hegel had written nothing but prefaces? or what if, instead of placing them outside the work as an hors d'oeuvre, he had inserted them here or there, for instance in the *middle* (as in *Tristram Shandy*) of the *Greater Logic*, between *objective logic* and *subjective logic*, or anywhere else? (Derrida, 1981: 49n)

Introductory Unscientific Prescript

I begin, or attempt to begin, with questions—not simply *my* questions but (also) questions of an other. The questions haunting the pages that fall between the *epigraphein* and the *epitaphos* are always questions of an other . . . a certain other that always questions.

> Indeed, what forces us at all to suppose that there is an essential opposition of "true" and "false"? It is not sufficient to assume degrees of apparentness and, as it were, lighter and darker shadows and shades of appearances—different "values," to use the language of painters? And if somebody asked, "but to a fiction there surely belongs an author?"—couldn't one answer simply: *why?* Doesn't this "belongs" perhaps belong to the fiction, too? Is it not permitted to be a bit ironical about the subject no less than the predicate and object? Shouldn't philosophers be permitted to rise above faith in grammar? (Nietzsche, 1966: 46–47)

My question, as well as the question of *(nota bene)* the other, is, then, a question of shades—shades of difference, a question that is, perhaps (endlessly) provoked by the glimpse of *difference as shade*. There are, of course, many shades of "shade": partial or comparative darkness; absence of complete illumination; especially the comparative darkness caused by a more or less opaque object intercepting the direct rays of the sun or other luminary; *shade of death;* comparative obscurity; the darkness of night; the growing darkness after sunset; the darkness of the nether world; the abode of the dead, Hades; the darker color expressing absence of illumination; those portions of a story, a literary work, or the like, which are designedly less brilliant in effect than others; a minutely-differentiated degree or variety; a dark figure cast upon a surface by a body intercepting light; an unsubstantial image of something real; an unreal appearance; something that has only fleeting existence, or that has become reduced to almost nothing; an inseparable follower or companion; the visible but impalpable form of a dead person, a ghost; cover afforded by the interposition of some opaque body between an object and light, heat, etc., especially shelter from the sun; a lace scarf for the head worn by women. *The Shades:* originally, a name for wine and beer vaults with a drinking-bar, either underground or sheltered from the sun by an arcade.[1]

Shades eternally return to disrupt and unsettle the following analysis. Is there something shady about philosophy? Does reflection always cast a shadow? Does shading constitute a blind (spot) that breaks the purportedly closed circle of reflection? Do shades short circuit the current/currency of the sun's/son's economy? Is the "bacchanalian revel" held in the nether world? Is the wine served in The Shades a *pharmakon*? Are these shades of difference the shades of death, the death of *(nota bene)* (Hegelian) philosophy? Questions of an other . . . a certain other, an "almost nothing" which, nonetheless, makes all the difference.

But why begin or attempt to begin an analysis of Hegel by re-citing Nietzsche? Few thinkers appear to be in more fundamental disagreement than Hegel and Nietzsche. Hegel, the thinker in whose System philosophy becomes scientific and knowledge absolute; Nietzsche, the thinker in whose aphorisms philosophy becomes fictive and knowledge perspectival. While Hegel is the philosopher of the Book *par excellence*, Nietzsche is a writer whose texts unravel every form of bookishness. Gilles Deleuze goes so far as to insist that "Anti-Hegelianism runs through Nietzsche's work as its cutting edge" (8). From this point of view, any reference to Nietzsche seems to be a misleading detour that needlessly delays a serious consideration of Hegel (and *vice versa*).

All of this can, however, be approached otherwise. Over against what has come to be a widely accepted understanding of the opposition between Hegel and Nietzsche, I propose to read Hegel through Nietzsche (and others). More specifically, I shall argue that a reconsideration of Hegel's "presentation of appearing/apparent knowledge {*des erscheinenden Wissen*}" in the "Introduction" to the *Phenomenology of Spirit* suggests unexpected similarities between Hegel's interpretation of "*das Werden des Wissen*" and Nietzsche's interpretation of interpretation. Appearances to the contrary notwithstanding, there is only a shade of difference between Hegel and Nietzsche. From this perspective, it becomes possible to appreciate the force of Jacques Derrida's suggestion that:

> The horizon of absolute knowledge is the effacement of writing in the logos, the retrieval of the trace in parousia, the reap-

propriation of difference, the accomplishment of what I have elsewhere called the *metaphysics of the proper* {*le propre*—self-possession, propriety, property, cleanliness}.

Yet, all that Hegel thought within this horizon, all, that is except eschatology, may be reread as a meditation on writing. Hegel is *also* the thinker of irreducible difference. He rehabilitated thought as the *memory productive* of signs. And he reintroduced. . . . the essential necessity of the written trace in a philosophical—that is to say Socratic—discourse that had always believed it possible to do without it; the last philosopher of the book and the first thinker of writing (1976: 26).

Liminary Shades

Beginnings always trouble Hegel. Philosophy, it seems, is subverted by either beginning or not beginning. On the one hand, if philosophy begins, *sensu strictissmo*, then the circularity that Hegel believes to be definitive of scientific knowledge is (from the beginning) breached. If, on the other hand, philosophy does not or cannot begin, then does it exist? Philosophy, in other words, can begin only by repressing the impossibility of (its) beginning. Hegel (but not only Hegel) faces a double bind: he must begin without really beginning. In an effort to resolve this dilemma, Hegel attempts to write a preface or an introduction to philosophy that is not properly a preface or an introduction but is, in some sense, already philosophy itself. Such a preface erases itself in its very inscription.

> Prefaces, along with forewords, introductions, preludes, preliminaries, preambles, prologues, and prolegomena, have always been written, it seems in view of their own self-effacement. Upon reaching the end of the *pre* (which presents and precedes, or rather forestalls, the presentative production, and, in order to put before the readers' eyes what is not yet visible, is obliged to speak, predict, and predicate), the route which has been covered must cancel itself out. But this subtraction leaves a mark of erasure, a *remainder* which is added to the subsequent text and which cannot be completely summed up within it. Such an operation thus appears contradictory, and the same is true of the interest one takes in it.
>
> But does a preface exist?
>
> On the one hand—this is logic itself—this residue of writing remains anterior and exterior to the development of the content it announces. Preceding what ought to be able to present itself on its own, the preface falls like an empty husk, a piece of formal refuse, a moment of dryness or loquacity, sometimes both at once. From a point of view which can only, ultimately, be that of the science of logic, Hegel thus disqualifies the preface. Philo-

sophical exposition has as its essence the capacity and even the duty to do without a preface (Derrida, 1981: 9).

My question (which is always already the question of an other) will be whether the mark inevitably left by erasure mortally wounds the dream of systematic philosophy.

Despite (or, perhaps, because of) their impossibility, Hegel writes and rewrites prefaces, forewords, and introductions. His most important (self-erasing) preface is the *Phenomenology of Spirit*. This introductory work is supposed to provide a "ladder" (14) with which one can progress from an "uneducated {*ungebildeten*} standpoint to knowledge"[16]. Hegel's preface, however, is not straightforward but is convoluted; it folds in on itself. At the edge of philosophy, thresholds multiply. Hegel's preface contains (or tries to contain) another preface as well as an introduction. The relationship of this preface within a preface to the book it foretells is as ambiguous as is the relationship of the entire book to the totality it predicts. While the *Phenomenology* is properly neither inside nor outside the System, the "Preface {*Vorrede*}" is properly neither inside nor outside the *Phenomenology*. The "Preface" is not really a preface to the *Phenomenology*. Hegel's remarks in the "Preface" are both more general and more specific than his concerns in the book as a whole. By anticipating the consummation of absolute knowledge, the "preface" looks beyond the *Phenomenology*. Furthermore, Hegel's prefatory comments represent an effort to place his work within its historical context. Wedged between the "Preface" and the book proper, the "Introduction" appears to be more closely tied to the *Phenomenology*. In the "Introduction," Hegel addresses vexing methodological difficulties posed by the investigation he is about to undertake. But it quickly becomes apparent that he remains preoccupied with the (pre)liminary problem of the boundary.

> It is a natural assumption that in philosophy, before we start to deal with its proper subject-matter, viz. the actual cognition of what truly is, one must first of all come to an understanding about cognition, which is regarded either as the instrument to get hold of the absolute, or as the medium {*das Mittel:* medium or mean} through which one discovers it. A certain uneasiness seems justified, partly because there are different types of cognition, and one of them might be more appropriate than another for the attainment of this goal, so that we could make a bad choice of means; and partly because cognition is a faculty of a definite kind and scope, and thus, without more precise definition of its nature and limits, we might grasp clouds of error instead of the heaven of truth. This feeling of uneasiness is surely bound to be transformed into the conviction that the whole project of securing for con-

sciousness through cognition what exists in itself is absurd, and that there is a boundary {*Grenze: boundary, frontier, limit, border, edge, threshold*} between cognition and the absolute that completely separates them (46).

The *Phenomenology* is inscribed along the limen that Hegel traces in the "Introduction." The end of the phenomenological sojourn is "true knowledge." Hegel explains that "the *goal* is as necessarily fixed for knowledge as the serial progression; it is the point where knowledge no longer needs to go beyond itself, where knowledge finds itself, where notion corresponds to object and object to notion. Hence the progress towards this goal is also unhalting, and short of it no satisfaction is to be found at any of the stations of the way" (50).[2] If the shadows of ignorance are to be dispelled and every shade of doubt erased, it is necessary to cross out the border separating cognition and the absolute and to render the medium between subject and object completely transparent. Such illuminating border crossing is the task Hegel sets for himself in the preface of his System. The way across this frontier is as long and as difficult as the "history" of consciousness. To "prepare the way" for the perfect reconciliation of subject and object, Hegel retraces the circuitous course that consciousness ineluctably follows in its progression from darkness to light. The object of the phenomenologist is nothing other than consciousness. Hegel's understanding of the phenomenological enterprise complicates the subject-object relationship. Inasmuch as phenomenology is the "science of the experience of consciousness {*Wissenschaft der Erfahrung des Bewusstseins*}," the object of investigation is itself divided between subjectivity and objectivity. The relationship of observing and observed consciousness can be summarized as follows:

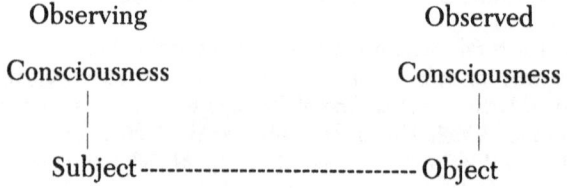

Even this account of the interplay of subjectivity and objectivity fails to do justice to the implicit complexity of Hegel's analysis. Although usually overlooked, it is important to distinguish the author from the reader of the *Phenomenology*. Throughout the book, Hegel tries to obscure this distinction by identifying with the reader by means of the editorial "we." There is, nonetheless, an undeniable difference between the author/teacher who is already a phenomenologist but (impossibly) is not yet a philosopher and the reader/pupil who no longer embodies "natural consciousness" but is not yet a phenomenologist. The reader is *neither* Hegel's observing *nor* observed consciousness. Readers can, of course, read only what is written—even when they read between the lines. Though the author of the book always seems to know more than he can (even on his own terms) possibly know, the actual writing of the *Phenomenology* remains irreducibly marginal. In spite of appearances to the contrary, the time and space of writing and reading lie *between* observing and observed consciousness—along the boundary that marks and remarks the shade of difference between subject and object. In view of these considerations, it is necessary to revise our graph of phenomenological reflection.

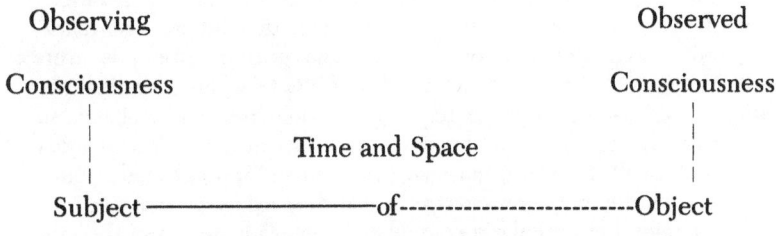

When understood in this way, Hegel's project in the *Phenomenology* becomes considerably clearer. This book, which, it is important to recall, is not properly philosophical, is designed to close the gap, heal the rift, and bridge the breach between subject and object. "In pressing forward to its true existence," Hegel maintains, "consciousness will arrive at a point at which it gets rid of its semblance of being burdened with something heterogeneous, with what is only for it, and some sort of 'other,' at a point where appearance becomes identical with essence, so that its presentation will coincide at just this point with the authentic science of spirit. And finally, when consciousness itself grasps this its own essence, it will signify the nature of absolute knowledge itself" (56–57). To appreciate the implications of Hegel's claim, it is necessary to realize that he defines spirit as "that which *relates itself to itself* and is *determinate*, it is other-being {*Anderssein*} and *being-for-self*, and in this determinateness, or in its self-externality, abides within itself; in other words, it is *in and for itself*" (14). In an important sense, Hegel is preoccupied with the problem of otherness throughout the *Phenomenology*. The full realization of spirit in absolute knowledge is possible only when alterity in all of its forms is overcome. Difference must be reconciled with identity to form an identity-in-difference in which there is "*pure* self-recognition in absolute otherness" (14).

The interpretation of knowledge as the sublation of all heterogenity creates a further methodological dilemma for Hegel. In order to retrace the experience of consciousness as it moves from less to more complete forms of knowledge, it would seem that the phenomenologist would have to employ criteria with which to distinguish and arrange various ways of knowing. If, however, the goal of the investigation is to lead the reader to absolute knowledge that no longer is "burdened with something heterogeneous," then the phenomenological guide cannot impose norms, standards, or measures in a heteronomous manner. To the contrary, the criteria of judgment that enable consciousness to progress must arise from *within* consciousness itself. Hegel attempts to solve this problem in the most important paragraph of his "Introduction."

> But the *Trennung*, or this semblance of *Trennung* {separation, division, severing, parting, dissociation, dissolution, disintegration, decomposition, or divorce}[3] and presupposition, is overcome by the nature of the object we {*nota bene*} are investigating. Consciousness provides its own criterion from within itself, so that the investigation becomes a comparison of consciousness with itself; for the difference {*die Unterscheidung*} made above falls within it. In consciousness one thing exists *for* another; i.e., consciousness regularly contains the determinateness of the moment of knowledge; at the same time, this other is to consciousness not merely *for it*, but is also outside of this relationship, or exists *in itself*: the moment of truth. Thus in what consciousness affirms from within itself as *being-in-itself* or the *true*, we have the standard that consciousness itself sets up by which to measure what it knows. If we designate *knowledge* as the notion, but the essence of the *true* as what exists, or the *object*, then the examination consists in seeing whether the notion corresponds to the object. But if we call the *essence* or the in-itself of the *object* the *notion*, but on the other hand understand by the *object* the notion itself as *object*, viz. as it exists *for an other*, then the examination consists in seeing whether the object corresponds to its notion. It is evident, of course, that the two procedures are the same. But the essential point to bear in mind throughout the whole investigation is that these two moments, "notion" and "object," "being-for-another" and "being-in-itself," both fall *within* that knowledge which we are investigating. Consequently, we do not need to import criteria, or to make use of our own bright ideas and thoughts during the course of the inquiry; it is precisely when we leave these aside that we succeed in contemplating the matter in hand as it is *in and for itself*' (53–54).

This passage underscores the importance of the question of *difference* in Hegel's argument. To overcome alterity, it is necessary to erase every trace of difference. We have seen, however, that there are many shades of difference. The two most recurrent differences in Hegel's phenomenology are the difference between observing and observed consciousness and the difference within observed consciousness. Both of these differences are, of course, variations of the difference between subject and object. Hegel attempts to accomplish the (impossible) task of simultaneously maintaining and effacing difference by arguing that the gap between subject and object is merely the "semblance of separation {*Scheins von Trennung*}." Each shape of consciousness that the phenomenologist examines both assumes and attempts to negate the difference between itself and its object. In Hegel's terms, "Consciousness simultaneously *differs* from something, and at the same time *relates* itself to it, or, as it is said, this something exists *for* consciousness; and the determinate aspect of this *relating*, or the *being* of something for a consciousness, is *knowing*" (52). From the point of view of observed consciousness, the object-in-itself is independent of the knowing subject and provides the criterion with which to determine the adequacy or inadequacy of knowledge. The presupposition of the exteriority and anteriority of the object of knowledge is the distinguishing feature of "natural consciousness." Hegel is convinced that the assumption of the original separation of subjectivity and objectivity inevitably leads to the frustration of the desire for knowledge. To enjoy the longed-for "satisfaction {*Befriedigung*}" that knowledge promises, it is necessary to heal the rift between observed consciousness and its object by bridging the gap between observing consciousness and its object (i.e., observed consciousness).

Observing consciousness recognizes what observed consciousness fails to notice: the object that appears to be independent of the subject and to constitute the *given* criterion of knowledge is actually *posited* by consciousness. "Consciousness," Hegel insists, "provides its own criterion from within itself" (53). Accordingly, the difference between consciousness and its other is, in the final analysis, no difference at all. The phenomenologist guides the reader along the way that consciousness has passed in its journey from its lowly "natural" state to the heights of absolute knowledge. The narrative structure of the book is organized in such a way that each stage of knowledge assumes coherence as an essential moment in the necessary unfolding of an organic totality. The completion of the book discloses the circularity of the entire analysis. The end returns to the beginning to reveal the identity of (the) Alpha and Omega. Observed and observing consciousness unite to celebrate the consummation of the wedding of subject and object.

> In this knowing, then, Spirit has concluded the movement in which it has shaped itself, insofar as this shaping was burdened

> with the difference of consciousness, *a difference now overcome* {emphasis added}. Spirit has won the pure element of its existence, the notion. The content, in accordance with the *freedom* of its *being*, is the self-alienating self, or the immediate unity of self-knowledge (490).

With the r(u)(a)pture of the hymen that had seemed to separate subject and object, absolute knowledge is born. Or so it seems.

Hegel's conclusion to the *Phenomenology* is not as conclusive as he would have the reader believe. In the last two paragraphs, he acknowledges that the beginning and end of his book are separated by space and time.

> The self-knowing spirit knows not only itself but also the negative of itself, or its limit: to know one's limit is to know how to sacrifice oneself. This sacrifice is the externalization in which spirit displays the process of becoming spirit in the form of *free contingent happening*, intuiting its pure self as time outside of it, and equally its being as space. This last becoming of spirit, *nature*, is in its existence nothing but this external externalization of its *continuing existence* and the movement which reinstates the subject.
>
> But the other side of its becoming, *history*, is a *conscious*, self-*mediating* becoming—spirit externalized into time . . . (492).

The time and space of the writing and reading of Hegel's prefatory *Phenomenology* are, in effect, time and space. In other words, "Time is the time of the preface; space—whose time *will have been* the Truth—is the space of the preface" (Derrida, 1981: 13) The time and space of the preface delay the appearance of philosophy proper. The philosopher, nonetheless, is forced to admit that delay is inevitable and detours are unavoidable. Hegel tries to turn delay and detour to philosophical advantage by taking away with one hand what he has just given with the other hand. The externalization of spirit, i.e., time and space, Hegel argues, "is equally the externalization {*die Entäusserung*} of itself" (492). This externalization of externalization is, in turn and by turns, the process of internalization through which spatial and temporal dispersion are recollected in the eternal self-becoming of the notion. "The Golgotha of absolute spirit" (Hegel: 493) "is the effacement of writing in the logis, the retrieval of the trace in parousia, the reappropriation of difference . . ." (Derrida, 1976: 26).

But what if the time and space of writing and reading cannot be easily effaced? What if erasure is always incomplete—forever leaves a mark? What if Hegel's difficulty beginning foretells the impossibility of concluding? What if the preface cannot be contained but spills over {*déborde*} into the work or the System? What if Hegel has written nothing but prefaces?

A Question of Rhetoric

In an effort to probe these questions, I return to my beginning, a beginning from which I have never really departed: the question of an other. If a certain other *always* questions, conclusions must, of necessity, remain inconclusive. And if conclusions are inconclusive, differences cannot finally be overcome. In the absence of definitive conclusions, we are left in "comparative darkness" with "almost nothing" . . . nothing but shades of difference.

In order to test the capacity of Hegel's heliocentric System to dispel the darkness of the nether world by allowing the reader to gaze at the sun/son without the intervention of shades, I would like to reread the central argument in the "Introduction" to the *Phenomenology* in semiotic terms. It is commonly acknowledged that every sign is comprised of a signifier and a signified, each of which can assume a variety of forms. For example, the signifier can be, among other things, either phonic or graphic. The signified, by contrast, can be either real (e.g., an object "in" the world) or ideal (e.g., an idea "within" the subject). In most cases, the signified serves as the seemingly independent criterion by which to judge the adequacy or inadequacy of the signifier. A sign is effective to the extent that it clearly re-presents the signified by means of a transparent signifier. With these distinctions in mind, it is possible to recase Hegel's argument.

> Consciousness provides its own criterion from within itself, so that the investigation becomes a comparison of consciousness with itself; for the difference made above {i.e., between consciousness and its object} falls within it {i.e., consciousness} . . . If we designate *knowledge* as the signifier, but the essence or the signified as what exists, or the *object*, then the examination consists in seeing whether the signifier corresponds to the signified. But if we call the *essence* or in-itself of the *object* the signifier, and on the other hand understand by the *object* the signifier itself as *object*, viz. as it exists *for another*, then the examination consists in seeing whether the signified corresponds to its signifier. It is evident, of course, that the two procedures are the same.

This formulation throws a different light on Hegel's position. The object of knowledge is not a "transcendental signified." To the contrary, "*The thing itself is a sign*. . . . The so-called 'thing-itself' is always already a *representamen* screened from the simplicity of intuitive evidence. The *representamen* functions only by giving rise to an *interpretant* that itself becomes a sign and so on to infinity" (Derrida, 1976: 49) The sign of consciousness is constituted as a signifier of a signified which, in itself, is a signifier. From this viewpoint, consciousness deals *only with signs*. Signs, Charles Sanders Peirce explains, "come into being by development out of other signs, particularly from icons and symbols. We think only in signs" (1932: 169). If we think only in signs and signs always develop out of other signs, then the "science of the experience of consciousness" is the science of signs. Contrary to expectation, phenomenology turns out to be semiotics. Elsewhere Peirce indicates the far-reaching implications of this insight.

> The science of semiotics has three branches. The first is called by Duns Scotus *grammatica speculativa*. We may term it *pure grammar*. It has for its task to ascertain what must be true of the representamen used by every scientific intelligence in order that they may embody any *meaning*. The second is logic proper. It is the science of what is quasi-necessarily true of the representamina of any scientific intelligence in order that they may hold good of any *object*, that is, may be true. Or say, logic proper is the formal science of the conditions of the truth of representations. The third, in imitation of Kant's fashion of preserving old associations of words in finding nomenclature for new conceptions, I call *pure rhetoric*. Its task is to ascertain the laws by which in every scientific intelligence one sign gives birth to another, and especially one thought brings forth another (1940: 99)

Hegel, *malgré lui*, implies the rhetorical nature of his undertaking. As we have seen, "Consciousness provides its own criterion from within itself . . ." What now has become clear is that the criterion consciousness gives itself is a sign that grows out of another sign. Consciousness is, therefore, a play of signs that are nothing other than signifiers of signifiers. Since no signifier can properly re-present the thing-in-itself, the activity of signification is inescapably fictive. In different terms, the criterion that consciousness gives itself is always, in some sense, an interpretation. As Nietzsche points out:

> No, facts is precisely what there is not, only interpretations. We cannot establish any fact "in itself": perhaps it is folly to want to do such a thing . . .
> Insofar as the word "knowledge" has any meaning, the world is knowable; but it is *interpretable* otherwise, it has no meaning behind it, but countless meanings.—"Perspectivism" (1968: 267).

Such an inconclusive conclusion is, of course, precisely what Hegel's philosophical System is constructed to avoid. The entire movement of the *Phenomenology* is from certainty to truth. Absolute knowledge is intended to be the antidote to the dangerous *pharmakon* of perspectivism. Such a remedy presupposes that the play of signification is not infinite but can, at some point, be stopped. Though Hegel emphasizes on the development of truth and, correlatively, the truth of becoming, there is finally something unbecoming about his view of knowledge. Absolute knowledge, he argues, removes all shadows of doubt by "inwardizing {*erinnern*}," "incorporating {*vereinigen*}," or "digesting {*verdauen*}" every other and domesticating all alterity. From this perspective (but is it anything more?), the philosopher is the high priest (perhaps even a sorcerer, exorcist, or magician) who sacrifices the uncanny {*unheimlich*} *Pharmakos* that unsettles every domestic economy. With the appearance of the question of the *pharmakon* and the *pharmakos*, we re-turn to the shady nether world of the limen. "The ceremony of the *pharmakos*," Derrida explains, is "played out on the boundary line between inside and outside, which it has as its function ceaselessly to trace and retrace. *Intra muros/extra muros*. The origin of difference and division, the *pharmakos* represents evil both introjected and projected. Beneficial insofar as he cures—and for that, venerated and cared for—harmful insofar as he incarnates the powers of evil—and for that, feared and treated with caution. Alarming and calming. Sacred and accursed (1981: 133).

The *pharmakos* . . . origin of difference and division. Hegel never really leaves the question of the boundary with which he begins his "Introduction." Nor is it clear that he ever answers the question of the boundary. In view of this uncertainty, it seems that the limen marks the site (or the nonsite) of the question that forever haunts (Hegelian) philosophy. In order to erase the boundary between subject and object, Hegel maintains, "The essential point to bear in mind . . . is that these two moments, 'Notion' and 'object' {signifier and signified, or signified and signifier}, 'being-for-another' and 'being-in-itself' both fall *within* that knowledge which we are investigating" (53). The question that and of remains concerns the nature of this "*within*." Is this "*within*" the product of an "*Er-Innerung*" that overcomes all difference and reconciles every other? Or does this "*within*" remain without? Is this remainder the interiority of exteriority that fissures the Hegelian System (as if from "within")?

Insofar as it inevitably entails the dyadic moments of signification, consciousness harbors an other that repeatedly disrupts its self-identity and breaches its closure. If signs are always signs of signs, then interpretations are always interpretations of interpretations. Nietzsche's aphorism provides a helpful gloss to Hegel's "Preface."

"Ends and means"   "Cause and effect"   "Subject and object"   "Acting and suffering"   "Thing-in-itself and appearance" as interpretations (not as facts) and to what extent perhaps *necessary* interpretations?" (as required for "preservation"— all in the sense of a will to power.) (1968:323)

Since "we think only in signs," interpretation is infinite, which is definitely not to say that it is absolute. The quest for secure knowledge is the search for what Kierkegaard calls an "archimedean point" that would stop *"das Werden des Wissens."* The claim to possess knowledge, Nietzsche contends, is an assertion of the will to power. When translated into Hegel's terms, this will to power appears to be a struggle for mastery. But what does the philosopher, what does Hegel struggle to master?

The philosopher writes in an effort to overcome alterity which paradoxically, can only be accomplished by mastering writing. The point of such labor becomes clearer when we recall that the time and space of writing and reading are nothing other than time and space. Thus the struggle to master writing is the struggle to overcome time and space. The end of the philosopher's book is the denial of death and the apotheosis of the philospher.

> *The goal*, absolute knowledge, or spirit that knows itself as spirit, has for its path the recollection {*die Eriennerung*} of spirits as they are in themselves and as they consummate the organization of their kingdom. Their preservation, regarded from the side of their free existence {*Daseins*} appearing in the form of continegency, is history; but regarded from the side of their comprehended organization, it is the science of knowledge: the two together, comprehended history {*die begriffne Geschichte*}, form the inwardizing {*die Erinnerung*} and the Golgotha of absolute spirit, the actuality, truth, and certainty of this throne, without which he would be lifeless and alone. Only from the chalice of this realm of spirits foams forth for Him his own infinitude (493)[4].

But a question (always) remains—the question of remains: Is Hegel's *Phenomenology* a book? Or does it remain a preface, a preface to the book to end all books (i.e., the *Encyclopedia of the Philosophical Sciences*)? If the *Phenomenology* is a preface, then it is more like a labyrinthian text from which there is no exit than a neat and tidy {*propre*} book in which beginning and end are one. While the book seeks closure by filling the space and closing the gaps of time, the text always remains open and is, therefore, endless. The infinite play of signification inscribes a boundless text. "To allege that there is no absolute outside of the text is not to postulate some ideal of immanence, the incessant reconstitution of writing's relation to itself. What is in question is no longer an idealist or theological operation which, in a Hegelian manner, would suspend and sublate what is outside discourse, logos, the concept, or the idea. The text *affirms* the outside, marks the limits of this speculative operation, deconstructs and reduces to the status of 'effects' all the predicates through which speculation appropriates the outside. If there is nothing outside the text, this implies, with the transformation of the concept of the text in general, that the text is no longer the snug airtight inside of an interiority or an identity-to-itself (even if the motif of 'outside or bust' may sometimes play a reassuring role: a certain kind of inside can be terrible), but rather a different placement of the effects of opening and closing" (Derrida, 1981:35–36).

The "outside" affirmed "inside" the text is the "almost nothing" of difference. Apart from shades of difference, there can be no consciousness (or life). Perfect light is indistinguishable from total darkness. Consciousness includes as a condition of its own possibility precisely the difference it struggles to exclude. the consummation of the wedding (of subject and object) for which Hegel longs is, therefore, forever delayed. In other words, always in other words, it is no more possible to overcome writing by writing than it is to stop time in time. These two are actually the same impossibility—the impossibility of *(nota bene)* writing. The terrible inside that philosophy can never properly interiorize is an irreducible outside that opens "the fault through which the yet unnameable of the beyond-closure lets itself be glimpsed {la faille par laquelle se laisse entrevoir, encore innommable, la lueur de l'outre-clôture} (Derrida, 1976:14). Gl . . .gl . . . a glimmer . . . a glimpse, no more, for shades are nothing (substantial), nothing other than a play of differences that recurs eternally as eternal recurrence. This is what the last philosopher of the book has *written*-written in spite of what he intended to say.

{*epitaphos*}

> The preface to the *Phenomenology of Spirit* had posited the equivalence of understanding, formality, the mathematical, the negative, exteriority, and death. It had also posited the necessity of their work, which must be looked at in the face. Now, calculation, the machine, and mute writing belong to the same system of equivalences, and their work poses the same problem: at the moment when meaning is lost, when thought is opposed to its other, when spirit is absent from itself, is the result of the operation certain? And if the *relève* of alienation is not a calculable certitude, can one still speak of alienation and still produce statements in the system of speculative dialectics? Or in dialectics, whose essence is encapsulated by this sytem, in general? If the investment in death cannot be integrally amortized (even in the case of a profit, of an excess of revenue), can one still speak of a work of the negative? What might be a "negative" that could not be *relevé?* And which, in sum, as negative, but without appearing as such, without *presenting itself, that is, without working in the service of meaning, would work?* but would work, then, as pure loss? (Derrida, 1982:106–7)

What is an epitaphos?

ἐπί *upon* τάφος, sepulcher, tomb. An inscription upon a tomb. Sepulcher: a tomb or burial-place, a building, vault, or excavation, made for the internment of a human body; *Whited sepulcher:* in biblical language, used figuratively for a hypocrite, or one whose fair outward semblance conceals inward corruption; *The Holy Sepulcher:* the cave in which Jesus Christ was buried outside the wall {*nota bene*} of Jerusalem. Tomb: a place for burial; an excavation in earth or rock for the reception of a dead body, a grave. Also, a chamber or vault formed wholly or partly in the earth, and, in early times, a tumulus or mound raised over the body; a monument erected to enclose or cover the body and preserve the memory of the dead; a cavity in an altar where relics are deposited; an altar-cavity.

There is always something cryptic about an epitaph.

> What is a crypt?
> All that can be said against a preface, I have already said. The place of what absence—of what of whom of what lost text—does the preface claim to take? Thus disposing and predisposing (of) a first word that does not belong to it, the preface—a crypt in its turn—will take the form of what preserves (and ob-serves me here), the irreplaceable . . .
> The crypt is always an internalization, an inclusion intended as a compromise, but since it is a parasitic inclusion, an inside heterogeneous to the inside of the Self, an outcast in the domain of general introjection within which it violently takes its place, the cryptic safe can only maintain in a state of repetition the mortal conflict it is impotent to resolve (Derrida, 1977:65, 70).

Inscribed upon a sepulcher or a tomb, the epitaph marks the h(o)(a)llow place of remains—the remains of death and of the dead. By citing (the remains of) the dead and (remaining) death, the writing of the epitaph re-cites the liminal nonsite of the shades. The purpose of the epitaph is, of course, to dis-spell the shadows and shades through an a-mortization that turns death to profit. When death pre-serves life, time and space are effectively overcome and the shades are put to rest: *requiescat in pace*.

> But the life of spirit is not the life that shrinks from death and keeps itself untouched by devastation, but rather the life that endures it and maintains itself in it. It wins its truth only when, in utter dismemberment, it finds itself (Hegel: 19).

It is, however, possible to read this epigraph *other* wise. to find oneself in death is to find death in oneself. *Erinnerung* recollects and internalizes death. The interiority of this uncanny exteriority transforms the pacifying R.I.P. into a terrifying rip, rift, tear, tear—an open wound "within" that never closes or heals, like a shadow or shade that blocks x-ray vision and spells death. Is Hegel's pre-face such a shade? If *The Holy Sepulcher* is a *Whited Sepulcher*, then is Hegel's epigraph to philosophy the epitaph of philosophy? A gl . . . gl . . . *glas?*"

I end, or attempt to end, with questions—not simply my questions but (also) questions of an other. The questions haunting the pages that fall between the *epigraphein* and the *epitaphos* are always questions of an other . . . a certain other that always questions.

Notes

[1] All definitions are taken from *The Oxford English Dictionary* (New York: Oxford University Press, 1971).
[2] Hegel is, of course, alluding to the stations of the cross.
[3] Miller's translation of *Trennung* as dissociation does not suggest the rich implications of Hegel's term.
[4] The final couplet is a variation of Schiller's *Die Freundschaft, ad fin.*

WORKS CONSULTED

Deleuze, Gilles
    1983   *Nietzsche and Philosophy.* Trans. H. Thomlinson. New York: Columbia University.

Derrida, Jacques
    1976   *Of Grammatology.* Trans. G. Spivak. Baltimore: Johns Hopkins University. *De le grammatologie.* Paris: Les Editions de Minuit, 1967.
    1977   "Fors." *Georgia Review* 31.
    1981   *Dissemination.* Trans. B. Johnson. Chicago: University of Chicago. *La dissemination.* Paris: Editions du Seuil, 1972.
    1982   *Margins of Philosophy.* Trans. A. Bass. Chicago: University of Chicago. *Marges de la philosophie.* Paris: Les Editions de Minuit, 1972.

Hegel, G.W.F.
    1977   *Phenomenology of Spirit.* Trans. A.V. Miller. New York: Oxford University. *Phänomenologie des Geistes.* Hamburg: Felix Meiner, 1951.

Nietzsche, Friedrich
    1966   *Beyond Good and Evil.* Trans. W. Kaufmann. New York: Random House.
    1968   *The Will to Power.* Trans. W. Kaufmann. New York: Random House.

Peirce, Charles Sanders
    1932   *Elements of Logic, Collected Papers of Charles Sanders Peirce.* Vol. II. Eds. C. Hartshorne and P. Weiss. Cambridge: Harvard University.
    1940   *The Philosophy of Peirce: Selected Writings.* Ed. J. Buchler. New York. Cited in *Of Grammatology*, p. 49.

FROM TEXTUALITY TO SCRIPTURE: THE END OF THEOLOGY AS "WRITING"

Carl A. Raschke
University of Denver

ABSTRACT

How can the text as historico-phenomenal artifact be understood as scripture? In what respects does the development of cultural hermeneutics as applied to the "sacred writing" raise anew the question of the transcendental status of Scripture?

The hermeneutical character of contemporary theology is derived from the move away from all forms of confessionalism toward the deeper "gnosis" of ontological comprehension. A hermeneutical theology maintains the semblance of the traditional preoccupation with the transmundane, while in fact it is bent upon exploring indefinitely the realm of the empirical. It is a scholastic kind of illuminism. The text becomes but a cipher for other texts.

The problem of scripture has its beginnings in the mystifications posed by the text. One of the root meanings of the word "text" is "to cover," "to conceal." Thus textuality is intimately associated with phenomenality. Deconstruction indicates the final moment in the progressive self-portrayal of the text. It is hermeneutics that has lost its enthrallment with history.

The canon is not what makes the text scripture. Within the Western theological tradition all valorization of the religious using the norm of scripture has been undertaken in terms of the metaphysics of presence. The very idea of scripture derives from the primitive realization that all language surpasses itself. The self-surpassing character of language is what makes possible an understanding of the essence of scripture. Language then recovers the infinite out of the finite, and it is a proper "hermeneutics of the infinite" that enables us to distinguish scripturality from textuality.

There can be no such thing at the grammatical level as "God's Word." Post-structural criticism demands that we discharge all claims of content, presence, subject, or kerygma as phantoms of discourse. Theology must recall Barth's reminder that all religious reflection must shatter against the divine negation, against the iconics of mere textuality.

. . . when rightly understood, the infinite significance of the Holy Scriptures is not in contradiction to its hermeneutical limitations.
—Friedrich Schleiermacher, *Hermeneutics*

Now to preach the kingdom of God is nothing else than to preach the gospel, in which is taught the faith of Christ by which alone God dwells and rules in us. But the doctrines of men do not preach about faith, but about eating, clothing, times, places, persons, and about purely external matters which are of no profit to the soul.
—Martin Luther, *Avoiding the Doctrines of Men*, 1522

I.

Even though they convey succinctly what the Reformation of the sixteenth century was fought over, Luther's words are strange to us. Stranger still is his carefully honed dialectic of "faith" and "doctrines of men." For has not, in fact, the post-Romantic epistemic mooring of all "faith statements" in historical and linguistic webworks of meaning thrown us back unconditionally on certain theological postures corresponding to such "doctrines"?

We know that if representations of ultimate reality are "projections" (Feuerbach) and theological locutions amount to "analogies" (Tracy) or "constructions" (Kaufman), then Luther's language of faith cannot be said to have any privileged semantic status, and the notorious "Protestant principle" is but a *caput mortuum*. The Protestant principle, nonetheless, retains its relevance if only because it backlights the fundamental dilemma of the theologian in the waning era of modernity—that is, the transcendental in contradistinction to the mere historical value of the *sacra verba*. Christian liberalism, especially during the past two decades, has sought to avoid the transcendental question by contriving a crude dogma of cultural perspectivism that has its earliest origins in Dilthey's method. In this connection it has become fashionable to say that theology is no longer constitutive or constructive, but "hermeneutical." Furthermore, a hermeneutical theology of this order is supposedly fashioned from the inexhaustible mirror play of textual strands, literary remains, and socio-linguistic ensembles—what the post-structuralists have felicitously, but vaguely, termed the "formation."

A hermeneutical theology is essentially a normative version of *Religionswissenschaft*; it draws together the aggregates of symbolical givens and determines their integral nature, which then becomes the basis for making judgments about the "divine display" through the apertures of historical particularity. The approach, again, was made routine during the Romantic period. We find its quintessential expression in Herder. Finally, the sentiment is consummated in Hegel's metaphysics of itinerant reason. At the foundational level such a hermeneutics is conceived as far more than the art of reading texts; it is an archaeology—and therefore an onrunning mediation—of the phenomenal world itself. It rests without doubt on Gadamer's "polarity of familiarity and strangeness" (262), serving thenceforth as a probe that goes behind all representations. Modern hermeneutics, finally, as Ricoeur has shown us, has its genesis in the nineteenth century quest for understanding not the letter, but the total *human* world in which literacy is generated as one among many puzzling signs and tokens. It "is necessary," Ricoeur notes, "to push the central *aporia* of hermeneutics further by considering the decisive development . . . of a greater *universality*, which prepares the way for the displacement of epistemology towards ontology" (1981: 48).

The hermeneutical character of contemporary theology, which was first actually codified in the later Tillich, can be derived explicitly from the move away from all forms of confessionalism, from theories of religious knowledge, toward the deeper "gnosis" of ontological comprehension. A hermeneutical theology, which germinated in nineteenth-century historicism and the sundry efforts at historical *Verstehen*, could only have emerged out of what was procedurally an anthropologically informed philosophy of *religion*. According to Tillich, "theology is the normative and systematic presentation of the concrete realization of the concept of 'religion'" (33). And religion is the manifestation via symbolic forms, such as myths, of the unity of life itself, of the "holy." A hermeneutical theology maintains the semblance of the traditional preoccupation with the transmundane while, in fact, it is bent upon exploring indefinitely the realm of the empirical. Such a theology is but a somewhat baroque taxonomy of religious emblems, a scholastic kind of illuminism. The text is but a cipher for other texts. And behind the texts lurks perhaps the abyss of unchartered "meaning" itself.

It is in this distinct setting that the so-called "problem" of the text arises. Classical theology has always been concerned with rendering its texts in a manner that was historically intelligible and epistemologically coherent. But it has only been in what has perhaps prematurely been dubbed the "post-Christian" epoch that the text qua text can be earmarked as an issue. The problem of the text, it may be argued, is both a logical concomitant and an evolutionary sequel to the loss of the significance of scripture. And with the loss of the sense of scripture vanishes Luther's dichotomy between faith and human doctrine. At the same time, however, it is only such a dichotomy that ultimately commissions us to resolve the problem of the text. In a word, hermeneutics as the curator of symbols and the regulator of texts must have proceeded somehow from the position that *particular* texts have scriptural integrity. What do we mean by this distinction? We must first make clear what is meant by scripture versus text.

II.

In an odd, but not entirely absurb, fashion the problem of scripture has its beginnings in the sundry mystifications posed by the text. A text is a complex presentation, an embroidery of appearances, as in the Greek etymon *texere*. "Text" is also connected orthographically to the term *tekhne*—hence "technics" or "technology." A third kind of archaic cognate is the term *tegere*—to "cover" or "conceal." Thus if some quasi-Heideggerian probe across the frontiers of language should come into service, we may descry that "textuality" is intimately associated with phenomenality. However, the phenomenality of the text is not the same as the phenomenality of the nature. Just as *techne* and *physis* constitute, for Heidegger, entirely different epochs in the sphere of ontology, so textual interpretation and natural history have respectively a different *episteme* (Foucault). The problem of the text, as Gadamer has indicated, actually emerges throughout the Romantic preoccupation with historical particularity and early nineteenth-century endeavor to find a metaphysical leverage for the investigation of culture. Hence, Ricoeur's multifaceted endeavor to meld hermeneutics with the human sciences is but the grand outworking of the previously unself-conscious Romantic enterprise.

The text shows itself as text once historical self-reflection has permeated the adventure of inscription and interpretation. Derrida's program of deconstruction betokens the final moment in the progressive self-portrayal of the text; it is hermeneutics that has lost its enthrallment with history, which is exactly what happened during the French structuralist interlude, and must fall back upon the solipsism of writing and reading. If hermeneutics purports classically to obtain a first-order system of representations for the second-order phenomenality of literature, then in Derrida the referential thrust is toward the temporal displacement of language itself, toward meaning that is alienated and not recovered. That is the precise significance of Derrida's view of deconstruction as "double science." Interpretation does not unmask the phenomenon; in a quite trenchant sense it leaves intact the "covering" *(teguement)* that is the text. What it does is to deracinate language and expose it as text so that its semantics now is no longer a function of metaphysics, but of what Derrida calls the "liminal space" that "is thus opened up by an inadequation between the form and the content of discourse or by an incommensurability between the signifier and the signified" (18).

In short, any hermeneutical exercise today is confronted by the sheer facticity of texts which, in turn, springs forth from the total default of innocence that has occurred since the completion of the modern cycle of historico-critical understanding. It is this understanding that has disclosed all texts as *techne*, as artifice. The act of canonization, which in an earlier age constituted a response to the suggestion of the "artificial" (i.e., apocryphal) and therefore merely "textual" character of certain religious documents, would be an otiose strategy. For canonization, like creedalism, presupposes an ideality anterior to the phenomenality of the inscription, a superior denotation for historically contingent writing. Canonization, which occurs in all literary ventures, rests on a deference to the primordial authority of discourse. But when history inundates the letter, the canon is washed out.

At the same time, the canon is not necessarily what makes the text a scripture. Luther surely did not desire to couple faith with scriptural authority because the latter had somehow been ordained as the axial reference point in the legacy of Christendom. Quite the contrary! For Luther, the proclamation of *sola fides* was endued with the passion for personal intimacy with the God of tradition whose face remain veiled by the literality of the canon itself. If Erik Erikson is correct in his classic appraisal of Luther's thought in relation to his biography, then the latter's tutoring in Occam's nominalism combined with his mystical and introspective tendencies is comparable to what could be found in the *devotio moderna* and made it impossible for him to treat "Scripture" as a realistic touchstone for theology (See Erikson). Instead, Luther could only appropriate the grammatological element in religious thought as something which abolished itself in order to secure the very *presence* of what could not be merely encoded in writing—the incarnate *logos*, the living Christ. If one reads Luther's polemics carefully, one obtains the distinct impression that the issue is not human versus divine prerogatives so much as it is the hermeneutical primacy of original language as opposed to the paltry mimesis of theological construction. This motive is clear in Luther's treatise of 1539 *On the Councils and the Church* in which he ridicules Catholic efforts since Augustine to "harmonize" the scriptures and states baldly that "a canonist is nothing but an ass." Scripture, for Luther, has what nowadays we might call a "primal" intent. According to Luther:

> Thus Scripture, too, must remain master and judge, for when we follow the brooks too far, they lead us too far away from the spring, and lose both their taste and nourishment, until they lose themselves in the salty sea, as happened under the papacy (212).

It would not be going too far to say that the Lutheran idea of Scripture has prevailed in German thought from Hamman's obsession with an *Ursprache* through Freud's notion of the overdetermination of speech to Heidegger's urging us toward "originary" language. Faith in the Lutheran sense is both an archaeology and an ontology; and it is this archaeology which converts the text into scripture, parlaying in the end into what Bultmann, the last great Lutheran exegete, termed the *Sprach-ereignis*, the "language event."

But it is our historicism as applied to textual problems that has rendered such an archaeology, let alone an ontology, suspect. Historicism has become our modern, post-dogmatic habit of canonizing the work of interpretation. And it is this canonization of scriptural wording in accordance with its historical usage, with its purely semiotic format, that has brought back the conciliar or pre-Reformation style of hermeneutics. Certainly if the conciliar style was not in the ascendancy, we would not have the current high-purposed but asinine attempts to rewrite the Bible in conformance with present wishes for genderless grammar. And the conciliar style can only be the culmination of a long era of historicist verdicts, which have effaced all vestiges of the text's originary significance in favor of its cultural import. "Scripture" can only be tampered with, and rephrased by, socially conscious church committees once it has been depotentiated as scripture, once it is perceived no longer as the *fons et origio* of faith, but as a temporally scarred palimpsest, as text *qua* text.

Historicism, however, is a spurious hermeneutic. Indeed, it cannot pass muster as a hermeneutic at all, inasmuch as it merely substitutes covalent chains of discourse for each other without accomplishing the "fusion of horizons" that Gadamer has shown is indispensable to all credible interpretation. Philology, for example, cannot yield that elusive aim we call "meaning" any more than vital statistics can give us an "event." Philology only discloses for us strands of historical syntax. For interpretation we require a *tertio comparationis*. And what we know as components of scripture demanding hermeneutical intervention are themselves constituted by different horizons, different *Vorbegriffe* (Gadamer), that cannot be stropped down into one set of linear assertions through the historicist reduction.

Still, within the Western theological tradition all valorization of the religious text using the norm of scripture has been essayed in terms of the metaphysics of presence. For that tradition scripture is the text understood as a manifestation of the trans-textual, of the *logos*. The very idea of scripture, which is not uniquely Christian, derives perhaps from the primitive realization that all language surpasses itself. The self-surpassing character of language has been the most important discovery of phenomenology; and it gives the lie to conventionalist, or sociological, theories of meaning which holds that words signify primarily by their function within a system of semantic transactions or operations. Scripturality, according to the linguistic model of phenomenology, is the nimbus surrounding the word in its immediate presentation. That is the fundamental insight behind Heidegger's delphic saying *Die Sprache spricht* ("language speaks"). Language "speaks," explains Merleau-Ponty, because "statements claim to unveil the thing itself; language goes beyond itself toward what it signifies" (81). The reification of the semantic act in which the letter is surpassed by the semantic objective, the reference by the referent, is the source of the metaphysics of presence. The text, if it has not been routinized, appears as God's word.

But the metaphysics of presence—or more specifically the theology of "God's word"—may be more closely related to the psychology of the numinous and the mystique of hieroglyphs than what actually compels faith. Luther may have been searching for the origins of true doctrine, but scripture itself has its genesis in something we call "revelation," in the saying of the unsaid. That is where the philosophy of Derrida currently assumes cardinal importance.

III.

Derrida alone and the "method" of deconstruction—contrary to its current modish pride of place in post-theological dabbling with theology (See Taylor, 1982)—can never be conscripted for the sake of preserving the *re-presentation* of essential meaning in the text, what during the Bultmannian era was innocently, but as a malapropism, known as the "kerygma." What Derrida has made both thematic and explicit is the recognition that textual studies by themselves are self-referring. All metaphysical, or "theological," projects must somehow be grafted onto them. Metaphysics since Aristotle has been the science of the identical. Deconstruction, which actually has its beginnings in Nietzsche's assaults on Platonic formalism and denotative semantics by the supplanting of the argument with parabolic anomaly, is the disclosure of *difference*. And the movement of difference, according to Derrida, occurs within the skein of repetitions, substitutions, word plays, and exchanges that emerges as the process of reading and writing, or convergently as "interpretation."

The text merely bends back upon itself in what Derrida refers to as "the dissimulation of the woven texture" that can "take centuries to undo its web." Thus it must be the true confession of all hermeneutical philosophy that "to a considerable degree, we have already said all we *meant to say*" (65). The unsaid is said in the very instant of displacement, whereby all literalism is overcome by the fact that writing renders impossible the rescue of presence. And the impossibility of rescue indicates that the text as the seemingly indeterminate web of writing suffices as the domain of the "sacred." It is Derrida's obsession with the text as text, and not as the threshold of the numinous, that has prompted various critics to identify his style as "Rabbinic." For Derrida, the text is established with the divorce of writing from speech, which harbors the illusion of presence. Thus, the destruction of that illusion, suggests Taylor, may engender "the possibility of . . . a writing that is in not in the service of speech but 'is' nothing other than scripture" (1984: 583). How can scripture be constituted, if it be understood, as does Taylor, as a kind of unbounded textuality in which presence has wholly vanished, in which there can be discerned no longer the Lutheran *revelatum?*

Is is here that we can draw a subtle but extremely critical distinction between the Lutheran concept of faith as appropriation of the kerygmatic content and the Reformed attitude of *finitum non capax infinite* that crops up particularly in the early Barth. The early Barth with his Kierkegaardian leanings is usually not as clearly demarcated in theological overviews from the later Barth of the *Kirkliche Dogmatik* as should be the case. Especially in Barth's *Epistle to the Romans* we find operative what I shall refer to as "the hermeneutic of the infinite," which serves in lieu of the kind of Lutheran/ Bultmannian hermeneutic of the immediate, deriving straightaway from the metaphysics of presence.

The hermeneutic of the infinite is contained expressly in the notorious Barthian principle of "KRISIS" where the time-tested structures and organons of human experience are divulged as blunt fabrications, where historical life itself—which was the protological "text" for, say, Dilthey in the nineteenth century move from epistemology to the study of culture—is apprehended as having "meaning as a parable of a wholly other world" (107). It is configured in the Kierkegaardian critique of the "speculative distraction" arising from what was then the neo-Hegelian fascination with cultural transforms, a distraction that fundamentally misses "the incommensurability that subsists between an historical truth and an eternal decision" (90). It is the principle of incommensurability bodied in the *finitum non capax*, or in the Kierkegaardian disavowal of historicism, that sets the backdrop for the passage from the mere hermeneutical enterprise to a confrontation with the *totaliter aliter*. For it is the presentation of *totaliter aliter* as what Steven Smith has termed the "argument to the other," a movement of discourse away from secure rules of inference to the entertainment of the paradoxical relation, that confirms the basis of the distinction between text and scripture.

Whether we are speaking of the classic document or the entire warp of representations, glyphs and ciphers comprising Foucault's *episteme,* the text, as the proper object of interpretation which achieves its transcendent dimension at the moment Derrida designates "difference," is forever indited within a matrix of signifiers. Scripture, on the other hand, is eternally open to an entirely divergent "order" of possibilities—Kierkegaard's "infinite qualitative difference." Therefore, when Taylor suggests that the deconstruction of the theological motive, which in turn abolishes the semantics of presence, must lead to a new avowal of "scripture," he is really talking about *ecriture* (writing as Derrida's "supplementary double," as the order of appearance, as mime) rather than *scriptura* (writing as the formal composite of language that "means" other than itself).

And so in a very important sense the distance between text and scripture seems at first glance to turn on the hermeneutical choice we currently have between the post-structural enshrinement of language as self-implicated process, the game of icons, and what is really a neo-Heideggerian theory of discourse as *incarnation*. If we examine the classical meaning of *scriptura*, we find that it refers to the densification of word and text into a public *de-scription*, the metamorphosis of mere writing into the document. Furthermore, the document becomes the repository of presence that stands wholly apart from the act of writing which gave it body. The document is charged with the sense of the *aliter*. That is why "scripture" has always been gilded and illuminated by monastic scribes. Scripture is the "book," and the book is not simply the material ensemble of inscriptions; it is a veritable theophany. "Book" is etymologically connected to "beech," an "edible tree" (cf. the Greek root *phago-*). Thus the book is the tree, the symbol of life, that is ingested as a sacrament. Reading in the classical context is akin to the celebration of the "mass," the assimilation of meanings, the consumption of the god, the transfer of presence. It is clear, then, that "deconstruction," which prophesies the "end of the book," is founded upon the Hebraic passion for iconoclasm, for de-situating holiness and making it a temporal disclosure. The semantics of presence is really the ritual of the temple, trenching upon the very institution of idolatry.

But scripture also has another connotation that can be placed midway between the classical model and the Derridaean force of *ecriture*. Even as a possible variant on the classical understanding, "scripture" can be construed not as *ecriture* so much as *oeuvre*. The notion of the *oeuvre* has heavily informed the less radical proponents of a post-structural hermeneutics, particularly Ricoeur. For Ricoeur, all language, as opposed to writing alone, figures into the *oeuvre* or "work" of discourse. The *oeuvre* is what gives language its foundation, its ontology. The Ricoeurian *oeuvre* is, henceforth, the Heideggerian *poiesis*, a coming to presence through language instead of the installation of presence in the book. The *oeuvre* is a "work" insofar as it constitutes an *outworking* of the transtemporal within the rhythm of language. As with the "scriptural" dimension of the Biblical "word," it is a manifestation of the *kairos*, the "fullness," within the flux of the historical. The *oeuvre* means that the text, which enjoys its own cultural privilege and autonomy, now parlays into a set of paradoxical references, which is actually a better way of grasping Ricoeur's idea of the "surplus of meaning." And these paradoxical references—vectored on the one hand toward the syntax of common sensicality and on the other hand toward the indeterminacy of the unspoken—establish the language of the text as scripture.

For words become "scriptural," as we have argued, not because they are already canon, but because they reveal in their immediacy what cannot be enclosed, or "inscribed," as part of discourse. Derrida's "mimesis" is an incomplete account of the self-surpassing properties of language, because it obscures the semantics of paradox as well as the hermeneutics of the infinite. Displacement is not equivalent in the ontological sense to transcendence. The current "theological"—or even "a-theological" in Taylor's sense—fascination with the program of deconstruction reflects an odd sort of neo-Wittgensteinian "bewitchment" with language itself, a kabbalistic enchantment with the letter.

But this enchantment can never be hermeneutics, nor theological work, nor the general resolution of the enigmas of language, for that matter. For such a resolution hinges on the realizing of the capacity of text to become *oeuvre*, "scripture" in its non-eidetic or post-canonical form. It was Ricoeur who, in fact, gave us prior to Derrida the word "deconstruction," designating in Continental thought the transit from Husserlian phenomenology to the critique of ideology, the dismantling of self-referential systems of subjective idealism and their replacement by the philosophy of language (1974). Moreover, it is the philosophy of language that, so far as the Ricoeurian effort to make language "mean more than it says" is concerned, leaves open the possibility of scripture. As Walter Lowe argues, the Reformed principle of *finitum non capax* is lodged at "the Ricoeurian center" (29–45); and that principle is what enables religious thinking to be emancipated from all forms of academic "superstition," including the hermeticism, psychologism, sociologism, positivism, subjectivism, and even the fashionable belletrism that has haunted us since the first annunciation of "end theology." If *hermeneutics per se* is engaged in the demystification of the text, then the hermeneutics of the infinite is what holds forth the option of regarding the text as scripture. For scripture is more than "writing," even though it is writing in both an historical and phenomenal sense that has constrained the discovery of the Kierkegaardian "paradox."

The paradox, the rupture of the "eternal," can only arise at the moment that the self-certainty of consciousness is "objectified," i.e. encounters itself as alterity, in the writing, in the word as text. It was Kierkegaard's fundamental realization *contra* Hegel that the "return" of the subject to itself through the dialectical negation is possible only in the mirror of reflection, not in "existence." For it is writing that brings "spirit" into existence. That is why Kierkegaard was perhaps preoccupied with himself as an "author." Once the self-presence of the writer is annulled in the inscription, there can be no negation except through further writing. What Kierkegaard actually discerned is that Hegel's "speculative sentence" is impossible as a sentence. The act of predication as an "othering" of the subjective content belongs within the domain of logical inference, which in turn depends upon the sequential, not circular, movement of writing, i.e., the self-limiting continuum of grammar. Hence for Kierkegaard, the theological radical, even the alleged canonicity of religious texts cannot be taken seriously. "The first dialectical difficulty with the Bible," wrote Kierkegaard, "is that it is an historical document; so that as soon as we make it our standard for the determination of Christian truth, there begins an introductory approximation process, and the subject is involved in a parenthesis whose conclusion is everlastingly prospective" (38).

Derrida's "supplement" is Kierkegaard's "parenthesis." The parenthesis follows upon the vanishing of the self-presence of the author. The crucial difference between Kierkegaard and Derrida, who are both essentially anti-Hegelian, is that for the former the self-presence of the author, "alienated" eternally from the text he composes, is the touchstone of *Existenz*. In the universe of "deconstruction," however, it is the text that manifests and the author who is disclosed as having no substance. Kierkegaard's parenthesis is set off by the paradox of the relationship between time and eternity. Derrida's "grammatology" yields the supplement that cannot be viewed in contrast, because the "subject" that has been replaced is now totally effaced and forgotten. Grammatology is the world of the text which stands by itself because the portals of the infinite have all been closed up. The Kierkegaardian paradox alone allows for the confirmation of a "scriptural" valency within both the religious and literary syntax. But we must ask ourselves: does the affirmation of text as scripture, which demands faith and not interpretation *simpliciter*, put to rout the entire "theological" program of modernity, which has sought to "make sense" out of the ancient *verbum Dei?*

IV.

In point of fact, there can be no such thing at the grammatical level as "God's word." Theological hermeneutics from Justin Martyr to Bultmann has been constituted as a privileged task because of the tacit assumption that there was such a "content" to be rendered intelligible. But if we have learned anything from post-structural criticism, it is that a proper iconoclasm within the theory of language demands we discharge all claims of "content," "presence," or "subject" as phantoms of discourse. The text remains the given; "scripture" is the hermeneutical discernment that the text as a finite system of inscription is somehow charged with the infinite. But that possibility can only be seriously countenanced if we understand that the study of religious and symbolical language, whether in the Wittgensteinian, the Heideggerian, or Derridaean idiom, is not another disguised mode of metaphysics, but a propaedeutic to "faith" in the most profound and incommensurable way. And it is the assertion of faith as the only genuine ground of a transcendental semantics that explains what we have meant all along by "the end of theology."

"Faith," of course, which was Luther's *bon mot*, has a greater force than any bare psychological attitude which resists the enclosure of the infinite, whether through metaphysics, anthropological reduction, or historicist trivialities. Ricoeur, for one, has given us what amounts to a theory of metaphorical disjunction that remains inner-textual. The theory offers a new philosophy of language free of Heideggerian obscurities as well as the kind of semiotic formalism so trendy in the last decade which accounted for every linguistic datum while explaining nothing. But a theory of metaphorical disjunction is not the same as a transcendental semantics. Contrary to T. M. Van Leeuwen's provocative profile, the Ricoeurian model leaves us with an ontology, but not an *eschatology*. For it is the nature of eschatology to outstrip all "grounds" of thinking, all starting points, even language itself. Ricoeur has not, in fact, been able to step out of the Heideggerian shadow, wherein *logos* and *ontos* intermingle, where mystery torturously climbs toward utterance, where "language" is designed according to its primordial and pre-inscriptive architecture as the "house of Being." Ricoeurian semantics is Romantic linguistics that has been hybridized with the science of grammar. It is saturated with the symbology of archaic striving, the Romantic Eros, the Nietzschean sort of *Urwille* which Heidegger recognized as the drive behind all metaphysics and which he, even with his quasi-Buddhist doctrine of *Gelassenheit*, was not able to "overcome."

As Van Leeuwen says of Ricoeur, "philosophy understands faith primarily in terms of the desire to be" (187). But that is to confuse *religion* with faith. The Barthian indictment of "religion" should be read carefully again by all "theological" writers. Religion, as we have known since Comte, is actually pre-metaphysical; at a purely semantic level, it is the return of the repressed. It is the Dionysian force that impinges upon the Apollonian coherence of the text. Hence, if we are to move beyond theology to writing not as mere text/techne, but as scripture, we must transcend the Nietzschean struggle between intelligence and opacity, between form and chaos. Our intelligence must not be an apology for the occult, which is precisely why a new "philosophical theology," or even a serious Biblical methodology, must absent itself from that curious and littered archaeological deposit we call "religious studies."

Perhaps such a theology in its fascination with the forms of language, experience, and of culture could recall Barth's long-neglected reminder that all "religious" reflection must shatter against the "No" of God. For the divine negation, which Barth has expressed dogmatically and, in an unconscious fashion, metaphorically, is what we mean by the hermeneutics of the infinite. And it is the hermeneutics of the infinite that comes to power only when theology is ending, when the parable has obliterated all Pharisaic and scribal (i.e., "academic") preconceptions, when the "Kingdom of God," and not the vanished author off the text, is present amid the grief of absence.

WORKS CONSULTED

Barth, Karl
    1986   *The Epistle to the Romans.* Trans. Edwyn C. Hoskyns. London: Oxford University Press.

Derrida, Jacques
    1981   *Dissemination.* Trans. Barbara Johnson. Chicago: University of Chicago Press.

Erikson, Erik
    1962   *Young Man Luther: A Study in Psychoanalysis.* New York: W.W. Norton.

Gadamer, Hans Georg
    1982   *Truth and Method.* New York: Crossroads.

Kierkegaard, Soren
    1968   *Concluding Unscientific Postscript.* Trans. David F. Swenson. Princeton: Princeton University Press.

Lowe, Walter
    1983   "The Case of Paul Ricoeur." In *Evil and the Unconscious.* Chico, CA: Scholars Press.

Luther, Martin
    1967   *Selected Writings.* Vol. iv. Ed. Theodore Tappert. Philadelphia: Fortress Press.

Merleau-Ponty, Maurice
    1964   *Signs.* Trans. Richard C. McCleary. Evanston: Northwestern University Press.

Ricoeur, Paul
    1974   *The Conflict of Interpretation: Essays in Hermeneutics.* Evanston: Northwestern University Press.
    1981   *Hermeneutics and the Human Sciences: Essays on Language, Action, and Interpretation.* Cambridge: Cambridge University Press.

Smith, Steven
    1983   *The Argument to the Other.* Chico, CA: Scholars Press.

Taylor, Mark C.
    1982   *Deconstructing Theology.* Chico, CA: Scholars Press.
    1984   "Altizer's Originality: A Review Essay." *Journal of the American Academy of Religion* 52.

Tillich, Paul
    1973   *What is Religion?* New York: Harper & Row.

Van Leeuwen, Theodor Marius
    1981   *The Surplus of Meaning: Ontology and Eschatology in the Philosophy of Paul Ricoeur.* Amsterdam: Rodopi.

THE QUESTION OF THE BOOK
RELIGION AS TEXTURE[1]

David L. Miller
Syracuse University

ABSTRACT

Wherein lies the authority and power of a text, whether it be the text of the Bible or any text? Such is the problematic which is probed by way of a clue from J. Hillis Miller concerning the intertextuality of all texts *(influence or influenza?)*. A confusion is discovered in the linguistic fantasy resident within the history of the idea of textuality *(weaving or potting?)*, and this muddle accounts for a theological shift from the notion of religion as the texture of life and meaning to religion as the content of belief and action. A reason for the shift is sought in the fundamental ambivalence of the original root metaphor *(warp or woof?)* with the result that the Occidental tradition concerning the "religions of the book" has produced a captivating perspective *(penal colony!)* with regard to the textuality of authority and power.

Influence or Influenza?[2]

That the question of the book is crucial to the politics of meaning in our time may be obvious and unnecessary to labor. I am thinking, for example, of terrorism. It has been now not even three months since we were sorely shaken by pictures on television's evening news: terrorist shootings in the airports at Rome and Vienna, the slaughter of innocents, absurd suffering beyond human ability to mean and imagine, this being only a drop in the bloody bucket of Near and Middle Eastern "wars and wars and rumours of wars," and surely "the end is not yet"! The Holy Land is riven, ripped apart by war perpetrated by literalistic and exclusivistic religious vision: your Book (Koran) against my Book (Torah) against her and his Book (the New Testament). Which Bible is the Bible? Surely, in the case of terrorism, the Book has too much power of a wrong sort, too much influence.

But, on the other hand, the book has also had too little influence. It is not only the case that there is a somatic respiratory infection presently epidemic in our land; there is, also, an influenza of reading. The title of a book from some years ago—*Why Johnny Can't Read*—says it all. Teachers and employers everywhere complain. Those who read cannot read. It is precisely the literate who are illiterate. Those who are influenced by books are not.

Influence or influenza, too much or too little!?—either way, and both ways, there is a sickness abroad that is somehow related to the question of the book. The politics of our problem's meaning makes the issue urgent. We have got our reading somehow wrong, and it is not healthy for the body politic.

But what *is* the problem of our problem? How can we quest for the problematic question of the book?

Ludwig Wittgenstein once suggested a way. He wrote: "A picture (*ein Bild*) holds us captive, and we cannot get outside of it, for it lays in our language, and language seems to repeat it to us inexorably" (Pt. I, pp 48, 48e). Perhaps this is the problem of the question of the book. Perhaps there is resident within our notion of "text" a picture, an image, a way of imagining the authority and power of books, a perspective. And perhaps this unconscious perspective may be discovered by mining the meanings of our linguistic ways of speaking and thinking about books, by digging for the picture which lays deep within the soil of our language, by descending into the imagery which captivates our understanding all the more by our not knowing its presence or whereabouts.

Some will feel that this searching for a perspective or world-view by researching the images resident within speech is a mere playing with words and, therefore, not worth the while, even if it were possible, especially in the light of the enormity and seriousness of the problem's political and social implications. But, in response to this criticism, Martin Heidegger has asked, "is it playing with words when we attempt to give heed to the play of language and to hear what language really says when it speaks?" Heidegger reminds us: ". . . it is not we who play with words, but the nature of language plays with us, ..." (118f, 130)

The idea in this saying—that we are not in full conscious control of language's meanings, but that our meanings are unconsciously shaped by langauge's imaginal structures—is not unlike the linguistic method for locating a problem that was urged by Wittgenstein. Words have histories. Deep within the story of any given term lies an image, a picture, a root metaphor. Even though *we* may have forgotten the picture resident in the word's idea when we "use" language, it is there, nonetheless, using us as much as we it. It is as if words, like people, have an unconscious; and, like many of us, they need therapy, a sort of therapy of the word, a making conscious of language's unconscious, a discovery of the fantasies secreted in the language of texts, fantasies which serve to sicken reality as the repressed patterns of signification return in the pathology of our everyday lives and social histories.

But—as the people say—"the proof of the pudding is in the eating." What insight into the question of the book, its influence and/or influenza, may be reaped from the field of language, from a therapy of the word? "By their fruits ye shall know them," says the Bible. So what is there to chew on in our language about the book?

Potting or Weaving?

Let us take the word "text," for an example, since the French word *texte*, which has given us our English word, has typically meant, not just any text, but the Scriptures in particular. So also the Medieval Latin term, *textus*, from which the French counterpart was taken, meant precisely and specifically "the Gospel." Nor does this word "text" countermand Wittgenstein's saying, since a picture, a strong image, indeed, lays hidden in this word's history.

In the classical use, say, by Quintillian, of the Latin word which, in the Medieval period, would come to mean "Gospel," *textus* meant "style," the "tissue of a literary work." Literally, the word is a past participial form of *tex-êre*, which means "to weave." So, a "text" is "that which is woven." Like a web or a tapestry, a text has and, in linguistic fact, is a "texture." When the people wanted to name what books do, when they wished to bring to articulation their sense of the influence and influenza of writings, they said simply: Weaving! This is the people's picture informing the question of the book.

But the story of the imagination of "text" does not end here. The perhaps unconscious fantasia of the people concerning the weavings of books—their function as spinning a web of meaning, a tapestry which gives texture to life—is itself a rich textile, a fabric containing threads of surprising hues.

Texêre—the Latin root—belongs to a family of four words, one of which is also Latin. The other two are Greek. The Greek brothers in this linguistic tribe are the terms *technê* and *tektôn*. The former means "manual skill" and the latter means "carpenter." They both indicate craft, and especially a craft connected with the body, with the labor of hands: handicraft. As one could guess, these Greek roots are the ancestors of the English words "technology," "technical," "architect" and "detective." It is not difficult to sense the connection with the meaning of "text," with the question of the book. Texts provide architectures of meaning, constructions concerning life; and, those meanings, if they are to be understood, must be detected, de-constructed, just as every text not only builds upon earlier designs of significations, but also de-structs former patterns and paradigms, dis-placing them with new solutions. Texts are Frank Lloyd Wright and Sherlock Holmes.

Sister to the two Greek family members, along with *texêre*, is the Latin word *tegêre*, meaning "to cover." In addition to providing the English language with the words "tegument" and "tile"—the one being a particular kind of "woven" connection and the other being a particular kind of "covering"—these Latin sisters have had somewhat odd English off-spring.

The word "toga"—a woven covering for the body—is one example. But perhaps more astonishing is the word "toilet." *Tegêre* ("to cover") was, by a circuitous route of philological transformations, the source of the French word *toile*, a word we have in English, meaning "linen" or "canvas," a woven fabric often used as a covering. The pristine meaning of *toile* seems to have referred to a large cloth, probably of rough texture, with ropes woven into the edges. The use of the French term went in two directions.

On the one hand, *toile* (English: "toil") indicated snares or nets fashioned from loosely woven materials with ropes attached. Later, it was the building in which such snares or traps were kept. And, still later, it was the work one does with these nets in these buildings (i.e., "toil").

On the other hand, the French word came to refer to the canvas cloth with ropes attached into which one could put clothes, like a suitcase or garment-bag. Similarly, it meant the robe one wore, with small rope-ties, while the hair was being cut or fashioned. Finally, *toile* meant the cloth-cover on the dressing table in the room where hair was fahioned and, at last, it was that table itself (i.e., the *toilette*). To be sure, in American English, "toilet" refers to another piece of equipment in the same room.

Although language's imagination has, in this instance, strange weavings, the connection with a sense for "text," the question of the book, can hardly be missed. Books and their meanings cover our nakedness like a Roman toga, civilizing our lives while covering our flaws and shame. Books, too, have been snares and traps for many nations and peoples, causing terrible toil and trouble, wounding labor. Perhaps we could even say, with not a little feeling, that books, like toilets, have often been containers for poisonous by-products, reservoirs of meanings which contaminate, like septic tanks filled to overflowing, fouling the ecology of life and mind. Too many books with too much influence, carrying contagious disease, as epidemic as influenza.

It is a far cry, one might have thought (and you may now be thinking!), from a finely woven tapestry to a stopped-up toilet. But that is just the point about "texts," the point shown in the history of language. The family of words to which our word "text" is related does *not* include, as is sometimes thought, the word *testa*, which is Latin for "earthen vessel" or "ceramic pot," and is related to other terms such as *testâceus* ("shell covered," like a crab) and *testûdo* ("tortoise shell"). It is all the more strange, then, that in the history of the people's imagination tapestries were hardened into toilets, into ceramic pots. But perhaps it is most noteworthy of all that this change took place in America!

The Bible: Seamless Garment or Earthen Vessel?

What's the point? The point is that there is a powerful picture in our language, a mighty perspective concerning the function of the written word, concerning texts and textuality, and, to be sure, not excluding the text of the Bible. In this perspective, texts are like weavings and are not like pottings. The power of a text, including the Biblical one, would be in the pattern of its fabric, as in a tapestry, a design which can shape a life meaningfully and one in which a person or a people can be trapped, as in a web or net. In the case of a religious text, this perspective implies that religiosity is in the texture.

The view of potters and potting is different. From the perspective of this image, texts would be containers or vessels, carrying fixed meanings within their walls, centered and secure, as on a potter's wheel. Texts—on this view—have their power in their content, in what they contain. So in the case of a religious text, the meaning is in what one does or what one believes, rather than in the texture of all doings and all contents of belief.

The importance of this distinction is seen and even felt when one remembers that the religions of the West, unlike the religions of the East, are all, as has often been said, "religions of the book." Judaism, Christianity, and Islam share this fantasy: namely, that the revelation of the divine, the highest and deepest meaning of life, is shown in a book. Torah, New Testament, and Koran: a text is the locus of ultimate reality and signification. If each of these texts is viewed, against the grain of the people's deepest unconscious intuition, as a vessel, a container holding the ultimate truth in its content, then it would seem inevitable that, at some point during the course of history, one of these fixed meanings would come violently into conflict with the others, and precisely to the degree that the believers who held the potting-perspective were passionate and faithful. The other possibility, of course, is that the book would have lost its influence altogether, not because the text was not powerful, but because the perspective required fixated constructions of the book's meaning which ultimately put people into conflicts, conflicts within the self, which never stands still, and conflicts with others, whose own text is not esteemed.

Or the matter could be put the other way about. When people and nations are at war over differing versions of truth believed in passionately, and when the locus of this truth is a text, the chances are that the conscious hermeneutical perspective which is in operation, against the unconscious instinct in the piety of the people's language, is that a text is a pot and not a tapestry. This is, of course, the case with Iranian or Palestinian terrorists, with Zionist fanatics, and with Christians who hold to a notion of Verbal Plenary Inspiration. Alan Watts once called this perspective "cracked pot." (11 and *passim*) probably because of its dangerous implications for the frail psyche of our fractured world.

It is not that the potting-perspective reads the Biblical text literally and a weaving-perspective reads it non-literally. The opposite is the case. A major problem with the viewpoint of so-called Fundamentalism and so-called Biblical Literalism, whether in Judaism, Christianity, or Islam—besides the fact that it is dangerous to the psyche and to the body politic—is that it is neither fundamental nor literal at all. When "text" is taken seriously, fundamentally, in its deepest and highest literal sense, it is, not potting, but weaving, not vessel or container, but texture and fabric. Biblical Literalists, who go by that name, whether in the Near East or in America, are not being literal at all. As Michael Fishbane has noted about the Bible, it is "text and texture" (xi-xii). Indeed, the Bible itself is not very sanguine about the potting metaphor and its perspective. The Psalmist is speaking about wicked persons when he says that God shall "dash them in pieces like a potter's vessel" (Psalm 2.9).

The vessel-perspective is cracked. The Bible contains nothing; it opens out. I am speaking about any Bible, the religious texts of all nations and peoples. It is all one rich fabric, with multifaceted patterns, shades, colorings, all weaving meanings endlessly through the life of text and through the texture of life, a thousand threads of significance, each important to the tapestry, none insignificant, all crucial to the whole picture. It is a powerful picture, this picture of the book.

Warped or Woofed?

If it is so perduring, so powerful, so present in the imagination of the language of the people, then how did we lose it?—this generous sense of text and religion, this sense which does not set us over against ourselves and others. Why did it have to go underground, into the unconscious of persons and language? What functioned to repress it? How is it that in our history sacred text has turned to terrorism and, at the same time, to a waning of the power of reading and writing? To use the figures we have been mining: How is it that tapestry has turned to toilet?

Perhaps it is because texts in fact spin two very different sorts of webs. Post-structuralist literary theorists have pointed to two sorts of weavings, a fundamental ambivalence in the function of texts. I should like to refer to this duplicity as the warp and the woof of the working of a textual fabric, and I should like, briefly, to call witnesses to both strands.

First, the woof. This is the good news! and a principle witness is

Roland Barthes. In a book entitled, *Image Music Text*, Barthes speaks of the "pleasure of a text"—its rich plural meanings, its complex self referential nature, the intertextuality in all texts, the very linguisticality of life and meaning—and he speaks of this utilizing the French word *jouissance* to bespeak the "pleasure" he intends. Julia Kristeva has explained this archaic French word by telling her readers that it refers to bodily pleasure, indeed, to sexual pleasure, this powerful pleasure of the reading experience, an experience that Kristeva calls "the desire of language," the erotics of writing. But, Kristeva insists, the sexual pleasure is of a particular sort: namely, that experienced by a woman. It is not pointed, focused, and once-for-all; rather, it is diffuse, undulating, and waving (see index entry for "jouissance" in Kristeva). So Barthes writes of this *jouissance* which both women and men experience with texts: "The Text is not a co-existence of meanings, but a passage, an overcrossing: . . . it answers not to an interpretation, not even to a liberal one, but to an explosion, a dissemination. The plural of the Text depends . . . not on the ambiguity of its contents, but on what might be called the *stereographic plurality* of its weave of signifiers. . . ." And then, having invoked language's fundamental figure, he explains: ". . . (etymologically, the text is a tissue, a woven fabric)." Whereupon Barthes notes in conclusion: "The reader of a Text may be compared to someone at a loose end" (159–64).

This notion of the endless "weave of signifiers" is reminiscent of a famous text from *A Midsummer Night's Dream*. "I have had a most rare vision," Shaespeare wrote. "I have had a dream, past the wit of man to say what dream it was. Man is but an ass if he go about to expound this dream. . . . The eye of man hath not heard, the ear of man hath not seen, man's hand is not able to taste, his tongue to conceive, nor his heart to report what my dream was. . . . It shall be call'd Bottom's Dream, because it hath no bottom." (IV, ii, 204ff) You will remember that Bottom, who really was a Weaver, had indeed become an ass, trying to confine meanings.

In addition to Barthes and Shakespeare, there is testimony from the side of contemporary theology. Charles Winquist has written a veritable paean to the sensual power of a text. His essay is called, "Body, Text, Imagination," and in it he invokes the textile metaphor, saying: "The materiality of fabric of the text is a sensuous weave precisely because it is never what it appears to be. It never contains itself" (41). But because it holds no-thing in it, a text can open everything outward. As Edmond Jabès has said: "The world exists because the book exists. . . . The book is the work of the book. . . . The book multiplies the book. . . . If God is, it is because he is a book" *(passim)*. This, so to say, is the woof.

There is also a warp, at least according to contemporary literary theorists. This is the bad news! and the first witness is responding directly to the saying, just cited, from the work of Jabès. It is Jacques Derrida who is speaking. ". . .the act of faith in the book," he admits to Jabès, "can precede, as we know, belief in the Bible. And can also survive it." But Derrida wants to ask a more fundamental question. He wants to know from where Jabès obtains his "unpenetrated certainty that Being is a Grammar . . . that the book is original, that everything belongs to the book before being . . . that anything can be born only by approaching the book, can die only by failing in sight of the book, and that always (there is an) impassible shore of the book being first." Surely this is implied by the view of the Bible in Judaism. Christianity, and Islam—as much as it is in the writings of Jabès. In the beginning is the Word, the Word of God, the Bible, the Book. But Derrida wonders and he writes: "But what if the Book was only, in all senses of the word, an epoch of Being, an epoch coming to an end . . . dead book (76f). To be sure, Marshall McLuhan had wondered the same thing many years before Derrida: namely, whether or not the medium of print technology, the Gutenburg Galaxy, was finished, being replaced by visual and aural media of human meaning, words replaced by images.

If indeed a book can no longer function to provide people with ultimate meanings, it may be a result, not of a failure of the weavings of text, but precisely because of their success, their excess. At least this is a possibility implied in the writings of Geoffrey Hartman. Indicating the same plursignification that Roland Barthes took to be the pleasure, the *jouissance,* of a text, Hartman notes the shadow-side: namely, that a text is constituted of ". . .a wilderness of passages that seem at first to lead nowhere except further into the bush (*Buch,* book, textuality)." Hartman then amplifies the "wilderness" of a text's multiple meanings by way of the metaphor of weaving, citing Coleridge, who lamented to his journal: "O Lord! What thousands of threads in how large a web may not a Metaphysical Spider spin out of the Dirt of his own Guts, but alas! it is a net for his own super-ingenious Spidership alone!" Hartman's concluding sentence is laced with a grim allusion. He writes: "A pointless pattern speaks to us, yet it may be Philomela's speaking picture, her 'voice of the shuttle'" (3–4, 156).

Philomela—in Greek mythology—was the daughter of the King of Athens. Her sister, Procne, was married to Tereus, who lusted for his wife's sister, and, finally, raped her. In order that the truth never be known, Tereus cut out Philomela's tongue and hid her in a dungeon. But, in order to get revenge, she requested from the serving-girl a needle and some yarn, with which she wove a tapestry whose picture told this story, a tragic fabric which she sent, by way of the servant, to her sister. Filled with grief, the women cut up Tereus' son, and fed the pieces to the father in his food. For their sin, their impiety, the gods transformed Philomela and Procne into song-birds in flight, into a nightingale and a swallow. The words are ended, tapestry finished. Only the music goes on, but, like the songs of the nightingale and swallow, it is sad.

Hartman's mythical allusion is telling, and its message is not unlike a third witness, after Derrida and Hartman, to the warp of a text's weave. Octavio Paz has also, like these others, spoken of the hermeneutic difficulty of a well-woven text. In reading, he writes, "it is necessary to unweave . . . even the simplest phrases in order to determine what they contain . . . Unweave the verbal fabric: reality will appear . . . (But) can reality be the reverse of the fabric? Language has no reverse. . . . Perhaps reality too is a metaphor." So, if reading is an unweaving of the weaving that constitutes a text, the reading is at the same time a new weaving of meanings, a texturing of a world. Paz speaks poetically of the puzzling experience of reading, where weaving is unweaving and where all is text. He writes: "Stains: thickets, blurs. Blots held prisoner by lines, the liane of the letters. . . ." (19, 35). With powerful texts, the reader is not in the clear, in the clearing; she or he is, rather, in the thicket, in the thick of it. So, Mark Taylor can entitle a recent theological essay, "Text as Victim," this title implying, not only something about what people do to texts as they attempt to unweave them in interpretation, but also what texts do to people, victimizing minds and hearts, taking prisoner with words and meanings, sentencing innocents by their sentences, unweaving a conventional world by weaving complex textures.

Such warp of text, shunted through textual woof, shows the question of the book. It shows why tapestry has turned to toilet, why the perspective of weaving is abandoned for one of potting.

There is ambivalence in the power of text: the pleasure of freedom, *and* the imprisonment in one's own anxiety in being unable to locate a single certain meaning; *jouissance* felt with passion throughout one's being, *and* lost in the wilderness; tegument, *and* toil; a linen cover for human nakedness, flaw, and shame, *and* a canvas net which ensnares our liberty; an architecture of signification, *and* a puzzle for the detective who risks the life and limb of sense; rich texture, *and* artificial technology. A text is all of these at once, and always.

No wonder the world has looked for containers, chamber pots, armour—like protective shells that crabs and turtles hide behind. No wonder the encrusted meanings of dogmatisms, of ideologies, and of fanaticisms have been bought wholesale at the high price of the very fabric of human generosity and the eros of meaning. It is, to be sure, understandable that a person or a people might trade a seamless garment for an earthen vessel, even without knowing this perspectival barter has happened. But what is difficult to grasp, perplexing in the extreme, and hardly healthy for our world, is why earthen vessels are then mistaken for golden bowls? why my book, with my construction of its meaning, is paraded, in military-style, infallible, over against the books of others? why human systems of meaning are granted divine status? Philosophers call this a category mistake. Theology calls it idolatry and sin. Psychologically and personally, sociologically and politically, cosmologically and ecologically, we can die from this pathology of perspective. Images can be hazardous to our health.

A Parable of the Book

It reminds me of a story, a story by Frank Kafka, a short story called, "The Penal Colony."[3]

An explorer—not unlike each one of us—is embarked on an adventure, but an adventure whose extent he cannot imagine at the beginning. He is visiting an island which is a penal colony whose inhabitants, those imprisoned here, do not know their sentences. They do not know of what they are accused. Yet in every case, as the story tells it, "guilt is never to be doubted."

This situation is, of course, remarkable enough, but even more shocking is the apparatus, the piece of technology, which had been assembled in this colony for the purpose of executing the sentences which were unknown to the accused. The machine was the special pride of the officer of the law, and he was eager to demonstrate its amazing function to the explorer, who was considerably reticent about learning, as well he might have been.

The apparatus had three parts. The lower part was called the "bed." It was where the prisoner lay to be executed. The upper part was called the "designer." It was from here that the whole working of the apparatus was governed, controlled, set in motion, determined, and ordered. Between the subject, recumbant on the couch of death, and the designer was the third part, called "the harrow." It was the function of the harrow to communicate the sentence to the victim, the sentence which would be the victim's end.

The harrow was constructed of many needles, with ducts of water accompanying each. These needles, controlled from the designer, would etch the sentence upon the body of the victim, with the water washing away the blood, and with the bed turning the body over and over, so that the weaving of the writing would cover the entire body. As the text puts it: "You have seen how difficult it is to decipher the script with one's eyes; but our man deciphers it with his wounds."

The explorer was as horrified at the sight of this inhumane apparatus as we are in hearing the story of the experience. All the more is this the case when we learn that the process goes on, writing deeper and deeper into the body, for twelve hours! Nor are we or the explorer convinced by the officer of the law who tells that in every case, after the sixth hour, that is, after the initial wounding impression, a peculiar radiance of enlightenment settles over the face of the one who is actually being tortured. And, in fact, in the explorer's experience, when the officer of the law had at last himself become victim of his own victimization, suffering the technology that he had imposed upon others, there was no sign visible, in the sixth hour, or in any hour, of "the promised redemption." What others had formerly experienced with this technique, now no longer seemed to work.

Perhaps this was because "the designer was badly worn." "It creaks a lot when working." The cogwheels no longer mesh properly. And yet, in spite of the horror, and in spite of the failure of the designer, as the text puts it, "the machine is still working and it is still effective in itself." . . . a terrible tale, a horrifying story!

But perhaps it is a parable of the problem of text in our time. People suffer the sentences of the book in their flesh. Women and men—harrowed like hell by the book—die from it, with no redemption in sight. The text, like the harrow, situated between God and mortals, supposedly bringing the divine message of the former to the latter, has become disconnected from the designer's control, and it continues to work its deadly work as if by habit, so that what formerly seemed a redemption has become a ghastly parody of crucifixing experience.

Do we live in a penal colony of text? imprisoned by books and our notions of them? suffering books in our bodies, the very body of our person and in the body-politic, yet having no sense of the wound?

However difficult the question of the book, however terrible the images and thoughts, it is crucial that we face them brutally. Our souls and bodies, our very world and the future of our world, are at stake. And, after all, is Kafka's story of "The Penal Colony" worse than the tales told on TV's news? Life is imitating art. The text has us in its grip. We are read by it.

NOTES

[1] This essay was originally given as The Loy H. Witherspoon Lecture in Religious Studies at the University of North Carolina, Charlotte, March 2, 1986.

[2] These terms used in connection with the problem of textual authority are taken from J. Hillis Miller, *The Linguistic Moment* (Princeton: Princeton University Press, 1985), pp. 57ff.

[3] I am indebted to Wolfgang Giegerich for bringing this story to my attention. His remarkable use of it is forthcoming in the following volume: *Eranos Jahrbuch 54 -1985* (Frankfurt: Insel Verlag, 1986?). See: Franz Kafka, *The Complete Stories*, ed. N. Glatzer (New York: Schocken Books, 1971), pp. 140–67.

WORKS CONSULTED

Barthes, Roland
    1977   *Image Music Text.* Trans. S. Heath. New York: Hill & Wang.

Derrida, Jacques
    1978   *Writing and Difference.* Trans. A. Bass. Chicago: University of Chicago Press.

Fishbane, Michael
    1979   *Text and Texture.* New York: Schocken Books.

Hartman, Geoffery
    1971   *Saving the Text.* Baltimore: Johns Hopkins University Press.

Heidegger, Martin
    1968   *What is Called Thinking?* Trans. F. D. Wieck and J. Glenn Gray. New York: Harper & Row.

Jabès, Edmond
    1976   *The Book of Questions.* Trans. R. Waldrop. Middletown: Wesleyan University Press.

Kristeva, Julia
    1980   *Desire in Language.* Trans. T. Gora, A. Jardine and L. Roudiez. New York: Columbia University Press.

Paz, Octavio
    1981   *The Monkey Grammarian.* Trans. H. R. Lane. New York: Seaver Books.

Taylor, Mark
    1982   "Text as Victim." In *Deconstruction and Theology.* New York: Crossroads.

Watts, Alan
    1970   "Western Mythology: Its Dissolution and Transformation." In *Myths, Dreams, and Religion.* Ed. J. Campbell. New York: E.P. Dutton.

Winquist, Charles
    1982   "Body, Text, Imagination." In *Deconstruction and Theology.* New York: Crossroads.

Wittgenstein, Ludwig
    1958   *Philosophical Investigations.* Oxford: Basil Blackwell.

FAILING SPEECH: POST-HOLOCAUST WRITING AND THE DISCOURSE OF POSTMODERNISM

Susan E. Shapiro
Syracuse University

ABSTRACT

Both post-Holocaust and postmodern writing share a preoccupation with the limits of representational discourse and employ many of the same figures of speech in order to inscribe these limits, this failure of speech. This paper asks if these two modes of discourse should be read as one, and if not, what other clues besides that of textuality might a reader follow in distinguishing them. What are the implications of the answers to these questions for understanding writings about the Holocaust, the critical function of the discourse of postmodernism, and the role of textuality in interpretation? These questions are raised with special reference to the writings of Paul Celan, Nelly Sachs, and Edmond Jabès.

"The Holocaust as Literary Inspiration" is a contradiction in terms. As in everything else, Auschwitz negates all systems, destroys all doctrines. They cannot but impoverish the experience which lies beyond our reach. . . . [How write about the event?] A matter of words. What kind of words? That, too, became a difficulty the writer had to solve and overcome. Language had been corrupted to the point that it had to be invented anew and purified. This time we wrote not with words but against words. Often we told less so as to make the truth more credible. Had any one of us told the whole story, he would have been proclaimed mad. Once upon a time the novelist and the poet were in advance of their readers. Not now. Once upon a time the artist could foresee the future. Not now. Now he has to remember the past, knowing all the while that what he has to say will never be told.

Acknowledgements: My thanks to Farrar, Strauss, and Giroux for permission to reprint and quote from the poems of Nelly Sachs' *The Seeker and Other Poems*, translated by Ruth and Michael Meed and Michael Hamburber and to Persea Books for permission to reprint and quote from the poems of *Paul Celan: Poems*, edited and translated by Michael Hamburger.

> What he hopes to transmit can never be transmitted. All he can possibly hope to achieve is to communicate the impossibility of communication (Wiesel, 1977: 7–8).

The failure of language to grasp or articulate the event is a recurrent topic in post-Holocaust writing. It is a problematic that cuts across genres. In some, especially poetry, the difficulty of speaking and the impossibility of communication are not only subjects; these failures permeate their very textuality. Muteness, silence and broken speech have not only become themes and motifs of post-Holocaust writing; the writing itself is made mute, silenced, broken. For how does one give testimony to an event that negates the very assumptions of discourse that make possible such telling? How can one tell about an event that shatters our assumptions about order (including social relations, conceptions of God, understandings of tradition, history and time) in discourse, the primary function of which is the ordering of human experience? This is one of the primary hermeneutical antinomies confronting those who write about, or in recognition of, the Holocaust[1]. Failing to testify to the event, however, is to condemn it to historical forgetfulness. The imperative to testify, thus, further intensifies this antinomy. Writing about the Holocaust becomes at once both impossible and necessary. One strategy of writing in recognition of, as well as despite this antinomy, is through its negative "constitution" of textuality. If all post-Holocaust writers "can possibly hope to achieve is to communicate the impossibility of communication," their testimony is ironically made possible through their inscription of this very failure in discourse[2].

In this paper, I will selectively consider the writings of Paul Celan, Nelly Sachs and Edmond Jabès with respect to their failing speech as itself testimony to the Holocaust, its character and effects. In configuring the limits of representational discourse, these writings differently exemplify the problematics of post-Holocaust writing and the preoccupations of postmodernism[3]. The central question of this paper is how we might read together post-Holocaust and postmodern writings, which seem to share not only many of the same suspicions about the limits of discourse, but whose very textuality appear to be similarly ruptured. Does this character of their textuality betray a common subject? Are post-Holocaust writing and the discourse of postmodernism to be identified? What are the implications of the answers to these questions for our understanding of the place of textuality in interpretation?

In the compass of this paper, my consideration in these terms of the poetry of Celan and Sachs is necessarily brief. I emphasize the confluence of, not the difference between their writings, so as to consider them in terms of the broader concerns of this paper. I then turn to a, necessarily, selective consideration of the writings of Jabes. I emphasize several themes that help locate the intersection of the Holocaust and postmodernism in his writings. The questions of how textuality functions as testimony and in interpretation are raised with respect both to post-Holocaust and postmodern discourses.

*

The poetry of Celan and Sachs are extreme cases of discourses whose failure is an "integral part of [their] testimony." As such, they offer insights that illumine, but in no way exhaust the problematics of post-Holocaust writing. Indeed, a privileging of one kind of writing will necessarily distort, not enlighten, understanding of the event and its effects. For the purposes of understanding the ways in which speech was silenced and language mutilated by the event, however, Celan's and Sachs' failures are exemplary.

For Celan, speaking is not only difficult. In different ways, and for a variety of reasons, it is dangerous.

> If one of these stones
> were to give away
> what it is that keeps silent about it:
> here, nearby,
> at this old man's limping stick,
> it would open up, as a wound,
> in which you would have to submerge,
> lonely,
> far from my scream, that is
> chiselled already, white.
>
> —"At Brancusi's, the Two of Us" (1980:239)

Stones appear often in Celan's writings, like other elemental forms such as ice and crystals, as essentialized experiences or meanings. Having been chiseled to their core, they hold a fragile, yet explosive possibility of communication and connection. The stones in this poem would wound if they spoke; indeed, one would then be submerged *within* the wound, alone, without recourse. This is a terrible possibility, even more because of the elemental tangibility of stones. By placing this wound not only in language, but "here, nearby," in our commonplace world (even though these stones, in particular, compose a sculpture), Celan embeds history and memory in nature, within the earth itself. Even if these stones "keep silent," they are a part of our landscape, and we may stumble upon them at any time. The world itself contains this testimony, enduring mutely, with dangerous and—as evidenced by some of his other poems in which, e.g., earthly stone turns to star—healing potencies.

Another danger of speech is that it may include too much and be too explicit, thus compromising that which is spoken.

> What times are these
> when a conversation
> is almost a crime
> because it includes
> so much made explicit?
>
> —"A Leaf" (Celan, 1980:287)

What times are these? There is a certain irony here that the verse barely contains. For what, during the Holocaust, would be the crime of a conversation as compared to the deeds of Nazis? Within and for the Nazi world, such conversation could only, perversely, be a crime as it unmasked *their* crimes. What times, then, are these? These are times after the event. For after the Holocaust, the crime of conversation is that it masks by telling so much. The Holocaust cannot be told, it seems, by being made explicit.

Language can be made more trustworthy by two opposing, but the complementary poetic acts. It can be etched or chiseled in order to cut away the inessential.

> Etched away from
> the ray-shot wind of your language
> the garish talk of rubbed-
> off experience—the hundred-
> tongued pseudo-
> poem, the noem.
>
> Whirled
> clear,
> free
> your way through the human-
> shaped snow,
> the penitents' snow, to
> the hospitable
> glacier rooms and tables.
>
> Deep in Time's crevasse
> by the alveolate ice
> waits, a crystal of breath,
> your irreversible
> witness.
>
> —"Etched Away" (Celan, 1980:189)

This austere, bleak aesthetic thus carves out an essential, elemental witness.

If cutting away rids speech of its excess, then a second poetic act, that of "speaking the shade," makes discourse more true by rendering it less explicit.

> Speak, you also,
> speak as the last,
> have your say.
>
> Speak—
> But keep yes and no unsplit.
> And give your say this meaning:
> give it the shade.
>
> Give it shade enough,
> give it as much
> as you know has been dealt out between
> midnight and midday and midnight.
>
> Look around:
> look how it all leaps alive—
> where death is! Alive!
> He speaks truly who speaks the shade.
>
> —"Speak, You Also" (Celan; 1980:85)

It is garrish talk that fails to "keep yes and no unsplit," in a vision that is blind to what "has been dealt out between/midnight and midday and midnight." Only in shade can the Holocaust be truly told. This shaded discourse is both ambiguous, in keeping yes and no unsplit, and shielded from the glare of explicit (split) speech. This shaded aesthetic absorbs dark meanings and protects them from overexposure. The poem continues with an even greater asceticism, however, as there are other dangers that arise from such unsplit speech. It is now necessary to further strip away discourse, combining in one poesis the two acts of cutting away excess and shading speech.

> But now shrinks the place where you stand:
> Where now, stripped by shade, will you go?
> Upward. Grope your way up.
> Thinner you grow, less knowable, finer.
> Finer: a thread by which
> it wants to be lowered, the star:
> to float farther down, down below
> where it sees itself flitter: on sand dunes
> of wandering words.
>
> —"Speak, You Also" (Celan, 1980: 85)

For Celan, it is impossible to rest in the moment of speaking truly. For even as the shade shows "how it all leaps alive—/ where death is!," it strips and tears away at speech itself. Celan's capacity for speech, thus, expands and contracts at the same time. Words grow in nuance; they are thickened with their shade. But the place where the poet stands, the vocabulary or topoi of his discourse, shrinks. Shading, then, is yet another way of trimming away the excess. But the dangers of this excision are that it cuts the very ground out from under the poet's feet. With this loss of "commonplaces," speech becomes both "less knowable" and "finer." It becomes even more symbolic, risking hermeticism and silence[4].

Ascent is necessary. Although precarious, upward is the only direction in which speech may continue. With nowhere left to stand, this ascent is no rapture, but a suspended groping over an abyss. And the holding thread grows increasingly thin.

As the grasped thread turns fine, however, it pulls the poet upward. There is a breathless turning point in the poem, around the word "finer," that demonstrates the successful ascent of the poet. Between the lines "Thinner you grow, less knowable, finer" and "Finer: a thread by which/it wants to be lowered, the star," the direction of the poem changes from ascent to descent. The perspective has shifted from the poet's dangerous groping heavenward to a star's gentle floating earthward. As the poet ascends by making his speech finer, so the star is lowered by a fine thread. In this "less knowable" and "finer" poesis, not only is speaking made true, but a reconnection—however tenuous or fleeting—is effected between heaven and earth, "star" and "sand."

In "Speak, You Also," Celan seems uncharacteristically hopeful (a relative term in this context). The last set of phrases in the final stanza of the poem, however, may be read more as a wish or a reverie than as an assertion or prediction of things accomplishable. Like the thread—language that becomes finer and less knowable in its ascent—this last set of phrases is nearly hermetic. Once the "you" in the poem becomes "star," the tone shifts from exhortation to musing, a more passive and imaginative observing. This is a tenuous (fine), even gracious moment, following upon stanzas of struggle and dangerous speaking. Speech finally ends and turns to sight. The turn from the tongue to the eye, from discourse to perception, is a motif that appears throughout Celan's poetry, although not usually as delicately.

Most of Celan's poems on this theme of speaking truly, however, do not end up with such connections between heaven and earth, although they often begin and/or end with a floating upward, suspended in the air. For the air is where the dead are and where testimony may, thus, best be given.

> To stand in the shadow
> of the scar up in the air.

> To stand-for-no-one-and-nothing.
> Unrecognized,
> for you,
> alone.
>
> With all there is room for in that,
> even without
> language.
>
> "To Stand" (1980:181)

This standing before and for the sake of the dead is a giving of a testimony that does not require—and may not even permit—language. For to stand in their place—the air—is a way of standing for, and testifying in behalf of, the dead. Two elements from this testimony become central to both Celan's and Sachs' poesies: silence and air. The air, the place of the dead, fills our lungs and makes it impossible to speak or breathe. The suffocation of breath in a poetics of expiration is constitutive of Celan's and Sachs' testimony to the dead. The failure of speech and the expiration of breath are two related and recurrent aspects of the textuality of their poems[5]. For how does one tell about an event that permeates our very speaking and breathing? Speech is stifled and breath is suffocated by that which these poets breathe in and seek to tell. And this expiration, their silenced, broken, choked-off speech, is their very testimony.

> How you die out in me:
>
> down to the last
> worn-out
> knot of breath
> you're there, with a
> splinter
> of life.
>
> —"How You" (Celan, 1980:247)

The motif of the testimony of exhaled breath is echoed in Sachs' poetry when she writes, e.g., "And what is released from the open wound of your breath!" (231) Although Celan's and Sachs' responses to this exclamation may differ, they share the sense that what is released from his breath and exhaled is death—expiration. As in the poem, "How You," the deaths of the victims of the Holocaust are brought to speech in the passing away of the poet's breath. As Alvin Rosenfeld remarks, "There is a terrifying mimesis at work in [Celan's] poems, so much so that as we read them we are almost forced to descend several degrees on the scale of animated being—to lessen our pulses, lower our rate of breathing, generally reduce our vital signs" (87). The readers of these poems, like the poet, mimetically recall this dying. As the exhalation of breath in the poem is mimetic of those who died in the Holocaust, so is the reader's lowered rate of breathing a repetition of the expiration in and of the poem. The effects of the Holocaust are communicated through this negative poesis, this "turning of breath."

The poetics of expiration runs counter to that of inspiration (Rosenfeld: 84–92). If inspiration (breathing-in) has been understood as the vital force animating, "inspiring" poetry, then the post-Holocaust poetry of Celan and Sachs is negative not only in its subject, but in its very poetic. In *Genesis*, God's *Ruach* (breath, wind, spirit, soul) brings to life human being from dust. The "dust" of the Holocaust, however, testifies to the dying-out, the expiration, of this breath. This counter-poesis is also a negative God-language. Sachs' poem, "Rescued," may be read in these terms.

> Rescued
> much falls
> into the baskets of memories
> for
> this night-age also
> will have its fossils
> the black-bordered mourning scripts
> of its crookedly grown dust.
>
> Perhaps
> our posthumous skies
> these pale blue stones
> will also
> practice healing magic
> laid down in other hells
>
> your dying words
> in the wind of woe
> in the cold team
> of the stretching limbs
> will
> breathe through ages
> and
> shape like a glassblower
> a banished form of love
>
> for the mouth of God—(279)

Although this poem is filled with a longing for rescue, for a "healing magic," the distance Sachs must go to even imagine such a fragile possibility demonstrates the magnitude of the wound suffered. She imagines, in this poem, a kind of *creatio ex nihilo*. It is by "your dying words" (God's? human being's?), from the breath of the dead, that a vessel may be shaped for the reanimating *Ruach* of God. However, this longing intensifies rather than diminishes our sense of the distance, the hiddenness, even the absence of God.

In another poem by Sachs, "Chorus of the Dead," we find further testimony against both a poetics and a theology of inspiration. Like Celan's "To Stand," it is written in the "voice" and for the sake of the dead.

> We from the black sun of fear
> Holed like sieves—
> We dripped from the sweat of death's minute.
> Withered on our bodies are the deaths done to us
> Like flowers of the field withered on a hill of sand.
> O you who still greet the dust as friend
> You who talking sand say to the sand:
> I live you.
>
> We say to you:
> Torn are the cloaks of the mysteries of dust
> The air in which we were suffocated,
> The fires in which we were burned,
> The earth into which our remains were cast.
> The water which was beaded with our sweat of fear
> We dead of Israel say to you:
> We are moving past one more star
> Into our hidden God. (51)

The second verse speaks against the first. "[Y]ou who still greet the dust as friend," must hear the testimony of the dead. The "cloaks of the mysteries of dust" are torn, the poetics and theology of inspiration have been suffocated, burned, and turned to dust in the gas chambers and ovens of the Holocaust. As in "Rescued," however, it is through the speaking of the dead, through a poetics of expiration, that a movement "into our hidden God" is imagined. Again, as in "Rescued," this startling and moving act of faith is not made without ambiguity. For in both Celan's and Sachs' poetry, this traveling further "Into our hidden God," like the pull beyond speech into silence, is difficult to distinguish from a return to darkness and death. It is nearly impossible to exclude from our reading of Celan's and Sachs' works, the denoument toward speechlessness in a number of their poems, and the endings toward which their lives were drawn, in suicide and madness. Their speech was, finally, weighted down and suffocated by that which it carried. This loss of words and of breath testifies to the failure of recovery. For as their displacement left them only language in which to "live," the waning of speech meant, it *was*, expiration.

The poetry of Celan and Sachs, thus, fails and expires as "an integral part of [their] testimony." In this failure, they are exemplary of a strain within post-Holocaust writing. The failure of discourse to represent, however, is a problematic not limited to such writing. It is a topos, as well, within what has most recently been termed "the discourse of postmodernism." In order to examine the relationship—i.e., the similarities and differences—between these two self-consciously failed discourses, I will consider the works of Edmond Jabès, whose writings have been designated as both post-Holocaust and postmodern.[6]

*

Jabès' *The Book of Questions* may be read in relation to the writings of Celan and Sachs. Like these poets, Jabès, displaced from land and country, dwells within and becomes language.

> This morning, words loot the flowers, and sentences crawl in the mud like worms. Nothing takes shape or form outside the word.
> The butterfly is entrusted with the name of the flower, the worm with that of the stem or trunk.
> I am butterfly and worm.
> This morning, nothing takes shape or form outside me.
> I am furrow and word. I am land, expressed.
>
>> ("More than a land, we need a language in common, our language, that of our ancestors, for our sons to propagate. It will return to them the loaded dice of their destiny."
>> —Reb Shames) (1976: 171–2)

For Jabès, the Holocaust is the most recent and dramatic sign of this displacement into language, of the separation of word from thing. He writes a story of the Holocaust that is broken-up and dispersed throughout the book, a story that is never whole, but given only in fragments. This fragmented story, especially those passages clearly alluding to the Holocaust, form a relatively small portion of the book. The following passage is one of the most direct allusions to the Holocaust in the text.

> When he thinks of his parents, they appear from the other bank. Between them, the red river which has carried so much mud; between them, all the mud the blood has carried. . . .
> He was cheated out of his parent's death. They were born for him—they died without him, perhaps for him. They died among their fellows, and their last glance was, no doubt, also for him.
> . . . Their relation began with "Yukel, come here. Don't do that, Yukel." (His earliest memories.) And it ended, one morning, with "We have to separate, Yukel. It's better to be prudent." (His last memory.)

> All memories are bound to death.
> He thinks of his sister dead in his arms, of the locked asphyxiated land, of all the dead who delight in Sarah's madness, of Sarah, dead in the life of grain and fruit (1976: 169–70).

Yukel Serafi and Sara Schwall, the two "protagonists" of Jabès' book, seem to share Celan's and Sachs' fate. They are victims of the Holocaust; Yukel commits suicide and Sara goes mad, becoming a "landscape of screams." But Yukel's and Sara's story is never told. It is only commented on.

Like all commentary, this fragmentary story is not to be found at the center of the text, but in its "margins." *The Book of Questions* is written as a commentary on another, invisible, unwritten book that it carries within itself.

> Shall I reveal the book within the book by its stifled echoes: a secluded existence on the margin of ours, a senseless story of God? (1983: 151)

This absent book both limits and makes possible writing. Reading the book is impossible, except by substituting one's own writing in its place. Commentaries fill the page and marginal notes become the text. The absent book, however, recedes beyond reach every time it is grasped. In its withdrawal, it marks the boundary that preserves writing by graciously condemning it to incompletion: Book without end, whose origin cannot be attained.

The emergence of the possibility of writing from lack—from the prior withdrawal of the impossible—is figured in Jabès' writings in a variety of ways. This boundary between life and death is both marked and erased in the figuration of writing as breathing. The possible and the impossible are also understood as interdependent, if not co-productive, in his commentary on Moses' breaking of the tablets of the Law. The commentary, like the other ways in which this relationship is figured, is itself troped through an altering of the terms of Lurianic Kabbalah. The impossibility of telling about the Holocaust is a final way in which the limits of discourse are inscribed. These different figurations of absence and writing, of the impossible and the possible, must each be examined and compared in order to understand the relationship between the Holocaust and postmodernism in Jabès' writing.

Like Sachs and Celan, Jabès joins together writing and breathing. Jabès has an asthmatic sensitivity to the "closure" of the book in narrative and by the exclusive designation of genre.

> ... this is why I dreamed of a work which would not enter into any category, fit any genre, but contain them all; a work hard to

> define, but defining itself precisely by this lack of definition; a work which would not answer to any name, but had donned them all; a work belonging to no party or persuasion; a work of earth in the sky and of sky on earth; a work which would be the rallying point of all the words scattered in space . . . ; the place beyond all place of an obsession with God . . . ; a book, finally, which would only surrender by fragments, each of them the beginning of another book (1983: 247).

Figures of strangulation and suffocation consistently appear in his writings about exclusive poetic forms and acts.

> A novel is the writer's triumph over the book, and not the opposite, because the novelist makes a strong entrance with his characters and, with them as go-betweens, gives free rein to his innumerable voices. The book is strangled by them, its voice choked by theirs (1983: 35–6).

Jabès writes in an aphoristic style in order to allow the book to breathe.

> Writing a book means joining your voice with the virtual voice of the margins. . . . This is why the aphorism is the deepest expression of the book: it lets the margins breathe, it bears inside it the breath of the book and expresses the universe at the same time (1983: 36).

In writing a book that "eludes all labels" and that "does not belong to any clan or class," Jabès wishes to write a book that is "closer to an anthology than to an epic," structured aphoristically rather than as a novel. The loose, open style of aphorism that "lets the margins breathe," is even discernible in the physical layout of his books. The margins are broad and there is extensive indenting, with luxuriant spacing within each paragraph and between the book's many quotations and fragmentary stories. The margins and white space intrude into the text, becoming a part of its textuality.

Jabès' figuration of writing in terms of breathing is both self-conscious and thorough. Consider the following quotation in which he speaks about writing, breathing, and asthma in response to a question about how the topographical layout reflects and "sets the rhythm of the work."

> As for this distribution of long and short passages, it's a question of rhythm. This is very important to me. A full phrase, a lyrical phrase, is something that has great breath, that allows you to breathe very deeply. There are other times when the work folds in on itself, and the breath becomes shorter, breathing becomes difficult. They say that Nietzsche wrote aphorisms, for example,

because he suffered from atrocious headaches that made it impossible for him to write very much at any one sitting. Whether this is true or not, I do believe that a writer works with his body. You live with your body, and the book is above all the book of your body. In my case, the aphorism—what you might call the naked phrase—comes from a need to surround the words with whiteness in order to let them breathe. As you know, I suffer from asthma, and sometimes breathing is very difficult for me. By giving breath to my words I often have the feeling that I am helping myself breathe. It's really quite incredible how you live with your writing. . . . If I say all this, it is only to show that we work with our bodies, our breathing, our rhythm, and that writing in some sense mimes all this. Writing works in two directions. It is both an expansion and a contraction. . . . It took me a long time to understand that *both* were valid, but that this was what style was all about, that this was the essence of writing. You have to write in the same way you breathe. . . . (Auster, 1985: 15–16)

While Sachs and Celan would agree that "You have to write in the same way that you breathe," they breathe and write differently than Jabès. Their writings are poetics of expiration, while Jabès' are asthmatic. For Jabès, breathing is difficult, but is not itself fatal, even if there must always be a final word and a last breath. Indeed, writing enables and enhances breathing. "Aphorism . . . surrounds the words with whiteness in order to let them breathe," releasing the stranglehold upon discourse. Although not a poetics of inspiration, Jabès figures writing as *both* inhalation and exhalation.

> The work I write immediately rewrites itself in the book.
> This repeatability is part of its own breathing and of the reduplication of each of its signs.
> If inspiration consists in filling your lungs with oxygen, expiration empties them of life, means gliding into the void.
> Thus we only hold on to the world by agreeing, in advance, to die.
> "The difficulty of writing," he said, "is only the difficulty of breathing in rhythm with the book" (1983: 323)

Death naturally follows life just as exhalation necessarily follows inhalation. But inhaling does not itself cause or bring death. For Jabès, the atmosphere in which the writer lives makes breathing difficult, not impossible.

> The writer lives in an atmosphere of letters ground fine.
> The air he breathes is heavy with the dust of words he puts his wits to recreating. Ill wind fills his lungs (1983: 332).

Writing and breathing are difficult because of the nature of language, the "dust of words," that fills the lungs. It is quite another dust "which creep[s] into our breath" in Sachs' writings.

> Daniel, Daniel—
> the places where they died
> have awakened in my sleep—
> there, where their torment passed from them as their skin wrinkled,
> stones have shown the wounds
> of their discontinued time—
> the trees have torn themselves up
> which with their roots
> clutch the metamorphosis of dust
> between today and tomorrow.
>
> Are the dungeons broken open
> by their suffocated cries,
> . . . .
>
> O the graveless sighs in the air
> which creep into our breath—
> Daniel, Daniel,
> where are you terrible dreamlight?
> The uninterpreted signs have become too many—(87)

This is, indeed, an "ill wind," but it is far more deadly than that which fills Jabès' lungs. The air we breathe is suffocating, not because of the "dust of words," but because it is filled with death and the dead. It is the sighs of those who were asphyxiated in the gas chambers and turned to smoke in the crematoria "which creep into our breath." It is impossible to breathe *this* air without choking. Further, for Celan and Sachs, this choking is fatal. Writing does not, finally, make space for breathing. Unlike Jabès, the figures of omission and the white space on the page do not allow recovery, by opening up a space within discourse for being. For Celan and Sachs, this absence, rather, signifies loss: loss of breath and, finally, loss of a sustaining discourse. Death and not being fills this empty space. Absence, therefore, is differently valenced and breathing differently figured in their writings. Ellipsis figures the absence of being in the poetry of Sachs and Celan, whereas, for Jabès, it tropes the being made possible by absence.

> In the book," he said, "writing means absence, and the empty page, presence.
> "Thus God, who is absence, is present in the book" (1983: 213).

Failing Speech

Although God is absence, the empty page in the book makes this absence present. And although, in Jabès' writings, being is figured through its relationship to death, death is itself figured as making possible life. Just as, for Jabès, "we only hold on to the world by agreeing, in advance, to die," the absence of God—the God of absence—makes human being possible.

> God, an obliterating tyrant? World and man perish where the Word rages.
> Our words testify above all to divine obliteration (1983: 214).

The relationship between God and human being, the Word and words, is commented on by Jabès, in his account of Moses' breaking of the tablets of the Law.

> In Exodus (32:31–33), Moses returned to the Lord on Mount Sinai and said: "Oh, this people have sinned a great sin, and have made them gods of gold. Yet now, if thou wilt forgive their sin—; and if not, blot me, I pray thee, out of thy book which thou has written." And the Lord said unto Moses, "Whosoever hath sinned against me, him will I blot out of my book."
> Could God sin against God? Could the Book have been His sin? But God is all virtue.
> The book, too, had to ask itself this question.
> God rules by His absence, and the book bears witness. Absence joined by that of man which in the book is only the words of his harrowing hopelessness to exist.
> "Whosoever hath sinned against me, him will I blot out of my book."
> Is the divine threat directed against the unbeliever who dared prefer a golden idol to the Tables of the Law, the book cut in stone?
> But when Moses, back down in the plain, harshly punished the sinners unworthy of mercy in order to slake, he thought, the wrath of God, was his hasty cruelty not a sin of unpardonable ignorance? A sin for which God made him pay by not letting him enter the Promised Land.
> Overwhelmed as he was by the Book of God, had Moses forgotten that he was its author? That from now on God could not help adopting in his renewed Word the word of man?
> When he punished the guilty in the name of God, did Moses not really slay them in his own? And did he not take revenge less for their insult to God than for that to himself?
> It is the book which remains at stake.
> Book given as pasture to future books, book at the heart of the covenant between Creator and inspired creature, covenant sealed by the word (1985a: 239–40).[7]

What does it mean to say that Moses was the author of the Book of God, "That from now on God could not help adopting in his renewed Word the word of man?" The Word requires the word just as God needs human beings in order to be read, in order to be.

> The Book of God owed it to itself to remain unique. But this was unthinkable from the start, because it would have remained a book without readers (Jabès, 1985a: 239).

Reading necessitates the breaking of the tablets.

> ("We read the word in the sunburst of its limits, as we read the Law through Moses' angry gesture, through the breaking of the divine Tables," he said. . . .
> By turning their back on the Tables, the chosen people gave Moses a master-lesson in reading. . . . And, rising up against the letter, their independence consecrated the fracture in which God writes Himself against God. . . .
> The destroyed book allows us to read the book. . . .) (Jabès, 1984: 39)

The word, thus, requires the breaking of the Word (breaking closure and completion into the openness of incompletion), just as human beings depend for their existence on the withdrawal—the death—of God.

> This frightening, crushing silence which in its finest moment, when God called on His people, divided and split in order to speak to itself, split into divine silence and the silence of the creature: this silence is what the broken Tables of the Law give us to meditate. Double silence which the inscribed word and silence of the outlived moment closed forever on its own hunger.
> God's language—language of absence, language of a language that has weathered fire and marble frost—is unalterable, as if spelled by death. Composed of eternal signs it refuses the life of whatever accent.
> Thus, because it cannot be heard, the name of God wants to be unpronounceable and sterilize the letter at the height of meaning. . . . (Jabès, 1983: 300–01)

The breaking of the tablets repeats a more primordial withdrawal of God, making a space for being.

> Could it be that all words are words of a sandlocked Word from which God has withdrawn precisely so that the distance he put between it and Himself should be the space allowed for the displacement to which he has subjected His people? . . .

> The book teaches us so in the evening of its silence. But is it possible that God tried to disappear a second time, aided and abetted by man? Unless it was to abolish the Resemblance he had wanted between man and His image, and He knew this could only be done within the image itself, as there is no language without it? (Jabès, 1985a: 232, 239)

It is, thus, the absence of God, His withdrawal and the breaking of His Word, that makes human being and language possible. The covenant (the tablets and the Word) must be broken by *both* God and human beings in order to preserve their difference, the distance between them that makes possible being, including the being of the absence of God. Breaking the Word of God, like His absence, thus, is construed in positive terms.

The relationship between God and human being, Word and word, is figured in Jabès' writings through an altering of the tropes of Lurianic Kabbalah. There are three "moments" in the process of creation in Lurianic Kabbalah. *Tsimtsum* is the primordial withdrawal of God into Himself, creating a space in which creation can then occur.

> According to Luria, God was compelled to make room for the world by, as it were, abandoning a region within Himself, a kind of mystical primordial space from which He withdrew in order to return to it in the act of creation and revelation. . . . The first act of all is not an act of revelation but one of limitation. Only in the second act does God send out a ray of His light and begin his revelation, or rather his unfolding as God the Creator, in the primordial space of His own creation. More than that, every new act of emanation and manifestation is preceded by one of concentration and retraction (Scholem: 261).

This second act of "revelation," however, goes askew with the Shattering of the Vessels *(Shevirat Ha-Kelim)* by the intensification of the Divine light. These vessels *(Kelim)* had been emanated for the purpose of containing the Divine light in the process of creating finite beings and forms. But in this process, the light was displaced and intensified, shattering the vessels receiving and containing this light, spilling and dispersing it in a cosmic catastrophe that requires a third moment, *Tikkun*, in order to mend creation. Some of the spilled light returned to the Godhead, but the rest of it remained dispersed as the waste of creation. It is this dispersed light, trapped within finitude, which must be released and returned to the Godhead in the process of *Tikkun*. In this third moment, human beings are essential. Human beings have the capacity to act in history and restore the harmony of creation. They do this by acting in accord with Torah. This act of mending, or restoration, is simultaneously the bringing of redemption and the completion of creation. Thus, "the process in which God conceives, brings forth and develops Himself does not reach its final conclusion in God. Certain parts of the process of restitution are allotted to man" (Scholem: 273–4).

It is this process of restitution, *Tikkun*, that Jabès undoes in his reading of Moses' breaking of the tablets. The completion of creation is rendered impossible through this shattering of the Law, the breaking of the Word, of covenant. This impossibility, ironically, continues creation by forbidding its completion. In an inversion of the valences of Lurianic Kabbalah, Jabès associates completion with the destruction of both God and human being, and incompleteness with their preservation. *Tikkun* is shattered in the necessity of the breaking of the tablets for the sake of both God and human being.

The three Lurianic moments of creation are valenced in positive terms in Jabès' writings. The withdrawal (exile) of God from His "sand-locked Word . . . so that the distance he put between it and Himself should be the space allowed for the displacement [exile] . . . [of] His people," is analogous to the moment of *Tsimtsum*. If *Tsimtsum* is understood by Luria as the exiling of God *into* Himself, then *Shevirath Ha-Kelim* (the Breaking of the Vessels) is to be understood as the exiling of God *out* of himself. For Jabès, these two exiles are complementary and positively valenced moments. These two moments occur together in Jabès' writing, configuring the following passages on creation.

> *Adding Energy means splitting an entity into its constituents. Withdrawing energy means regaining the entity, the point* (1984: 37).
>
> *("God was the first to break the silence," he said. "It is this breakage we try to translate into human languages."*
> *"Vowels make us see, make us hear. Vowels are image and song. In our ancestors' script, vowels are points.*
> *"God refused image and language in order to be Himself the point. He is image in the absence of images, language in the absence of language, point in the absence of points," he said.)* (1984: 15)
>
> *A slightly larger space within a word—the separation into syllables, for instance—an unexpected crack, a letter broken or dropped into the void give rise to such play within the word that it is drawn into a series of metamorphoses and destroyed in the process* (1984: 17).

Dissemination, rather than containment of exile is the "point" of Jabès' writing. The moments of *Tsimtsum* and *Shevirath Ha-Kelim* are not completed or overcome in *Tikkun*, but are, rather, preserved together as sustaining creation. His displacement of *Tikkun* in the breaking of the tablets, like the substitution of reading (following the Book) by writing (creating one's own book), finalizes and makes thoroughgoing the trope of exile. Exile is endless. In this incompletion, exile has "redeemed" us from Redemption. The breaking of the tablets (the abolishing of the Resemblance "between man and His image" from "within the image itself") ironically brings this "redemption."

> . . . A book whose words we need to cancel to let it return to its white plurality (1984: 19).

> "*. . . as if, suddenly, I could only speak through the silence of the spaces left empty by their difference.*"
> "*Their difference?*"
> "*Some basic incompatibility between man and his words, something that keeps them apart. Could it be that they are condemned to walk together, but have only the road in common? Exile within the exile.*" (1984: 35)

The figuration of the shared condition and fate of God, writing, human being and Judaism in terms of exile and finitude, thus, is made possible for Jabès in his alteration of the tropes of Lurianic Kabbalah. Their figuration by exile and finitude is made possible in *Tsimtsum*, sustained and disseminated in *Shevirath Ha-Kelim*, and finalized and preserved in the deconstruction of *Tikkun*.

These altered Lurianic tropes figure, as well, both the Holocaust and post-Holocaust writing in terms of exile. As Maurice Blanchot suggests, the ruptures of writing and history are equated in Jabès' work.

> [T]he rupture is marked not only by poetic fragmentation at its various levels of meaning, but is also questioned, suffered, re-grasped, and made to speak, always twice, and each time doubled: in history, and in the writing at the margins of history. . . . A rupture suffered in history, where catastrophe still speaks, and where the infinite violence of pain is always near: the rupture of violent power that has tried to make and mark an entire era. Then, the other, the original rupture, which is anterior to history and which is not suffered, but required, and which, expressing distance in regard to every power, delimits the interval where Judaism introduces its own affirmation: the rupture that reveals "*the wound. . . .*" For this interval, this gap, previously affirmed in relation to the pressure of things and the domination of events, precisely marks the place where the word is established, the word that invites man to no longer identify himself with his power. The word of impossibility. And then we understand that the meditation of the poet Jabès on the poetic act and its demands can be coupled with the meditation on his recent and ageless ties to the Jewish condition. (48–9)[8]

Although the Holocaust is clearly alluded to in Blanchot's description of "A rupture suffered in history," this rupture is displaced by a more primordial wound, "the original rupture, which is anterior to history and which is not suffered, but required." "[E]xpressing distance in regard to every power," this original rupture "precisely marks the place where the word is established, the word that invites man to no longer identify himself with his power. The word of impossibility." This original rupture is figured as *Tsimtsum*. In equating these two ruptures, of writing and history, the negative effects of the Holocaust are displaced by the positive ethical effects of the primordial wounding of discourse.

The Holocaust is figured here in terms of separation and death: as exile. Because exile is the "Jewish condition"—indeed, the condition of all being—the Holocuast is not a *novum*. It is eclipsed by the primordial exile or wound, i.e., *Tsimtsum*, that "delimits the interval where Judaism introduces its own affirmation." Not only, then, is history read in terms of the conditions of writing, but rupture and exile are reread from catastrophe to affirmation. Exile is the mediating (i.e., displacing) term in this translation from history suffered to writing and being made possible. Now we may "understand that the meditation of the poet Jabès on the poetic act and its demands can be coupled with the meditation on his recent and ageless ties to the Jewish condition."

> Six million burned bodies divide ours in two by the horrible image they perpetuate.
>
> Who could ever measure the extent of a suffering which has forgotten even its origin in order to remember nothing but its innocence?
>
> No, a Jewish theme will not be enough to make a book Jewish. The Jewish tale is much less in the anecdote, the confession, the painting of a milieu than in writing. You cannot tell Auschwitz. Every word tells it to us (Jabès, 1985b: 28).[9]

If language fails to refer, for Jabès, it nonetheless tells. Writing is the best testimony to Auschwitz because the rupture, the dispersion of words, itself witnesses. Although language cannot representationally testify, "Every word tells it to us."

What kind of witness is this that does not refer? Do Jabès' words witness the inadequacy of discourse to represent the Holocaust in—and as—particular, as do the poems of Celan and Sachs? Should we, in other words, consider Jabès' postmodernism as fundamentally informed by the antinomies of representation that underlie post-Holocaust writing? Is it the Holocaust that accounts for the textuality of Jabès' writings, the persistent failure, e.g., of narrative telling?

One reading of Jabès would eschew all attempts to separate the two questions of referentiality and textuality from each other, even momentarily. This reading would collapse all questions of the subject into questions of writing. To ask the question of reference as if one could disentangle it from that of writing would, in this view, be impossible. The question of reference must itself be asked within discourse, out of which one cannot step to gain a view both of writing and its subject. In this interpretation of Jabès' postmodernism, the more reflexive the reading, i.e., the more the subject becomes writing itself, the more one may understand the discursive or narrative conditions for the possibility/impossibility of reference. Questioning the subject of discourse, then, becomes available only through this reflexive doubling of discourse. In this way, the question of the subject of discourse is itself subject *to* discourse, to the question of the conditions of writing.

What happens to the subject of the Holocaust when it is, thus, subjected to the question of the conditions of discourse? Can this subject, indeed, can any subject, make a claim that in particular might raise questions as to the nature of discourse and the conditions of its communicativeness? On this reading of Jabès, distinctive claims about or made by the Holocaust cannot be seriously raised. For the conditions of writing do not vary with the subject of discourse; these conditions, rather, are understood, by Jabès, to be a part of creation itself.

The Holocaust is not understood by Jabès as a particular historical event as much as a sign and repetition of "the suffering of the Jewish people" and the primordial withdrawal of the Word. The Holocaust is figured in terms of exile and "every word tells it to us" because writing also is displaced. Only words of exile can tell the Holocaust as the exile of the Word[10].

This figuration of the Holocaust by exile, however, erases its distinctiveness by making it identical with the "Jewish condition," with the withdrawal of the Word, indeed, with writing itself. All of these exiles are, finally, the same. Further, exile is positively valenced as that which makes writing and being possible. By so thoroughly assimilating exile and otherness to the very conditions of discourse, alterity external to discourse is domesticated or made impossible. If the Other always already figures writing, then discourse is insulated from the shocks and challenges of that which is other than writing. That which is other than writing is domesticated in terms of the otherness within and of writing. These two modes of otherness are read, ironically, as the same. Only by remarking the limits of the constitution of the conditions of writing by alterity—exile and otherness—can textuality itself be marked by an alterity which is not already prefigured by the conditions of inscription. Only then can assumptions about the conditions of discourse be challenged, not simply confirmed or dramatized.

The two aporias of representation, that of telling the event of the

Holocaust and of narrative and referential discourse generally, are construed as one and the same in Jabès' writing. Is there only one abyss against which discourse resists, however from different regions and for different reasons? No matter what the occasion of telling, do all discourses testify only to the shared, not the different conditions of their inscription? Are all breaks, gaps, and interruptions of discourse only about the limits of discourse to refer beyond itself? Or, are the failures of discourse to refer occasioned differently, with differing epistemological results? In other words, to what extent may and should we let the different subjects of discourse guide us in our understandings of textuality—or is textuality itself always the primary, controlling subject of both reading and writing?

This comparison of post-Holocaust and postmodern writing suggests that the clue of textuality alone is not sufficient, although it is crucial for interpretation. As both post-Holocaust and postmodern writings are, to a certain extent, about the textual conditions of the impossibility of testimony and narration, they both employ some of the same figures of discourse[11]. But these figures, as I have demonstrated, are differently turned in Celan's and Sachs' poetry than in Jabès' writing because of the differences in what their texts seek to tell. These differences in figuration, thus, are not only textual; they inhere in what these texts are about. Although writing and the Holocaust are entwined in the texts of all three authors, Jabès' books seem to be more about how the conditions of writing configure the Holocaust and Celan's and Sachs' poetry emphasizes how the Holocaust alters the very conditions of writing. Jabès' figuration of the conditions of discourse makes it impossible for him to recognize the Holocaust as a *novum*, whereas it is precisely in these radically new terms that it figures the conditions of writing in the poetry of Celan and Sachs. Assumptions about textuality and reference cannot, finally, be disentangled from different understandings of the Holocaust[12].

Edward Kaplan claims that "The reality of the death camps pervades the Jabès text and prevents us from the separating the gas chambers from the negative utopia of language (124). Although Celan, Sachs and Jabès, e.g., each link testimony and textuality, is this relation mutually implicating? If it is impossible to separate "the gas chambers from the negative utopia of language," is it, thereby, impossible to separate the negative utopia of language from the gas chambers? Not only can we, but we *must* make this separation. The differences between, e.g., an asthmatic poetic and a poetics of expiration, and their different valencing of absence and death, must be recognized in these terms. Despite the entanglement of writing and the Holocaust in all of the texts examined here, this separation must be made, else we risk trivializing the testimonial character of the textuality of post-Holocaust writing by aestheticising it, and we risk losing, as well, the critique of writing and thinking that is made available

Failing Speech   87

by such "negative utopias of language" as exemplified by the discourse of postmodernism. In these terms, finally, the writings of Celan and Sachs and those of Jabés should be recognized as distinct, if related forms of discourse, distinguished by what they are about—whether or not they succeed in their representation—as well as in their textuality.

NOTES

[1] For a more complete explication of this problem, see Shapiro (1984), pp. 3–10.

[2] Wiesel's formulation of this hermeneutical antinomy is one of many possible strategies. I am emphasizing the constructive function of confessing the impossibility of communication as rhetorically making possible testimony. Wiesel's remarks here are not to be construed as simply denying the possibility of communication and testimony altogether. To read him thus would belie the negative dialectical character of his statement. The failure of speech is inscribed by post-Holocaust writers in a variety of ways, one of which is the use of *aporia* (talking about the impossibility of speech), as in Wiesel's formulation. The limits of discourse to represent the Holocaust are figured as well in *ellipsis* (omission) and *aposiopesis* (the breaking off of speech as if unwilling or unable to go on) in the writings of Celan and Sachs considered here.

[3] I employ the term "postmodern" here, in part, because of its ambiguous inclusion of aspects of both modernism and post-structuralism. See, especially, Huyssen (1981), (1984), Foster (1983), and (1984). Jabès' writing have been variously construed as modernist, post-structural and postmodern. In considering Jabès' writings here, the term "postmodern" is used to include this range of interpretation. The question I ask in this paper is whether postmodern discourse can be distinguished from post-Holocaust writing, not whether postmodernism can be differentiated from modernism or post-structuralism.

[4] While much of the criticism of Celan's poetry during the 1960's stressed his hermeticism, some recent interpreters emphasize the importance of communication, of the addressed *du*, in the making and reading of Celan's poems. See, especially, Felstiner (1982), (1983) and (1984). My allusion to Celan's hermeticism is not to suggest that he did not wish to communicate, to speak to a *du*. Rather, it is intended as a description of the often elliptical nature of his writings as reflecting the difficulties of his subject, not a wish to finally conceal or seal the meanings of his words from his hearers and readers. Thus, while I agree with Felstiner's assessment of Celan's desire to communicate as constitutive of his writing, I am emphasizing here the ways his poems also betray the difficulties of such speaking.

[5] See, especially, the lucid and sensitive analysis of Rosenfeld (1980), pp. 82–95. The term "poetics of expiration" is Rosenfeld's.

[6] Auster (1985), p. 3, e.g., considers "the central question of [Jabes' book to be]: how to speak what cannot be spoken. The question is the Jewish Holocaust, but it is also the question of literature itself. By a startling leap of the imagination, Jabès treats these as one and the same. . . ." Lang (1985) both grants and adeptly critiques this identification in Jabès' writings. Beyond representation and intransitive writing, he understands Jabès as unsuccessfully "Writing-the-Holocaust." The implication of Lang's interpretation is that to put the weight upon textuality alone in giving testimony to the Holocaust is an intrinsically flawed undertaking, with negative ethical consequences. My purpose in this paper is to examine the similarities and differences between post-Holocaust and postmodern writing by following the clue of textuality and asking how it constitutes both the possibility and impossibility of testimony. Megill (1985) unpersuasively identifies Jabès' and Derrida's writings as both "aris[ing] from this experience of extremity. The risks that Derrida takes as a writer," he suggests, "seem at least partly comprehensible when viewed from this perspective. . . . The shock of separation, the unbridgeable distance between origin and end—these join Jabès, Derrida, and Judaism. . . . It is no accident

that he places 'the Nazi repetition' alongside 'the poetic revolution of our century,'" pp. 317–19. Megill's argument rests on a mistaken identification of Jabès' and Derrida's positions and on the absence of the Holocaust as an explicit subject in Derrida's writings. This argument from *ellipsis*, from the failure to designate the Holocaust, is weak at best. If the absence of the Holocaust as an explicit term or subject qualifies a text as post-Holocaust, on the grounds that one cannot talk about or represent the event, the argument is reduced *ad absurdum*. One must question, rather, why it is that Megill "find[s] it in some ways satisfying to see [Derrida's work] as if it, too, arises from this experience of extremity," p. 319.

[7] In another passage with similar import, Jabès writes, "The believing Jew cannot go toward God except through the Book, but the commentary on the original Text is not a commentary on the divine Word. Only on the human word dazzled by the latter like a moth by the lamp. . . . The book bears witness to this conflict which no page can resolve. Any yet God lives only in the human word, and man is inspired and destroyed by it. Shared torment.," (1985), "There is such a thing as Jewish writing," b/pp. 28–29.

[8] See Kaplan's (1985) reading of this passage in reference to the Holocaust, p. 118.

[9] See, also, Lang (1985) for a critique of this view.

[10] This is to distinguish the subsumption of the Holocaust under exile from same of its exilic effects, including that of an exile both into and from language. See, esp., Felstiner (1982).

[11] See note 2 above for figures. These figures are present in both post-Holocaust and postmodern writing, as evidenced in the writings examined here.

[12] Indeed, one might argue that certain hermeneutical assumptions make attending to the claim of the Holocaust difficult, if not impossible. The case for the helpfulness of postmodern discourse in this regard is not aided by Derrida's (1986) reading of Celan and the question of the date: "And I will not speak here of the *holocaust*, except to say this: there is the date of a certain holocaust, the hell of our memory, but there is a holocaust for every date, somewhere in the world at every hour. Every hour is unique, whether it comes back or whether, the last, it comes no more, no more than the sister, the same, its other *revenant*, coming back," p. 336. On the difficulties within Gadamer's hermeneutics for attending to the Holocaust, see Shapiro (1984).

WORKS CONSULTED

Adorno, Theodor
    1967   *Prisms*. Trans. by Samuel Weber. London: Neville Spearman, Ltd.
    1983   *Negative Dialectics*. Trans. by E.B. Ashton. New York: Continuum Publishing Company.

Auster, Paul
    1977   "Story of a Scream." *New York Review of Books*, April 28, pp. 38–40.
    1985   "Book of the Dead: An Interview with Edmond Jabès." *The Sin of the Book: Edmond Jabès*. Ed. by Eric Gould. Lincoln: University of Nebraska Press, pp. 3–25.

Blanchot, Maurice
    1985   "Interruptions." *The Sin of the Book*. Ed. by Eric Gould. Lincoln: University of Nebraska Press, pp. 43–54.

Celan, Paul
    1971   *Speech-Grille and Selected Poems*. Trans. by Joachim Neugroschel. New York: E.P. Dutton.

1980	*Paul Celan: Poems*. Ed. and trans. by Michael Hamburger. New York: Persea Books.

Demetz, Peter
1972	*Postwar German Literature*. New York: Schocken Books.

Derrida, Jacques
1978	"Edmond Jabès and the Question of the Book." *Writing and Difference*. Trans. by Alan Bass. Chicago: University of Chicago Press, pp. 64–78.
1978	"Ellipsis." *Writing and Difference*. Trans. by Alan Bass. Chicago: University of Chicago Press, pp. 295–300.
1986	"Shibboleth." *Midrash and Literature*. Trans. by Joshua Wilner. Ed. by Geoffrey H. Hartman and Sanford Budick. New Haven: Yale University Press, pp. 307–47.

Ezrahi, Sidra Dekoven
1980	*By Words Alone: The Holocaust in Literature*. Chicago: University of Chicago Press.

Foster, Hal
1983	"Postmodernism: A Preface," *The Anti-Aesthetic: Essays on Postmodern Culture*. Ed. Hal Foster. Port Townsend, Washington: Bay Press, pp. ix–xvi.
1984	"(Post)modern Polemics," *New German Critique* 33:67–78.
1985	*Recodings: Art, Spectacle, Cultural Politics*. Port Townsend, Washington: Bay Press.

Felstiner, John
1982	"Translating Paul Celan's Last Poem." *American Poetry Review* (July/August):21–7.
1983	"Translating Paul Celan's 'Du sei wie du.'" *Prooftexts* 3:98–108.
1984	"Translating Paul Celan's 'Jerusalem' Poems." *Religion & Literature* 16(1):37–47.

Glen, Jerry
1973	*Paul Celan*. New York: Twayne Publisher.

Guglielmi, Joseph
1974	"Exile and the Law (Kafka and Jabès)." *European Judaism* 1:38–9.

Gould, Eric
1985	"Introduction," "Godtalk." *The Sin of the Book: Edmond Jabès*. Ed. by Eric Gould. Lincoln: University of Nebraska Press, pp. xiii–xxv, 160–170.

Habermas, Jurgen
1983	"Modernity—An Incomplete Project." *The Anti-Aesthetic: Essays on Postmodern Culture*. Ed. by Hal Foster.

Huyssen, Andreas
1981	"The Search for Tradition: Avant-Garde and Postmodernism in the 1970s." *New German Critique* 22:23–40.

1984 "Mapping the Postmodern." *New German Critique* 33:5–52.

Hamburger, Michael.
    1982   *The Truth of Poetry: Tensions in Modern Poetry from Beudelaire to the 1960s.* New York: Methuen.

Jabès, Edmond
    1976   *The Book of Questions.* Trans. by Rosmarie Waldrop. Middletown, Conn.: Wesleyan University Press.
    1977   *The Book of Questions II and III: The Book of Yukel. Return to the Book.* Trans. by Rosmarie Waldrop. Middletown, Conn.: Wesleyan University Press.
    1983   *The Book of Questions IV, V and VI: Yael, Elya, Aely.* Trans. by Rosmarie Waldrop. Middletown, Conn.: Wesleyan University Press.
    1984   *The Book of Questions VII: El, or the Last Book.* Trans. by Rosmarie Waldrop. Middletown, Conn.: Wesleyan University Press.
    1985a   "The Question of Displacement into the Lawfulness of the Book." *The Sin of the Book.* Ed. by Eric Gould. Lincoln: University of Nebraska Press, pp. 227–44.
    1985b   "There is such a thing as Jewish writing. . . ." *The Sin of the Book.* Ed. by Eric Gould. Lincoln: University of Nebraska Press, pp. 21–31.

Kaplan, Edward
    1985   "The Problematic Humanism of Edmond Jabès." *The Sin of the Book.* Ed. by Eric Gould. Lincoln: University of Nebraska Press, pp. 115–30.

Lang, Berel
    1985   "Writing-the-Holocaust: Jabès and the Measure of History." *The Sin of the Book.* Ed. by Eric Gould, Lincoln: University of Nebraska Press, ppl 191–206.

Langer, Lawrence
    1975   *The Holocaust and the Literary Imagination.* New Haven: Yale University Press.

Levinas, Emmanuel &
Starobinski, Jean
    1973   "Jabès and the Difficulty of Being Jewish." *European Judaism* 2:20–22.

Megill, Allan
    1985   *Prophets of Extremity: Nietzsche, Heiddeger, Foucault, Derrida.* Berkeley: University of California Press.

Neher, Andre
    1981   *The Exile of the Word: From the Silence of the Bible to the Silence of Auschwitz.* Trans. by David Maisel. Philadelphia: Jewish Publication Society of America.

Palmer, Michael
    1983   "Words Written in Sand." New York Times Book Review, August 21, pp. 13, 22.

Rosenfeld, Alvin H.
    1980   *A Double Dying: Reflections on Holocaust Literature*. Bloomington: Indiana University Press.

Sachs
    1970   *The Seeker and Other Poems*. Trans. by Ruth and Michael Meed and Michael Hamburger. New York: Farrar, Strauss, and Giroux.

Scholem, Gershom G.
    1941   *Major Trends in Jewish Mysticism*. New York: Schocken Books.

Shapiro, Susan E.
    1984   "Hearing the Testimony of Radical Negation." *Concilium* 175 (10):3–10.

Stamelman, Richard
    1985   "Nomadic Writing: The Poetics of Exile." *The Sin of the Book*. Ed. by Eric Gould. Lincoln: University of Nebraska Press, pp. 92–114.

Steiner, George
    1974   *Language and Silence: Essays on Language, Literature, and the Inhuman*. New York: Atheneum.

Waldrop, Rosmarie.
    1973   "Edmond Jabès and the Impossible Circle." *Sub-Stance* 5/6: 183–96.

Weightman, John
    1976   "The Problem of the Absent God." New York Times Book Review, May 23, p. 31.

Wiesel, Elie
    1977   "The Holocaust as Literary Inspiration." *Dimensions of the Holocaust*. Evanston, Il.: Northwestern University.
    1983   "Does the Holocaust Defeat the Artist?" New York Times, April 17, p. 12

Young, James
    1987   "Interpreting Literary Testimony: A Preface to Rereading Holocaust Diaries and Memoirs." *New Literary History*, Winter, 1987 (forthcoming)

FINITUDE, DEATH, AND REVERENCE FOR LIFE[1]

Carol P. Christ
San Jose State University

ABSTRACT

We live daily with the threat of nuclear extinction. *One* of the root causes of this threat is our loss of connection to the earth, our failure to fully embrace a life which is finite and ends in death. Since Plato, most Western philosophies and theologies have shared a desire to escape the limitations of change, finitude, and death. The finite has been opposed to the infinite and human reason has been understood as that which binds us to the infinite and separates us from nature. Many feminist theorists have challenged the classical dualisms which view emotion, body, nature, and woman as threats to human reason. In her visionary, mystical, poetic, and deeply philosophical book *Woman and Nature*, Susan Griffin images our connection to this changing and finite earth and challenges us to re-think our spiritual and philosophical heritages, offering clues to our survival, the survival of earth.

Modern culture has little connection with the earth—or, rather, normally fails to perceive a connection with it. But for the Greeks the earth embodied divinity (Scully: xi).

At any moment this earth and all who live upon it could be destroyed in nuclear war. I believe that one of the reasons we face nuclear destruction is that we do not recognize our connection to the earth. We fail to acknowledge our own finitude and death, and the potential finitude and death of the earth. We must acknowledge our finitude and death, and our connections to the earth, if we are to survive. Our religious and philosophical traditions since Plato have attempted to deny finitude and death, and hence have prevented us from fully comprehending our connections to this earth. We must challenge these traditions and provide alternatives. Feminist thinkers who remind us of our finitude and mortality and who name our connections to this earth have much to contribute to our survival.

Jonathan Schell defines the crisis we face in *The Fate of the Earth:*

> We live, then, in a universe whose fundamental substance contains a supply of energy with which we can extinguish ourselves (106)

> As for the destruction of all the life on the planet, it would be not merely a human, but a planetary end—the death of the earth (7).

Not content with merely describing the problem, Schell also attempts to evoke in us a sense of our deep connection to earth and the life forms on it:

> We not only live on the earth but also are of the earth, and the thought of its death, or even its mutilation, touches a deep chord in our nature (7).

I live daily with the knowledge Schell so eloquently expresses, that at any moment this earth which I love could cease to be. While I write, the sound barrier breaks overhead like the crashing of thunder on a sunny day. I rush to the window and look out: the sky is clear. I do not see the nuclear warheads streaking over San Francisco. The knowledge that we could destroy this earth weighs heavily on me. I can imagine the end of our way of life (indeed insofar as the American way of life is patriarchy and war, I hope for its end). I can imagine my own death and do not really fear it. I can even imagine that the time of the human species could end just as the time of the dinosaurs ended (even this thought is not entirely negative for me, when I think of how much greater a chance for survival the rest of the earth would have without us). But it fills me with enormous pain and anger to think that I am part of a species which may be responsible for the death of all the life on earth.

I find it difficult to comprehend the fact that I share this earth with those who can calmly calculate the risks of nuclear war and find them acceptable. I wonder if these scientists and politicians share my sense of connection to this earth, or whether in their hearts they despise their bodies, their lives, their families and friends, their mortality.

As a thealogian, I share with Gordon Kaufman the conviction that "there is no question that the possibility of nuclear holocaust is the premier issue which our generation must address (14). I agree further with Kaufman that as interpreters of our religious heritage:

> we must be prepared to enter into the most radical kind of deconstruction and reconstruction of the traditions we have inher-

ited, including especially their most central and precious symbols (13).

One of the ways our religious and philosophical systems have contributed to the threat of extinction we face is that they have cut us off from our connection to nature and from the full experience and acknowledgement of our finitude. I believe that our political leaders can think about fighting a nuclear war only because they don't really think they (and almost all other human beings and life forms) will die. They imagine a nuclear war to be "survivable" despite all the evidence to the contrary. Most of us are probably familiar with the story that became the title of Robert Scheer's book *With Enough Shovels*. Scheer reports that a government official told him that the way to survive a nuclear war is to dig a hole, climb into it, and pull a door down over it. The absurdity of this scenario, which reportedly was taken from a Russian survival manual, should not blind us to the fact that all schemes to survive a nuclear war are just as absurd (18–19).

Paradoxically the denial of finitude and death may express an even more profound failure of our culture, the failure to affirm life as it is lived, this life, on this earth, in these bodies. The underside of the denial of death may be despair about the meaning of life which ends in death. And thus the very politicians who assert that "we" will "survive" nuclear war may not really care whether we do.

It might be argued that the denial of finitude and inevitable death expresses an affirmation, not a denial of life. But this life which is bounded by finitude and death is the only life we know, the only life we can know for certain to exist. To deny finitude and death is to deny the limitations of life as we know it, in favor of an idea of life without death. I believe that we must learn to love this life which ends in death. This is not absolutely to rule out the possibility of individual survival after death, but it is to say in the most certain of terms, that we ought not interpret our task in this life in light of such a possibility. Our task is here.

Feminist thinkers and thealogians have a great deal to say about these issues. In *Woman and Nature* Susan Griffin evokes that "deep chord" of connection which we feel to the earth when she writes:

> This earth is my sister; I love her daily grace, her silent daring, and how loved I am *how we admire this strength in each other, all that we have lost, all that we have suffered, all that we know: we are stunned by this beauty,* and I do not forget: what she is to me, what I am to her (219).

Like Griffin I know "this earth is my sister." I feel and know my connection to earth more deeply than I feel or know anything. My spirituality stems from my sense of connection to this earth, to its cycles of changing seasons, to ocean, rivers, mountains, trees, grasses, birds, deer, roses, daffodils, and to my grandparents, to my mother, my father, my family, my friends, my dog, and to all the others whose lives have been intertwined with mine on this earth. With Alice Walker I pray: "Surely the earth can be saved for [these]" (70).

I believe that the inability to reverence our connections to the earth has deep roots in our culture, roots which go back at least to Plato, and which are intimately bound up with the denial of finitude and death. The finite is defined as "having boundaries; limited; capable of being bounded, enclosed, or encompassed; being neither infinite nor infinitesimal; existing, persisting, for a limited time only; impermanent, transient" (Morris: 493). In this definition is encompassed the major reason finitude has been denied in most of the philosophies and theologies influenced by Plato. For Plato that which is limited by time or space is imperfect. In *The Symposium* Plato argued that our true home is not this finite, imperfect world. He described the journey of the soul from love of beautiful bodies, to love of beautiful souls, to love of beautiful laws and institutions, to love of science and knowledge, until finally, the soul ascends to the vision of the good which is described as:

> that wondrous vision which is the very soul of the beauty he has toiled so long for. It is an everlasting loveliness which neither comes nor goes, which neither flowers nor fades, for such beauty is the same on every hand, the same then as now, here as there, this way as that way, the same to very worshipper as it is to every other.
>
> Nor will his vision of the beautiful take the form of a face, or of hands, or of anything that is flesh. It will be neither words, nor knowledge, nor a something that exists in something else, such as a living creature, or the earth, or the heavens, or anything that is—but subsisting of itself and by itself in an eternal oneness, while every lovely thing partakes of it in such sort that, however much the parts may wax and wane, it will be neither more nor less, but still the same inviolable whole (Hamilton and Cairns: 562).

For Plato "the Good" is not affected by time (it does not come into being or die) and it is not essentially affected by relationships (it is an inviolable whole). The vision of the Good as totally transcendent of finitude is fundamental to Platonic philosophy. Susan Griffin aptly characterizes the Platonic vision when she writes:

> It is decided that matter is transitory and illusory like the shadow on a wall cast by firelight; that we dwell in a cave, in the cave of

our flesh, which is also matter, also illusory; it is decided that what is real is outside the cave, in a light brighter than we can imagine, that matter traps us in a darkness. That the idea of matter existed before matter and is more perfect, ideal (5).

Griffin alludes to Plato's *Republic* where it is alleged that just as the shadows on the wall of a cave are poor reflections of physical objects, so our physical bodies are poor reflections of ideas or forms which are eternal.

Since Plato, Western thinkers have shared a dualistic philosophy in which mind and body are perceived as separable, and in which the body and nature (because impermanent, finite) have been perceived as less than the mind and the realm of ideas (imagined to be eternal, infinite). The contrast between finite and infinite is at the heart of Platonic dualism. Change and dependence are considered impediments to the soul's journey. In Platonic thought it is asserted that man is not essentially finite, that his mind or soul partakes in the infinite. (I use the male generic here and elsewhere in describing dualistic thought, not only because this way of thinking is the product of male minds, but also because philosophers and theologians have never been certain that women have minds or souls with the same rational capacity as the minds of men.) In denying finitude, man has proposed that he is not limited by time or space. When we are aware of our bodies, we are aware of limitation: we cannot be everywhere and we will surely die. We cannot live in our bodies without eating, drinking, sleeping, and going to the bathroom. We know our bodies to grow and change, whether we want them to or not, no matter how we try to deny it. And one day our bodies will die. We will not live forever. And yet man has sought to deny that he is limited by his body. He has asserted that his mind or soul is eternal. He has attempted through ascetic practices to deny that he is his body, in order to free his soul. He has even denied that he came from his mother's body. "I think, therefore I am," he has said, and he tells himself that he is not even certain that other minds exist.

Much Christian theology is built on the denial of finitude and death. The Platonic vision of the Good is immaterial, unchanging, and essentially unrelated to any other entity became the philosophical basis for Christian theology's doctrine of God. In classical Christian theology, God is declared totally or absolutely transcendent of creation, the earth, and all creatures in it. God's absolute transcendence becomes the basis for doctrines such as God's aseity, or inability to be affected in his essential nature by what happens to creation, God's omnipotence, or total power, God's omniscience, or knowledge of everything, etc. The doctrine of God's absolute transcendence, like Plato's notion of the Good, correlates with a theology in which this earth, the body, and this life are despised, and in which the spiritual goal is to transcend the flesh and its desires and to seek a life after death in which the limitations of finitude are overcome.

It is sometimes asserted that the doctrine of the incarnation is an affirmation of finitude, and thus that Christianity cannot properly be accused of denying finitude. The incarnation, the doctrine of God's full presence in the body of Christ; is said to be an affirmation of the body. That God entered into this life is said to be an affirmation of it. That God died on the cross is said to indicate acceptance of death. But at best the incarnation is a partial affirmation of finitude. The doctrine of the incarnation was developed by church fathers influenced by Platonism, who believed that the finite and the infinite are essentially opposed. For them, as for Kierkegaard, it was the highest paradox that the divine could be fully present in the human flesh. There would be no paradox if the finite were understood to be the natural home of the spirit or the divine. Because they polarized the finite and the infinite, the church fathers could not fully affirm the finitude.

Nor could they affirm death. The denial of finitude within Christianity is encompassed in the phrase "he is risen." Without addressing the complex theological disputes about the nature of the resurrection, let me state the obvious: the statement "he is risen" is a denial that death marks the end of individual life. The hopes of Christians throughout the centuries have been based upon the expectation of an individual life after physical death in which the limitations of finitude are overcome.

The Christian doctrine of original sin asserts that since the fall, since Adam and Eve, we no longer have the choice not to sin, or, as it is often put, "we cannot *not* sin." Whatever we do, this doctrine states, is tainted with evil. This doctrine imposes an infinite standard on our finite lives. We are made to feel guilty for being human, and told to long for a salvation which will release us from bondage to the finite. According to traditional theology, "the wages of sin is death." Because Adam and Eve sinned, death has entered into the world as punishment, it is said. Instead of being understood as an ordinary, and accepted, part of life, death is set up as an enemy of life, as something to be feared and avoided. This is a colossal mistake. To understand death as punishment for some defect is completely to misunderstand the nature of life. Death is implicit in life. And we would do better to recognize and accept that fact. The cycles of nature include birth, fruition, and decay. We all die so that others may live. This is neither punishment nor sacrifice. It is simply the way things are.

Asceticism, the practice of self-denial, is a reflection of the Christian denial of finitude. Extreme ascetics deny themselves food, sleep, sex, comfort, baths. The number of vermin falling from an ascetic's body was once said to be a way of determining his holiness (Daly: 37). Self-flagellation was also practiced. The theory behind asceticism is dualism.

Finitude, Death, and Reverence for Life

It is said the body is at war with the soul, and that by denying the body, one frees the soul.

While extremes of asceticism are frowned upon in most circles today, celibacy is still required of Catholic priests and nuns. The ascetic attitude toward the body has been reaffirmed in Pope John Paul II's teachings on sexuality, marriage, and celibacy. While these teachings take a more positive attitude toward sex within marriage than some earlier theologians did, they nonetheless affirm the traditional view that celibacy is a higher calling than marriage.[2] Though Protestantism abolished the celibate ideal, ascetic attitudes remain. Many Protestants are taught that pleasure is a sin, and are urged to practice mental asceticism by constantly dwelling upon their imperfections.

Apocalypticism takes the denial of finitude and death a step further. The apocalyptic vision alleges that the whole finite world will come to an end, but affirms that God will create a new order. The gospel of Mark states the apocalyptic view, "There will be such a distress as until now has not been equalled since the beginning when God created the world, nor will there ever be again. . . . Heaven and earth will pass away, but my words will not pass away." (13:19, 31) The Book of Revelation likewise envisions the destruction of this earth. "Then I saw a new heaven and a new earth, and the first earth had disappeared, and now there was no longer any sea." (21:1) These writings are inspired by a mentality filled with disgust for this earth and this life. To envision destruction of this earth and its recreation by God is to imagine that the limitations of finitude and death could be transcended in a new creation. The new fundamentalist movement which has had a great deal of influence on American politicians and policy makers accepts and promulgates the apocalyptic vision, explicitly tying the possibility or even inevitability, of nuclear war to God's apocalyptic will.

Modern science is also the product of a culture which denies finitude and death. Carolyn Merchant in her brilliant book *The Death of Nature*, shows that prior to the advent of modern science in the sixteenth and seventeenth centuries, people viewed "the earth as geocosm . . . as a nurturing mother, sensitive, alive, and responsive to human action." Because earth was viewed as being alive, it was understood that there were limits to man's attempts to control or master her. Human beings understood themselves to be part of a finite system; there were limits to their ability to control nature. As Merchant establishes, this view of nature as a finite system was not compatible with modern science. She writes that "the changes in imagery and attitudes relating to the earth were of enormous significance as the mechanization of nature proceeded. The nurturing earth would lose its function as a normative restraint as it changed to an inanimate dead physical system" (22–23) Scientists declared the earth "dead matter" to be controlled by "man." Modern science is based upon the correlative notions that the powers of the human mind are unlimited, and that the mind can fully control and manipulate nature.

Modern medicine expresses the assumptions of modern science. Many doctors believe that they are omnipotent, that they can conquer the limitations of the flesh. Elizabeth Kubler-Ross wrote this about the medical profession:

> We believed that we could transplant kidneys, then livers, then hearts, then brains. People would no longer die. We [could] deep freeze them in a deep freeze chamber and 50 years from now, we [could] defrost them when we [had discovered] a cancer cure and they [would] live happily ever after.

Kubler-Ross adds, "I am not making up stories" (46). Doctors believe that their powers to control the body are not finite, and that the body is not finite.

The nuclear mentality is built on the denial of finitude. It is believed that man in his infinite wisdom can control forces far more powerful than himself. Plutonium 239, one of the substances created in nuclear power plants and used in the making of nuclear bombs, is deadly even in small amounts. Its radioactivity could contaminate the earth for 500,000 years (Caldicott 67). Even if all nuclear bombs were dismantled and all nuclear power plants were closed tomorrow, we would still have to find a way to safely store radioactive material for half a million years. Scientists assume that when the time comes other scientists will find a way to clean up the mess they have created. They deny that the time is now: today containers in which nuclear waste is being stored are leaking into the ground and into the ocean. Scientists fail to contemplate the possibility that there is no way to control a deadly substance for 500,000 years. They do not accept finitude, their own, or that of the earth. The fragility of the ecosystem, the limitations of our minds and our power to control, are denied. The very real possibility that the human race and most complex species of plants and animals would be destroyed in a nuclear war is not faced.

Politicians share the denial of finitude. The architects of nuclear policies imagine that nuclear war can be justified in order to preserve an abstraction called "our way of life." Robert Scheer asked the following question to Eugene Rostow, one of the architects of American nuclear policy:

> Would it be fair to say that you feel that the dangers inherent in the arms race, the dangers of accidental war, the dangers brought about by more and more weapons piling up, are a less

serious threat to peace than the danger of not controlling the Soviets and of having the Western alliance break up?

To this question Rostow answered, "That is absolutely correct." He acknowledged that the damage that would be brought about by a nuclear war would be "worse" than that caused by the two world wars, yet he stated that Soviet expansionism posed a greater threat (210). Apparently he has deceived himself into believing that a nuclear war is different only in magnitude, not in kind, from World War II. Louis O. Giuffrida, appointed by Ronald Reagan in his first administration to run the Federal Management Agency said this to ABC News about the consequences of nuclear war. "It would be a terrible mess, but it wouldn't be unmanageable" (Scheer: 3). He apparently expects to be around afterwards to clean up the "mess." Ronald Reagan told Scheer that nuclear war is survivable. "It would be a survival of some of your people and some of your facilities [so] that you could start again" (241). He evidently did not comprehend the significance of the fact that a single one megaton bomb is 80 times the size of the Hiroshima bomb, and would gut or flatten an area the size of the city New York (Schell: 47) and that it is highly unlikely that only one bomb would be dropped. He apparently did not wish to know that any areas of the U.S. not immediately vaporized, exploded, or burned by nuclear bombs would be poisoned by radiation, that all the major hospitals would be destroyed. He apparently did not know that this earth is finite. Ronald Reagan has since declared that he believes that a nuclear war is not survivable, yet his policies continue to bring us ever closer to the brink of disaster. Caspar Weinberger's statement to Scheer was more frightening. In his conversation with Scheer about nuclear war, he admitted that he expects this world to come to an end. "I have read the Book of Revelation, and yes, I believe the world is going to end—by an act of God, I hope . . . I think time is running out, but I have faith" (xi). Weinberger seems not to take seriously the threat to survival posed by nuclear war, since he believes God is planning to bring this world to an end in any case.

These men have not allowed consciousness of the finitude of life on this earth to affect their thinking about nuclear policy. They deny that nuclear war is likely to mean the end of civilization, the end of humanity, the destruction of all but a few species of plants and animals. Jonathan Schell's vision of the survivors of a nuclear war as a "republic of insects and grasses"[3] seems to me to be a more realistic assessment of the consequences of nuclear war. According to Schell, the short and long term effects of nuclear war would probably mean the destruction of all the complex species of plants and animals. Yet, those who are making the decisions about the life and death of our planet seem to believe that they are not finite, and that human life and all life is not capable of being "bounded, enclosed, or encompassed." Most frightening are those who contemplate total destruction but imagine that such might be the will of God.

It is easy to dismiss these men as madmen. Indeed they seem to have lost touch with reality. But these men are not aberrations within Western civilization. They are its products and their visions of reality are considered sane within a culture founded on the denial of finitude and death, a culture which clings to ideas about life, to ideologies, rather than to life itself. I am not suggesting that Platonic dualism as represented in theology and philosophy is the sole cause of these men's views. But the cultural habit of denying finitude and death which is deeply embedded in Western thought makes it easier for them to deny that nuclear war could destroy almost all the life on this planet.

I agree with Gordon Kaufman that in face of potential nuclear destruction "we must be prepared to enter into the most radical kind of deconstruction and reconstruction of the traditions we have inherited" (13). I believe the crisis of our times calls upon us to point out the roots of our peril in the denial of finitude and also to begin to depict a religious vision which is compatible with the preservation of this finite earth.

I believe that we must envision a spirituality which acknowledges finitude and death and which encourages us to affirm rather than deny our connections with the earth and all life on earth. From the perspective of our religious heritage it might seem that such a spirituality is a contradiction in terms. What is spirituality, it might be said, if not an answer to questions we have about finitude and death? What is religion if not a call to deny our limitations, to strive for a "more perfect way"? The spirituality we need for our survival, I would argue, is precisely a spirituality which encourages us to recognize limitation and death, a spirituality which calls us to celebrate our connections to all that is finite.

There are many resources for such a religious vision. The indigenous preurban traditions of Africa, Asia, America, and Europe all have much to teach us about a spirituality that connects us to earth and to finitude. Feminist thinking and spirituality also have much to say about the overcoming of the Platonic legacy of the denial of finitude.

Feminist thinkers remind us that our ideas about finitude, the body, and nature are very much bound up with our ideas about women. As Rosemary Ruether, Mary Daly, and others have shown, in Western philosophy and theology, women are associated with the negative side of the Platonic dualisms. Women are associated with the body, nature, and finitude, while males (and the male God) are associated with the mind, the spirit, and the infinite. These attitudes, which are prevalent in Western philosophy and theology, reach their apex in the following allegation found in the *Malleus Maleficarum*, the book used as a "hammer" against "witches": "All witchcraft comes from carnal lust which in women is insatiable" (Summers: 47). The root of the equation of women with the body, nature, and finitude can be found in the fact that those doing the equating were men. Male theologians, philosophers, and scientists have viewed women's cycles of menstruation, pregnancy, childbirth, lactation, and menopause as manifestations of our carnal nature, while conveniently denying their own bodily processes (such as birth, aging, and death, not to mention the uncontrollability of the penis) which just as definitively mark them as carnal. Recognizing the damage that has been done to women by dualistic philosophies which equate us with the despised body, some feminist thinkers have begun to question the equation of women with that which is despised. We have asserted that women's rational and spiritual capacities are equal to men's. And some feminist thinkers have also begun to question the dualistic patterns of thinking which separate mind and body, spirit and nature, finite and infinite.

One of the thinkers who has questioned dualism in her writing is Adrienne Rich. In her book *Of Woman Born: Motherhood as Experience and Institution,* Rich is forced by her position as a thinker who is also a mother to question the dualistic patterns which equate women with the body. She chooses to affirm both her mind and its creative capacities *and* her body and its creative capacities as equally relevant to her task of understanding motherhood. She therefore acknowledges herself as an embodied female thinker. She cannot accept the denial of the body in the work of some feminist thinkers who affirm women's minds. She writes that she understands why "many intellectual and creative women" have "minimized their physicality" in their affirmation of women's rationality. But she urges feminist thinkers to move beyond dualism when she writes:

> feminist vision has recoiled from female biology for [obvious] reasons; it will, I believe, come to view our physicality as a resource . . . we must touch the unity and resonance of our physicality, our bond with the natural order, the corporeal ground of our intelligence (39).

When Rich writes that we must learn to "think through the body" (and I assume she means all of us, not just women), she is fully aware that she is proposing a fundamental break from the dualism of Western thought. She is saying that we must recognize that all thought is finite. Thus she is denying the Platonic view that the mind can separate itself from the body in order to perceive and participate in the unconditioned.

Susan Griffin is another feminist writer whose work challenges the underlying metaphysic of Western thought. In *Woman and Nature* Griffin documents "how man regards and makes use of woman and nature," (3) showing how man has categorized both woman and nature as inferior to himself, as matter to be shaped and controlled by his mind and will. The central movement of Griffin's book occurs when woman strips off this false naming. When she recognizes that she is more than matter to be shaped by man's will, woman finds herself in a cave where she has a vision. Susan Griffin's vision in "The Cave" provides us with a model for a spirituality based on the acceptance of finitude and death. Griffin's vision provides a clear alternative to Plato's. In her vision the ego is transcended, but the earth and the body are not transcended. Socrates' vision as recorded by Plato was of the union of the soul with that which is unchanging, independent, and immaterial. Susan Griffin's vision is of the connection of the body and spirit to that which is changing, dependent, and material. Socrates wanted to transcend the body and nature; Susan Griffin experiences deeply her connection to body and nature. To Socrates the shadows on the wall of a cave are a metaphor for the illusory nature of material reality. In Griffin's vision the cave *is* nature speaking to woman:

> *the shape of this cave is a history telling us with each echo of the sound of each wave rushing against its sides:* "I was not here before; my shape changes daily. I was sand. I was mountain. I was stone. I was water, I was shellfish and sea anemone and sea snail, I was fish, eel, urchin. I was plankton. I was seaweed and sea grass. Here I am black and polished and round, here I am yellow, here I am covered with moss, here I gleam with a purple reflection when the light lies across me, here I curve outward, here I sink back.
>
> "When the water approaches me, the shape of the wave is changed. And when the tide ebbs, you will see, I, too, have changed" (160–61).

The voice in this passage is the voice of the cave, speaking to us, telling us that it changes daily, that it is constantly transforming. The cave is made of the bodies of sea animals and sea plants long ago returned to mineral form, transformed to sand, transformed to rock. The cave would not be cave without water flowing in, wearing the rock away. The cave tells us that all is ever changing, transforming. Change is its essence, it is not permanent, it is connected to everything. When I read Griffin's words, I recognize the cave's voice is also my voice. *I* was not here before; my shape changes daily. *I* was sand. *I* was mountain. *I* was stone. *I* was water, *I* was shellfish . . . Here *I* am black and polished and round, here *I* am yellow . . . I come from earth, my body is made of water, minerals, plant and animal life, one day my body will become food for other animals, my molecules will become something other than what they are today. Like the cave, I am not permanent, I am changing and continually changed, I am connected to everything.

Later Griffin expresses these thoughts more explicitly. "We know ourselves to be made from this earth. We know this earth is made from our bodies" (226). She challenges the Platonic longing for permanence when she writes, "everything moves, everything changes" (224). She bridges the gulf between "man" and "nature" when she insists:

> we are nature. We are nature seeing nature. We are nature with a concept of nature. Nature weeping. Nature speaking of nature to nature (226).

When she says "we are nature," Griffin challenges the classical legacy which insists on a categorical distinction between the human mind and what is called nature, namely finite, embodied, impermanent reality. Griffin rejects religious and philosophical traditions which place "man" half way between "angels" and "animals." When she says "we are nature," Griffin is not saying, as the Romantics might say, that the human ego encompasses the whole. Her suggestion is much more humble. Rather she is asking us to consider that we are as much a part of nature as are plants, stones, and other animals. Griffin acknowledges that we "see" nature (a capacity we share with most other animals), that we have a concept of nature (a capacity which may be uniquely human) and that we speak of nature. But she does not conclude that we are set apart from nature by virtue of having a concept of it. Rather she insists that "we are nature." This statement sounds paradoxical to us because the idea that nature is one thing and we are another is deeply embedded in our thinking. Griffin is asking us to reconsider one of the fundamental and unquestioned assumptions of our thought. It would be a mistake to conclude that Griffin "reduces man to nature." In asserting that we are nature, Griffin asks us to accept our finitude and our temporality. Like the cave, we are changing and continually changed. We too are made from other creatures, one day our bodies will become food for other creatures, our molecules will become something other than what we are today. But Griffin does not deny our ability to perceive, to think, to conceptualize. Rather than reducing us to "brute" nature, Griffin asks us to expand our concept of nature to include all that we are. It is important to stress this point for it is easy to misread feminist thinkers like Griffin as denying human capacities for self-reflection and limited freedom to shape our relation to the earth. I believe rather that Griffin is calling us to redefine self-consciousness and limited freedom within rather than in opposition to our fundamental grounding in nature.

In *Diving Deep and Surfacing* (20–23), I discussed visions like

Griffin's as examples of nature mysticism, and I named nature mysticism as one of the sources of women's spiritual vision. In so doing, I confronted the fact that nature mysticism (if it is discussed at all by theorists of mysticism) is denigrated as an inferior form of mysticism. This is because nature mysticism has been defined as union with the finite world, while so-called "higher mysticism" has been defined as union with the infinite, that which utterly transcends the finite, sometimes called the Void, or God. In my book I argued that nature mysticism is an important source of spiritual insight. Now I ask us to consider whether there is any reality which is "higher" than the finite, the earth, that which changes. I believe that we cannot know such a reality if it exists, and that it is destructive of the reality we do know to focus on an imagined reality which is superior to the finite, embodied, reality we do know.

During the past two summers, while visiting the alleged birthplace of Sappho, I had visions similar to Griffin's. My visions came in the cave at "Minerve's point" in Skala Erresos. I share these visions because I take seriously theology's starting point in our own experience. I believe we will be faithful to that starting point only when we reflect on our own experience as well as that of other women. This vision in Lesbos is not the only nature mystical experience I have had, but it is one of the most intense. I refer to the cave as "She" in the words that follow, because for me (as for Griffin) the cave resonated with my knowledge that caves once were known as the womb and birth canal of earth, her opening.

She appears to me while I am floating in the embrace of the azure sea, rising up from the water in the shape of an enormous vagina. I swim her mouth and climb over anemone and urchin covered rocks to her opening. I see that iron ore has stained her mottled granite and sandstone folds the color of blood. I am startled yet comforted by a strong smell of salt and fish within. Watching the water flow in and out of her, I feel drawn to her center. I climb back and lean into the crevice. As my body relaxes, I feel a surge of energy, the life force flowing through me. My rhythms merge with hers, the shapes of the rock become the shapes of my body pulsating with energy, flowing into the sea. When I stand up I feel dizzy.

Near the cave is a tiny white church, dedicated to Panagia, All Holy Mary. I know the church is here because people knew the cave to be Panagia, All Holy Mother. I am struck by the contrast between the enormous cave formed by the sea, changing with it, and the small church enclosed against the sea, constantly in need of repair. And I know which place for me is the more holy.

Though these visions come to us through women, visions such as these do not belong to women exclusively. They offer a vision which is essential to us all. These visions in caves contain a clue to a spirituality which can reawaken our sense of our connection to all living things, to

Finitude, Death, and Reverence for Life   107

the life force within us and without us. If we experience our connection to this finite and changing earth deeply within ourselves, then we must find the thought of its destruction or even mutilation intolerable. When we deeply and fully affirm this finite changing earth as our true home and accept our own inevitable death, then we must know as well that spirituality is the celebration of our connection to all that is and is changing. Then we will also know that there is no cause or ideology more precious than life itself. Such visions might undergird our survival. With every bone in my body, I pray, "surely the earth can be saved for us (Walker: 79).

NOTES

[1] Earlier versions of this essay were presented at the 1983 meetings of the American Academy of Religion, as part of the Davidson Lectures at Carleton University in Ottowa in March, 1984, as part of the Fifth Annual Religious Studies Colloquium at California State University in Fullerton in April, 1984, as part of the Celebration of 100 Years of Women's Education and the Celebration of the Arts at Bucknell University in March, 1985, and as the 11th Antionette Brown Blackwell Lecture on Women and Religion at Vanderbilt Divinity School in March, 1985.

[2] See, for example, John Paul II, "Address to a General Audience about Marriage and Celibacy," Osservatore Romano (English edition) 27 (741) July 5, 1982, 3ff.

[3] This is the title of the first chapter of *The Fate of the Earth*.

WORKS CONSULTED

Caldicott, Helen, et al.
    1984   *Nuclear Madness: What You Can Do!* Brookline, Mass.: Autumn Publishers.

Christ, Carol P.
    1980   *Diving Deep and Surfacing: Women Writers on Spiritual Quest.* Boston: Beacon Press.

Daly, Mary
    1978   *Pure Lust: Elemental Feminist Philosophy.* Boston: Beacon Press.

Griffin, Susan
    1978   *Woman and Nature: The Roaring Inside Her.* New York: Harper & Row.

Hamilton, Edith and
Chairns, Huntington, Eds.
    1966   *The Collected Dialogues of Plato Including the Letters.* New York: Pantheon Books.

Kaufman, Gordon
    1983   "Nuclear Eschatology and the Study of Religion." *Journal of the American Academy of Religion* LI/1 (March)

Kubler-Ross, Elizabeth
    1980   "Lighting Candles in the Darkness." *WomanSpirit* 8/31 (Spring).

Merchant, Carolyn
    1980   *The Death of Nature: Women, Ecology, and the Scientific Revolution.* San Francisco: Harper & Row.

Morris, William, Ed.
    1973   *The American Heritage Dictionary of the English Language.* New York: American Heritage Publishing Co., and Houghton Mifflin.

Rich, Adrienne
    1976   *Of Woman Born: Motherhood as Experience and Institution.* New York: W. W. Norton.

Scheer, Robert
    1982   *With Enough Shovels: Reagan, Bush, and Nuclear War.* New York: Random House.

Schell, Jonathan
    1982   *The Fate of the Earth.* New York: Avon Books.

Scully, Vincent
    1979   *The Earth, the Temple, and the Gods.* Rev. Ed. New Haven: Yale University Press.

Summers, Montague, Trans.
    1971   *The Malleus Maleficarum of Heinrich Kramer and James Sprenger.* New York: Dover Publications.

Walker, Alice
    1984   *Horses Make a Landscape More Beautiful.* New York: Harcourt Brace Jovanovich.

LIVING EARTH AND LIVING CHRIST
Thoughts on Carol P. Christ's "Finitude, Death, and Reverence for Life."

John Dominic Crossan
DePaul University

"Much Gesture, from the Pulpit—
Strong Hallelujahs roll—
Narcotics cannot still the Tooth
That nibbles at the soul"

Emily Dickinson (Johnson: 2.384–85)

We speak of Text and for Carol Christ that text is the earth. We speak of Textuality and for Carol Christ that textuality is the earth's most possible destruction by those who cannot accept their own finitude.

My thoughts upon reading her essay are less upon that textuality than upon that text. I leave aside the textuality of nuclear catastrophe, not because I disagree with her about its horror but because I agree too much to have anything to add to her own words. What commentary is needed on the apocalyptic pornography of Weinberger's admission, "I have read the Book of Revelation, and yes, I believe the world is going to end—by an act of God, I hope . . . I think time is running out, but I have faith."

What I want to think about is her text. I wonder where does the literal and the metaphorical meet in her text of earth. I also wonder where does the romantic and the mystic meet in her text of earth. Let me try it very slowly and carefully, step by step.

1. The Living Earth as Text.

Carol Christ quotes from Susan Griffin's, *Woman and Nature*, concerning woman and nature, "*we are stunned by this beauty,* and I do not forget: what she is to me, what I am to her." The uneasiness begins right there for me. There seems to be no terror in that beauty. There is no sense of the earth's serene and magnificent indifference. What the earth is to me is one thing. What I am to the earth is quite another. The earth would destroy me with the same unconcern it would destroy itself. Let me be very clear on this. I know that I will one day cease to be and I accept that moment's random unexpectedness. I do not think that gives me a right to my suicide or others a right to my murder. Neither do I think that humans have a right to cosmic suicide and planetary murder within some nuclear nightmare. But I also know that the earth may well destroy itself or that some hurtling star or freezing sun may one day do it just as efficiently. And I do not expect the heavens to weep for that eventuality. To love the earth, to embrace the universe, means to accept that sublime unconcern but not to emulate it.

My initial uneasiness with a too romantic vision of the earth and of nature continues throughout Carol Christ's paper and becomes intensified by the conclusion, by her account of Lesbos. I admit immediately that, for me, any nature mysticism must be one not only of beauty but of terror, or, with apologies to Yeats, of a terrible beauty. I have spent a decade of summers on a small Mediterranean island, not Lesbos but Ibiza, and am absolutely seducible by the beauty of white wall and purple bourgainvillea, ancient olive and spreading fig, wild thyme and wilder rosemary, azure sky and glistening sea. But I also remember and include in that seduction a day in late August of 1977 in a villa which stepped down the cliff from a road above it towards the sea below. It had hardly rained all summer and the earth was bone dry. The rain began as a monsoon downpour at about 3 A.M. that Sunday morning. By dawn, with the rain continuing unabated, there was a river flowing down the road. Two hours later the road was flowing down the river. The metallic earth, totally unable to absorb so much so fast, smoothly translated continual rain into instant river. The road-river above us was soon sending a small but definite tributary down through the villa, coming in on the level above and streaming out on the level below. Boulders, larger than our little Seat 600, had already been loosened from the cliffs above us and coming down on what had once been a road. We spent the day watching the valley below turned into a flood, the beach below turned into an estuary, and the boats below turned into matchsticks. Around 5 P.M. the downpour stopped as suddenly as it had begun and a rainbow came up over a sea turned brown with the topsoil it had absorbed. A small terror, surely, and certainly no Santorini. But still part of nature, part of earth, part even of a smiling Mediterranean island.

I have, therefore, two main problems with Carol Christ's reading of her text of earth, and the first is much more clear to me than the second. First, I think her nature mysticism is more a nature romanticism or even a nature narcissism. Baudelaire said that after he found nothingness, he found beauty. I see romanticism, in Baudelaire's terms, as beauty without nothingness. Otto talked of *fascinans* and *tremens*. I see romanticism as *fascinans* without *tremens*. What is of serious concern here is this. A revered madonna may be but the other side of a raped prostitute. So also may a romanticized earth be but the other side of a ravished nature. Second, and this is more difficult to articulate, I think her nature mysticism is a much too literal reading of the earth. My own presuppositions are that humans need to accept their own fragility and mortality but also that they need to participate in phenomena they experience as infinite, eternal, and immortal. These phenomena may be family or tribe, group or institution, state or nation, religion or sect. But they are not literally infinite, eternal, immortal. They can never be more than fictions of the infinite, images of the eternal, metaphors of the immortal. It is not clear to me that Carol Christ reads her earth metaphorically rather than literally. She never contemplates how the earth might blow itself to bits from out its own molten core. It is as if, apart from nuclear catastrophe, the earth is eternal. I hope that is not unfair. If one speaks only against nuclear obscenity, one need hardly discuss that question. But if one speaks of nature mysticism, how can one avoid it? Does the earth "care" if it (or we) relocate its atoms elsewhere in the universe?

2. The Living Christ as Text.

The fairness of that last criticsm, that Carol Christ reads her text of earth not only too romantically and narcissistically but also too literally, may be warranted by the way she, quite rightly in my opinion, complains that a literal Christian reading of the resurrection is a rather crude denial of one's finitude. She says: "The denial of finitude within Christianity is encompassed in the phrase 'he is risen.' Without addressing the complex theological disputes about the nature of the resurrection, let me state the obvious: the statement 'he is risen' is a denial that death marks the end of individual life. The hopes of Christians throughout the centuries have been based upon the expectation of an individual life after physical death in which the limitations of finitude are overcome." I find such a literal reading of Christ's resurrection and our participation in it as unseemly as a similar reading of the earth's continuation and our participation in that. My next step, then, is to test some texts concerning the resurrection to see if a literal reading is the only one possible. If that were the situation, I would agree that it represents a rather crude denial of human finitude and could only be justified as narcosis, that is, as something which obliterates intolerable pain when no other alternative is present.

(a) *Earthly Jesus in Unearthy Mode.*

Soon after the middle of the first Christian century some of Paul's Corinthian converts scoffed at the idea of bodily resurrection, for Christ, for themselves, or for anyone else ever. "But some one will ask, 'How are the dead raised? With what kind of body do they come?'" (1 Cor 15:35).

Paul's answer is quite fascinating. It is not the simple and obvious one that a God who could create the world could surely reconstitute a physical body. In fact such an understanding of resurrection is flatly contradicted: "I tell you this, brethren: flesh and blood cannot inherit the kingdom of God, nor does the perishable inherit the imperishable" (15:50). Instead, Paul moves slowly through metaphor into paradox. (15:42–44):

> "What is sown is perishable, what is raised is imperishable. It is sown in dishonor, it is raised in glory. It is sown in weakness, it is raised in power. It is sown a physical body, it is raised a spiritual body."

Paul must use this strategy of a paradoxical "spiritual body" because there are *two* values of equal worth to be preserved. First, Christ is in complete and total continuity with Jesus, therefore, he cannot be a disembodied spirit but must be a spiritual body. Second, this personal continuity is accompanied by a modal transformation. It is, one might say, *earthly Jesus in unearthly mode*. Paul speaks of this mode as being imperishable, glorious, powerful, and spiritual.

Paul challenged any future theology of resurrection with metaphor and paradox, with how to hold on equally to (1) spiritual and (2) body. James M. Robinson in his powerful, provocative, and persuasive SBL Presidential Address showed very clearly what happened as theology faced the challenge of this metaphorical paradox. He makes two main points. First, he suggested that two separate trajectories developed out of that original Pauline paradox. "Although orthodoxy and heresy could on occasion accomodate themselves to language actually developed to implement the emphasis of the other alternative, by and large they divided the Pauline doctrine of luminous bodiliness between them: Orthodoxy defended the bodiliness by replacing luminousness with fleshliness, heresy exploited the luminousness by replacing bodiliness with spiritualness" (1982: 17). Second, he proposed that the orthodox emphasis is a later reaction to the earlier heretical interpretation, or, at least, that it arose as that earlier vision was itself drawn inexorably towards heresy. "Our prevalent view that the church was launched by Easter experiences such as we find at the end of the canonical gospels must as a result be replaced by a recognition that they are secondary to an original luminous visualization of Christ's appearances, replaced as that original Christian experience played more and more into the hands of the trajectory from Easter to Valentinus. Over against that option, emerging orthodoxy, on the trajectory from Easter to the Apostles' Creed, expressed the reality of the bodily resurrection by emphasizing, in spite of supernatural vestiges, the human-like appearance of the resurrected Christ: the resurrection of the *flesh*" (1982: 16). I am completely persuaded by Robinson's arguments and presume them throughout the rest of this paper, but I will formulate it in my own somewhat different way. I emphasize that Paul presented any future resurrection theology with metaphor, paradox, and mystery, in speaking of what Robinson calls "luminous bodiliness" and I call, staying closer to Paul's own language, "spiritual body." The earliest theological responses split, quite simply, along the two possible trajectories or emphases already present in that paradoxical core.

(b) *Unearthly Jesus in Unearthly Mode.*

On the one hand, there was the trajectory of Gnostic Christianity which, in my terms, solved the Pauline paradox of *earthly Jesus in unearthly mode* by emphasizing *unearthly Jesus in unearthly mode*. This was done primarily by rendering the risen Jesus both luminous and heteromorphous. The *luminous* Jesus appears for example, in the *Letter of Peter to Philip* (CG VIII,2) from Nag Hammadi (134:9–18; Robinson, 1977:395; see Meyer: 105–43):

> "Then a great light appeared so that the mountain shone from the sight of him who had appeared. And a voice called out to them, saying, 'Listen to my words that I may speak to you. Why are you asking me? I am Jesus Christ who is with you forever.'"

This is underlined even more obviously in the *Sophia of Jesus Christ*, a text known before (BG 8502,3) and also from Nag Hammadi (CG III,4). It reads (91:10–23; Robinson, 1977:207–8; see Perkins: 39):

> "The Savior appeared not in his first form, but in the invisible spirit. And his form was like a great angel of light. And the likeness I must not describe. No mortal flesh can endure it, but only pure (and) perfect flesh like that which he taught us about on the mountain called 'Of the Olives' in Galilee."

The *heteromorphous* Jesus appears, for example, in the *Apocryphon of John*, another text known both before (BG 8502,2) and from three separate copies at Nag Hammadi (CG II,1, III,1, IV,1). It includes a reference to the light theme but emphasizes more the heteromorphous nature of Jesus (CG II.1:30–2:15; Robinson, 1977:99):

> "Straightway, [while I was contemplating these things], behold the [heavens opened and the whole] creation [which is] under heaven shone and [the world] was shaken. [And I was afraid, and behold I] saw in the light [a youth who stood] by me. While I looked [at him he became] like an old man. And he [changed his] form (again), becoming like a servant. There was [not a plurality] before me, but there was a [likeness] with multiple forms in the light, and the [forms] appeared through each other, [and] the

likeness had three forms. He said to me, 'John, Jo[h]n, why do you doubt, and why are you afraid? You are not unfamiliar with this likeness, are you? That is to say, be not timid! I am the one who [is with you (pl.)] for ever. I [am the Father], I am the Mother, I am the Son. I am the unpolluted and incorruptible one."

It is not immediately obvious to me that Paul would have disapproved of these formulations in themselves. At least a luminous and possibly even a heteromorphous Jesus might have seemed a legitimate way of describing, if one had to do so, what a "spiritual body" looked like. But the dangers and directions, tendencies and temptations of those texts may well be pulling already towards *unearthly Jesus in unearthly mode*. This is certainly clear in a section such as "John's Preaching of the Gospel" from the *Acts of John* 87–93 (Cameron: 89–91). This section concerns Jesus in his earthly life before the crucifixion and he is already *even then* both luminous and heteromorphous. His luminous nature is described only during the transfiguration (90):

"And we saw [on] him a light such that a man, who uses mortal speech, cannot describe what it was like . . . (And I saw that) his feet were whiter than snow, so that the ground there was lit up by his feet."

But the heteromorphous aspect is mentioned repeatedly. It is first mentioned as a feature of Jesus after the resurrection (87):

"'The Lord appeared to me in the tomb in the form of John and in that of a young man.'"

This is then explained as having been *always* a feature of Jesus. First, his appearance kept changing (89–90):

"For when he had chosen Peter and Andrew, who were brothers, he came to me and to my brother James, saying 'I need you; come with me!' And my brother said to me, 'John, what does he want, this child on the shore who called us?' And I said, 'Which child?' And he answered me, 'The one who is beckoning to us.' And I said, 'This is because of the long watch we have kept at sea. You are not seeing straight, brother James. Do you not see the man standing there who is handsome, fair, and cheerful-looking?' But he said to me, 'I do not see that man, my brother. But let us go, and we will see what this means.' And when we had brought the boat to land we saw how he also helped us to beach the boat. And as we left the place, wishing to follow him, he appeared to me again as rather bald-[headed] but with a thick flowing beard, but to James as a young man whose beard was just beginning."

Second, his solidity or corporality also changes (89,93):

> "And he had another strange (property); when I reclined at table he would take me to his own breast, and I held him (fast); and sometimes his breast felt to me smooth and soft, but sometimes hard like rock . . . I will tell you another glory, brethren; sometimes when I meant to touch him I encountered a material, solid body; but at other times again when I felt him, his substance was immaterial and incorporeal, and as if it did not exist at all."

Third, in case one has not already got the point, the earthly Jesus had two other mysterious features (89,93):

> "But then there appeared to me a yet more amazing sight; I tried to see him as he was, and I never saw his eyes closing, but always open . . . And I often wished, as I walked with him, to see his footprint in the earth, whether it appeared—for I saw him raising himself from the earth—and I never saw it."

In *Acts of John* 87–93 the docetism potentially latent or possibly even present in descriptions of the luminous and heteromorphous risen Christ is explicitly accepted as having always been a feature even of the earthly Jesus. This is certainly *unearthly Jesus in unearthly mode* and the Pauline paradox of spiritual body here appears as solved or dissolved into the permanence of disembodied spirit.

(c) *Earthly Jesus in Earthly Mode*

On the other hand, there was the resurrection trajectory of Catholic Christianity which, in my terms, solved the Pauline paradox of *earthly Jesus in unearthly mode* by emphasizing *earthy Jesus in earthly mode* and thereby offsetting forcibly and even crudely Gnostic Christianity's response of *unearthly Jesus in unearthly mode*. This can be seen in two steps.

First, there are vestigial remnants of the luminous and heteromorphous Christ still present in the intracanonical texts. The luminous Christ is still visible in the Transfiguration of Mark 9:3: "and his garments became glistening, intensely white, as no fuller on earth could bleach them." I proposed elsewhere that Mark, whose ending at 16:8 allowed no resurrection apparitions whatsoever, deliberately relocated this resurrection vision into the earthly life at 9:2–8 and had Jesus command the disciples not to disclose it until after the resurrection in 9:9–10 so that it would be clearly understood as proleptic parousia and not proleptic resurrection. For Mark, the risen Christ does not appear or intervene, not even and especially not even to save his own until the imminent parousia (1978; 1985:165–74). The heteromorphous Christ is still visible in those places where he appears presumably in human form but is not recognized: to the two disciples on their way to Emmaus in Luke 24:16, "but their eyes were kept from recognizing him"; to Mary at the tomb in John 20:15, "supposing him to be the gardener"; to the seven disciples near the beach in John 21:4, "yet the disciples did not know that it was Jesus." Finally, and be it luminous or heteromorphous, there is the ability of the risen Christ to appear in a closed room in John 20:19,26 and to disappear from another in Luke 24:31. This is all, and it is very little, that still survives of the luminous and heteromorphous Christ in our present intracanonical texts.

Second, and this is far more important, there is the almost crude insistence on the reality of Jesus' risen body in the resurrection tradition of Catholic Christianity. The two emphases here, corresponding to the twin emphases just seen in Gnostic Christianity, are that Jesus *can eat* and that Jesus *can be touched*. Both are present in Luke 24:36–43:

> "As they were saying this, Jesus himself stood among them. But they were startled and frightened, and supposed that they saw a spirit. And he said to them, 'Why are you troubled, and why do questionings rise in your hearts? See my hands and my feet, that it is I myself; handle me, and see; for a spirit has not flesh and bones as you see that I have.' And while they still disbelieved for joy, and wondered, he said to them, 'Have you anything here to eat?' They gave him a piece of broiled fish, and he took it and ate before them."

Although it might be possible to read the meals of Luke 24:30 and John 21:13 as eucharistic presence, that one in Luke 24:42–43 is simply a graphic underlining of the risen Christ as *earthly Jesus in earthly mode*.

A second example comes from the *Epistula Apostolorum* (Cameron: 131–62), a polemical work of second-century Catholic Christianity opposing Gnostic Christianity from within its own formal arsenal. Jesus appears (11–12; Cameron 137–38):

> "And we doubted and did not believe. He came before us like a ghost and we did not believe that it was he. But it was he. And thus he said to us, 'Come and do not be afraid. I am your teacher . . . whom you, Peter, denied three times . . . and now do you deny again?' And we went to him, thinking and doubting whether it was he. And he said, 'Why do you . . . doubt and . . . are you not believing . . . I am he who spoke concerning my flesh, my death, and my resurrection. And that you may know that it is I, lay your hand, Peter, (and your finger) in the nailprint of my hands; and you, Thomas, in my side; and also you, Andrew, see whether my foot steps on the ground and leaves a footprint. For it is written in the prophet, "But a ghost, a demon, leaves no print

on the ground.'" But now we felt him, that he had truly risen in the flesh."

A third and final example comes from Ignatius, *To the Smyrnaeans*, but here there is an attempt to emphasize both physical and spiritual realities. Ignatius confesses (3:1–3; Lake:1.254–55):

> "For I know and believe that he was in the flesh even after the Resurrection. And when he came to those with Peter he said to them: 'Take, handle me and see that I am not a phantom without a body.' And they immediately touched him and believed, being mingled both with his flesh and spirit. Therefore they despised even death, and were proved to be above death. And after his Resurrection he ate and drank with them as a being of flesh, although he was united in spirit to the Father."

We have come a very long way from Paul's "I tell you this, brethren: flesh and blood cannot inherit the kingdom of God, nor does the perishable inherit the imperishable" in 1 Cor 15:50. We have come so far that John 20:29 negated this whole touching process with "Blessed are those who have not seen and yet believe."

3. Living Earth and Living Christ as Texts.

This response does not discuss the comparative merits of the living Earth or the living Christ as ultimate texts. That is a separate and even more important question. My comments have more to do with how one reads than what one reads. On the one hand, I think that Carol Christ has read her text of living Earth not mystically but romantically and even narcissistically. On the other, I think she is quite right in criticizing Christianity for reading the text of the living Christ romantically and even narcissistically rather than mystically. As an alternative to such a literal reading of the living Christ, I proposed an emphasis on Paul's magnificent paradox of Christ's "spiritual body," a mystery involving both total continuity and modal transformation. It is, in other words, the total Jesus that abides but in a mode of radical otherness. The first theologies which faced this paradox of the *earthly Jesus in unearthly mode* slowly solved it by changing it first to *unearthly Jesus in unearthly mode* along a Gnostic trajectory and then to *earthly Jesus in earthly mode* along a Catholic trajectory. Despite the magnificent warning in John's story of doubting Thomas, this latter theology hardly took very seriously Paul's aphorism, "I tell you this, brethren: flesh and blood cannot inherit the kingdom of God, nor does the perishable inherit the imperishable" in 1 Cor 15:50.

It is necessary, therefore, in reading either the text of the living

Earth or the text of the living Christ to know the difference between, on the one hand, a metaphorical, paradoxical, or mystical reading, and, on the other, a literal, romantic, or narcissistic one. I know no better guide in learning those distinctions *for both those texts* than the poet cited as this paper's epigraph.

WORKS CONSULTED

Cameron, Ron (Ed.)
    1982   *The Other Gospels*. Non-Canonical Gospel Texts. Philadelphia: Westminster Press.

Crossan, John Dominic
    1978   "A Form of Absence: The Markan Creation of Gospel." Pp. 41–55 in Vol. 1 of *Semeia* 12–13: *The Poetics of Faith. Essays Offered to Amos Niven Wilder*. 2 vols. Ed. William A. Beardslee. 2 vols. Missoula, MT: Scholars Press.
    1985   *Four Other Gospels*. Shadows on the Contours of Canon. Minneapolis, MN: Winston/Seabury.

Johnson, Thomas H. (Ed.)
    1955   *The Poems, of Emily Dickinson*. 3 vols. Cambridge, MA: The Belknap Press of Harvard University Press.

Lake, Kirsopp (Trans. & Ed.)
    1912–13   *The Apostolic Fathers*. LCL 24–25. Cambridge, MA: Harvard University Press.

Meyer, Marvin W.
    1981   *The Letter of Peter to Philip*. Text, Translation, and Commentary, SBLDS 53. Chico, CA: Scholars Press.

Perkins, Pheme
    1980   *The Gnostic Dialogue:* The Early Church and the Crisis of Gnosticism. New York: Paulist Press, 1980.

Robinson, James M. (General Editor)
    1977   *The Nag Hammadi Library in English*. Ed. Marvin W. Meyer. New York: Harper & Row.

Robinson, James M.
    1982   "Jesus: From Easter to Valentinus (or to the Apostles' Creed)." *JBL* 101:5–37.

FROM SCRIPTURE TO TEXTUALITY

Kent Harold Richards
The Iliff School of Theology

ABSTRACT

Raschke's "From Textuality to Scripture" invites reflection on the problem of the text. The loss of scripture was in some sense brought on by this problem. However, the movement from text to scripture must be accompanied by a movement from scripture to text. These movements permit the dependence and independence of scripture and text in a way which any single movement does not permit.

> Save that from yonder ivy-mantled tow'r
> The moping owl does to the moon complain
> Of such as, wand'ring near her secret bow'r
> Molest her ancient solitary reign.
>
> Thomas Gray

1. Introduction
1.1 English poetry is replete with examples of the unspoken texturing the spoken. The quatrain from "Elegy Written in a Country Churchyard" yields an example. The earliest and latest of the several known versions read as quoted. Other versions voice the phrase "sacred bower" not "secret bower."
1.2 The dimly lit graveyard scene supports the sense of sacred, as does "bower." The "ancient solitary reign" moves toward sacred as well. But how remarkable for an owl to have an "ancient solitary reign," let alone a "sacred bower." Surely no attempt is made to disclose the secretiveness of the owl's position. So the selection was not made to highlight the hidden perch of a bird. However, the final verdict of "secret" over "sacred" should be applauded. Bower gathers up a myriad of poetic, antique ambiguities—an abode, the woman's boudoir and the arbor. The secret develops a sense of sacred power to which the owl relates. Thus, in

order to create the sacred, the "secret" was selected. The sacred is opened to the unenclosed through the secret.

1.3 Just at a time when much of biblical studies seems rejuvenated by the text, it is difficult to allow any hearing of Raschke's title, "from textuality to scripture." It is as though the sacred scripture were to displace the secret, and without any real gain. One might argue that the "hermeneutics of the infinite" is possible only when scripture is given up and the text is all that remains.

1.4 With that said, I must go beyond the slogans found in both Raschke's and my comments. I think there are some common grounds, but the issues for the two of us from our different backgrounds (theology and biblical studies) suggest different emphases. In an effort to engage the discussion I have resisted the use of biblical texts. Raschke's article is directed to the text problem, not just the Bible. His textual concerns are not merely flippant speculation but are deliberative, ethical probes. My first objective is to state briefly some of my understandings of Raschke and then turn to several reflections.

2. Understandings of Raschke

2.1 The superficial reader might suspect that Raschke is advocating a return to some kind of neo-orthodoxy what with the old familiar names of Barth and Kierkegaard, not to mention the opening invocation from Luther. Do not be fooled. Here there is no hidden Jacob in the hairy covering of Esau.

2.2 Luther sets the stage admirably to demonstrate that the loss of scripture's significance arises when historicism's contextual longing left the text conned. Luther's finely "honed dialectic of 'faith' and 'doctrines of men'" provide at least one commissioning for us to resolve the "problem of the text." The resolution is not likely to take place through an understanding of text which necessitates the peeling back of the layers. For the text does not present itself as something which needs rescuing. The text does not provide the "threshhold of the numinous." The text says all it really "meant to say." The text provides the disclosure of difference a la Derrida.

2.3 It is at this moment of difference when through no "secure rules" one may entertain the iconoclastic possibility of the text becoming scripture. Said another way, the moment it is realized that the text provides no freeway to the transcendent—that is, it contains a kind of incapacity—then the text both struggles toward the unenclosed and retains its independence from scripture. Raschke emphasizes that the only way to affirm the text as scripture is to recognize the study of language for what it is "...not another disguised mode of metaphysics, but a propaedeutic to 'faith' in the most profound and incommensurable way." The radical and, I think not unfairly stated, eschatological dimensions of Raschke's position become evident. He seeks to exceed all starting points and grounds of thinking, including language. He repeats the Barthian warning of confusing religion with faith. He urges us to transcend the "Nietzschean struggle between intelligence and opacity, between form and chaos." And eloquently concludes that the hermeneutics of the infinite comes to power ". . .when the 'Kingdom of God' . . . is present amid the grief of absence."

3. Reflections

3.1 It is impossible to read Raschke without a sense of participation in his longing for a generative, constructive theology. Equally sensed is the nonsense expressed by Foucault's *Madness and Civilization* where insanity is exposed as the mirror of rationality. As a non-theologian but fellow traveller, I am recollected into a task which must not be trivialized through compartmentalizing. Theologians are not the only ones who will lose if the constructive task fails. Those of us in biblical studies, even if the work is thought of as propaedeutic, share in the failure.

3.2 I am concerned along with Edward Said that the task before us break out of the intellectual ghetto where critics only speak to each other. And the literary critics to whom Said is speaking are no more or less guilty than biblical scholars and theologians. I am not embarrassed to speak of the difficulty of reading these articles by my theologian colleagues. Our disciplines have taken quite different roads. Coming together in the discussion of text and scripture presents an opportunity which should not be fumbled. If there be any reason to search for an archaeology or eschatology, it surely resides in the surplus of meaning written in our twisted texts.

3.3 A further related and more specific reflection rests on the radicality of Raschke's suggestions. How does one exceed all starting points? In a poetic and metaphoric fashion one can approximate this point, but where, when we bring ourselves with all the trappings of the past? An entrée "for historical and descriptive studies that work within a semantics of meaning in the collecting of images and in the conservation of our linguistic and experiential inheritance" (Winquist: 75–76) must come forth. Interpretation occurs at the hinge (Ricoeur) between language and experience where the diverse "methodologies of hesitation" (Winquist) meet.

3.4 Finally, I am asking for a hinge on which we not only make the move from textuality to scripture but from scripture to textuality. Raschke's proposals regarding the first move have warrants. He articulates the necessity of distinguishing text and scripture. He understands the necessity of textuality for scripture. The move from scripture to textuality calls for additional comment.

3.5 Several points need underscoring. I am not contending that "Literary criticism has become a kind of substitute theology" (Handelman: xiii). The connection between the criticism of sacred and secular texts is indisputable. The renewed interest in rabbinic exegesis among some modern literary critics (Barthes, Bloom, Derrida, Lacan) is obvious. "Rather than rabbinic exegesis having influenced contemporary criticism, it may be that the newest criticism has actually taught us to appreciate midrash anew" (Stern: 204). Hartman reminds us that any of our imitations of former modes of interpretation are little more than archaizing fabrications unless we believe in the authority of the sacred text and by extension the critical text (Hartman: 176). However, authority for the rabbis precedes the text, rather than proceeding from the text. I think it essential not to equate theology and literary criticism.

3.6 The move from scripture to text is not to divine the text, but to leave open the perpetual incompleteness of it. Some of us in biblical studies have gained a sense of freedom as the Bible lost its divine position. Contextual and historical studies provided a release. Any kind of hurried step, back or forward, into scripture must be accompanied by careful understandings of the various "stages in imagination" (Crossan).

3.7 Equally undesirable is the scripturalization of text. To say that the text is the Holy Scripture for its critics (Handelman: 79) is to misunderstand the difference between text and scripture. While they may seek each other, the seeking occurs in the paradox of their present absence.

3.8 The presence of the text discloses what cannot be enclosed in its presence and may participate in becoming scripture. In becoming scripture one realizes the approximation and may return to the text discerning its incompleteness. To put it another way, the study of language is not disguised metaphysics; it may be propaedeutic; and it anticipates a return. The movement from text to scripture and scripture to text is not a circle but a helix. The introduction of this movement from scripture to text is not intended as a final movement or even one which merely involves circling.

3.9 The issue is that these movements encompass both reorientation and disorientation. The simple identification of either with just one of the movements of foretelling which movement will reorient or disorient involves a forgetfulness of their dependence and independence.

4. Conclusion

4.1 I conclude with a text which after all is the focus of my concern. George Elliott's *Fever and Chills* is a book length poem about a man initiating an affair with his best friend's wife. The man is also his wife's best friend. Half unconsciously and half deliberately he sets out to test the limits. What can he get away with in this world? The poem ends with the affair ending. Both the spouses know about the affair and the families have been shattered. The man is in the hospital.

> Before he had quite recovered,
> Susan was to join her husband.

> The night before she left, they met.
> He desired her because he thought
> He ought to. For the first time, his
> I want you failed to generate
> Hers. She lay with face averted
> And helped him make what had been love;
> She thought he wanted to. Even
> Then, their bodies could not fail.
>
> His wife, who did not reprove him,
> Also did not forgive him, but
> She wanted him back, and he went.

4.2 In voicing the text we need not choose between one, two, three, or an infinite number of thoughts. Rather we are called upon to trace the difference of repetition in the helix.

WORKS CONSULTED

Bloom, Harold
    1975   *A Map of Misreading*. New York: Oxford University Press.

Crossan, J. Dominic
    1981   "Stages in Imagination." In *The Archaeology of the Imagination*. The Journal of the American Academy of Religion Thematic Studies 48/2.

Derrida, Jacques
    1978   *Writing and Difference*. Chicago: University of Chicago Press.
    1981   *Dissemination*. Chicago: University of Chicago Press.
    1982   *Margins of Philosophy*. Chicago: University of Chicago Press.

Foucault, Michael
    1973   *Madness and Civilization: A History of Insanity in the Age of Reason*. New York: Vintage Books.

Handelman, Susan A.
    1982   *The Slayers of Moses: The Emergence of Rabbinic Interpretation in Modern Literary Theory*. Albany: State University of New York Press.

Hartman, Geoffrey
    1980   *Criticism in the Wilderness*. New Haven: Yale University Press.

Raschke, Karl
    ——   "From Textuality to Scripture: The End of Theology as 'Writing'." *Semeia 40*

Riceour, Paul
    1974   *The Conflict of Interpretations*. Evanston: Northwestern University Press.

1977   *The Rule of Metaphor.* Toronto: University of Toronto Press.
Said, Edward
1982   "Opponents, Audiences, Constituencies and Community. *The Politics of Interpretation.* Edited by W. J. T. Mitchell. Chicago: University of Chicago Press.
Snodgrass, W. D.
1977   *In Radical Pursuit.* New York: Harper Colophon Books.
Stern, David
1984   "Moses-cide: Midrash and Contemporary Literary Criticism." *Prooftexts* 4:193–213.
Winquist, Charles
1981   "The Archaeology of the Imagination: Preliminary Excavations." In *The Archaeology of the Imagination.* Journal of the American Academy of Religion Thematic Studies 48/2.

TEXT AND CONTEXTUALITY IN REFERENCE TO ISLAM

Richard C. Martin
Arizona State University

ABSTRACT

Poststructural criticisms of essentialist notions of religion and of language studies have increased during the past few years. Among the critics are some historians of religions and theologians who have attempted to deconstruct work done within their respective disciplines. The purpose of this paper is to explore whether and to what extent post-structuralist criticism in general and deconstruction in particular offer appropriate models for reformulating how history of religions might deal with the textuality of world religions. The paper argues that while certain aspects of textuality as understood in deconstructive thought are useful, deconstructive theology is at base a type of fideism and not helpful. It further argues that in Islamic societies the Qur'an can and should be thought of not merely as an isolable text, but also in its intertextual and intercontextual play in Islamic culture.

Textuality has . . . become the exact antithesis and displacement of what might be called history. Textuality is considered to take place, yes, but by the same token it does not take place anywhere or anytime in particular. It is produced, but by no one and at no time. It can be read and interpreted, although reading and interpreting are routinely understood to occur in the form of misreading and misinterpreting.

Edward W. Said, "Secular Criticism,"
The World, the Text, and the Critic.

Some historians of religions and theologians argue—correctly in my view—that religious studies should abandon essentialist notions of religion and of textuality. the label given to this trend is poststructuralism. In its most revisionist form, deconstruction, this kind of discourse expresses itself as a gloss on the writings of the French philosopher and critic, Jacques Derrida. More broadly, poststructuralist criticism questions the different epistemological privileges traditionally claimed in the humanities, social sciences, and even the so-called hard sciences. At issue cross-culturally are Western ethnocentric views of culture and society which are implicit in such areas of social science discourse as theories of modernization and secularization.

The purpose of this paper is to explore whether and to what extent poststructuralist criticism in general and deconstruction in particular offer appropriate models for reformulating how historians of religions might deal with the textuality of world religions. The views and criticisms presented below have a pragmatic justification in the case of Islam. I will contend that in Islamic societies the Qur'an can and should be thought of not merely as an isolable text, as Muslims and orientalists normally construe it, but also in its intertextual and intercontextual play in Islamic cultures. First, however, are more general issues concerning how history of religions relates to the poststructuralist discourse about religion.

That the problematic of "text and textuality" has been generally misconstrued in the human sciences is a fundamental complaint among deconstructionists. The decision of the editor to invite scholars familiar with the textual traditions of other religions to join this discussion among aficionados of deconstructionist theology arises from a longstanding concern in religious studies about the gap between theology and *Religionswissenschaft*. The incorporation of the views of historians of religions in this project is remarkable *a fortiori* because poststructuralist theologians seem to advocate the *Destruktion* and deconstruction of historical and religious studies, as these have been pursued in the human sciences, without providing constructive alternatives. Grounds for possible areas of agreement among the contributors as a whole have not been explored or even mentioned by the more dedicated deconstructionists. For some of them the point would seem to be that the "writing" of texts refers at best only within the field of writing itself, and not to extratextual realities, and therefore that the academic study of human cultural forms, such as religion, and including theology, has nothing to do with history and society. Clarification is needed, therefore, of the points of contact between history of religions and deconstructionist theology as well as of the lines that must inevitably be drawn between them.

Some aspects of textuality as defined by poststructuralist critics have come up for discussion in Islamic studies recently. Orientalism—writing about Islamic texts and history by Western specialists—has a provocative critic in Edward W. Said, who is among the very few poststructuralist critics to argue that criticism should be pursued beyond the boundaries of the Euro-American textual tradition. Insofar as both Said's critique of European orientalism and the deconstructionist theologians' rejection of rival notions of contemporary theology appear to have some common ground in poststructuralist criticism—primarily in their similar modes of criticizing the Western human sciences—the relationship between these two projects is worth considering. Are common hermeneutical strategies applicable to the multiple textual traditions of world religions? Can these strategies be disabused of Euro-American ethnocentrism to such an extent that religious studies can be disentangled from the interests of religion, business, and the state—the patrons of higher learning in the modern world? The presumption here is that if deconstructing orientalist and theological writing corrects certain basic mistakes then the issue of "textuality" might achieve greater articulation in religious studies.

The pessimism expressed below about the lack of proposed interpretive strategies among and across religious textual traditions by deconstructionists is not due alone to the fideism *qua* fideism to which the deconstructionist theologians resort, for the claim of ineffable sources is commonly found among proselytizing and revivalist religions. The risk lies rather in promulgating deconstruction as a textual strategy to be placed in the service of fideism by eliminating historical and textual grounds for the comparison and analysis of meaning systems. I propose instead to apply speech act theory to the problem of the meaning of discourse in text/context matrices and to modify the cultural idealist assumptions of the human sciences with reference to some of the different assumptions of historical materialism, which in many respects is more compatible with poststructuralist than with other modes of criticism.

A chief concern of this paper, then, which is argued in reference to the Islamic evidence, is the relation of text to context. Relying on the Western intellectual tradition for their evidence, deconstructionist theologians argue for decontextualizing the "Word of God" from the texts which presumably express it, and these from human discourse about texts (Western metaphysics, hermeneutics, and especially theology). Another kind of argument against contexts is Jacques Derrida's critique (Derrida, 1977) of J. L. Austin's theory of speech acts (Austin, 1962). Derrida argues that the concept of "context" in Western linguistics and language philosophy is incoherent; he has set out to deconstruct and eliminate "context" in favor of his own notion that "writing" (the intertext, great text) is the only tangible object for critical inquiry. The determination of cultural rule-bound situations in which meaning is established between speaker/writer and addressee/reader is not just practically, but theoretically (nearly) impossible, Derrida holds. The position taken in this paper is that speech act theory can be modified and applied in religious studies, although a careful reading of Derrida reveals why the historian of religions needs more than Austin and Searle to construct a hermeneutics of religious situations. In order to deal with

Derrida's claim that the conditions of a context are never absolutely determinable or "saturated" (1977: 174), I shall propose a concept of contextual analysis which I call "polyunsaturated."

Finally, understanding textuality in Islam rests on a consideration of Islamic religious conceptions and uses of language, scripture and writing—in both their unique cultural and theological formulations and in the implications of their relationship to the general problematic of text and contextuality.

I. A POSTSTRUCTURALIST ASSESSMENT OF ISLAMIC STUDIES

It may seem ironic for an "Islamicist" to approach the problem of textuality in partial reference to the works of Edward W. Said who, more trenchantly than anyone else, has questioned the intentions and cross-cultural impact of virtually the entire tradition of Euro-American scholarship on the (Muslim) "Oriental" World (Said, 1978a). Yet, the projects of the deconstructionist theologians and of Said share the quality of focusing critical attention on scholarly approaches to writing about religions—Christianity, Islam—as objects of knowledge in the academy. Following Derrida's deconstruction of Heidegger, deconstructionist theologians contend that the history of Western theological writing and religious hermeneutics have been faulted by what Derrida refers to as Platonic logocentric epistemologies and a metaphysics of presence (see Raschke's article in this volume and Derrida, 1976: 6–26; 166–67). In the manner (at least partly) of Foucault, Edward Said has focused his attention on the past two centuries of orientalist constructions of and dominion over (i.e., "discourse" about) an Oriental/Islamic reality through colonialism and the creation of institutions that study the Orient and "represent" it in the Romanticist mode of textual philology (Said, 1979: 1–28). Neither theological deconstruction nor Said's excavation of orientalism are isolated voices in the marketplace of ideas about history, textuality and hermeneutics. Poststructuralist criticism should be taken seriously if for no other reason than the fact that Michel Foucault and Jacques Derrida have a growing number of disciples on both sides of the Atlantic.

Poststructuralist criticism of the human sciences is rooted in the iconoclastic tradition of Nietzsche, Kierkegaard, Heidegger, Barth, Barthes, Foucault, and Derrida, *inter alia*, although Said is far less adoring and uncritical of Derrida than are the deconstructionist contributors to this volume. For Said, a vital function of humanistic criticism in today's world is for it to operate "between the dominant culture and the totalizing forms of critical systems." In his view, "the realities of power and authority—as well as the resistances offered by men, women, and social movements to institutions, authorities, and orthodoxies—are the realities that make texts possible, that deliver them to their readers, that solicit the attention of critics" (Said, 1983: 5). I would contend that among the realities that make texts possible is religion, or rather religious communities, which are also textual communities in one form or another. Choosing to identify himself as literary critic much closer to Foucault than to Derrida, as noted above, Said believes that texts occupy geographical, historical and, most importantly, political space; reading them apart from those spaces—as Derrida consistently attempts to do, sometimes with brilliance—leads to a view of texts and writing that has nothing to do with knowledge of the world, of human societies, or of how texts and writing (discourse) operate as instruments of history and culture. Indeed, Said believes that even Foucault's critique of the turn toward discourse in the human sciences since the eighteenth century is too blanched and unconcerned with the effects of particular writers and texts (Said, 1978a: 23) and too ethnocentric in the scope of its criticism (Said, 1978b).

I agree in part with Said's appreciative but incisive critiques of Derrida and Foucault; Derrida, because the deconstruction of the notion of the "context" of a text prevents one from saying anything more informative or more interesting about the Islamic uses and meanings of texts than the deconstructionist theologians have said thus far about Judeo-Christian texts; and Foucault, because the historian of religions needs a theory of textuality not confined to the history of thought in Northern Europe since the sixteenth century. The task of the historian of religions is to focus specifically on the texts that affect and effect religion and the uses of texts, which change, in the cultural/historical contexts of religious groups. The view expounded here is that, in the present academic milieu, religious studies should find a natural alliance with an approach in the humanities which raises important questions about the dominant culture and the totalizing forms of criticism. The phenomenological residue in much of religious studies, which continues to counsel the use of "empathy" (Dilthey's *Einfuehlung*) for understanding the religious situation under study and which continues to assume that religious systems are fundamentally and always integrative and good for human society, is itself subject to criticism, as Mary Douglas has cogently argued (Douglas: 26). Indeed, because the position advanced in this paper requires coming to terms with the social-historical world in which texts operate, the problem of textuality is closely related to social science research, where contextual determinants of social behavior are often studied in relation to cultural symbolism and value systems.

A revisionist view of social anthropology from a neo-Marxist perspective is given by Michael Kearney in *World View*. Kearney defines world view as a form of macrothought which consists of "those dynamically interrelated basic cognitive assumptions of a people that determine much of their behavior and decision making, as well as organizing much of their body of symbolic creations—myth, religion, cosmology—and ethnophilosophy in general" (Kearney: 1). Western social science, particularly in anthropology, where analyses of local world views have been undertaken, has been based on a humanistic variety of "cultural idealism" in which, Kearney says: ". . . human behavior and history in general are explained as a result of the appearance and interaction of ideas. Most of cultural anthropology is a variant of this tradition: personality, themes, patterns, structures, and the like are assumed to shape behavior. Attention is focused on these mental constructs and not on how they appear and evolve as a result of changing environmental and social conditions" (Kearney: 11). As a correction to cultural idealism Kearney proposes a historical materialist approach to world view analysis. In his own words:

> Historical materialism, while being neither an empiricist nor rationalist theory of knowledge, does give prime importance to material and social conditions as the origin of any particular self-consciousness and of knowledge in general. But this is only a starting point in the analysis, for the question immediately arises: to what does the environment in which this idea arose owe its nature? In the case of human beings, the answer is that to a very great extent this shaping environment is formed by previous human activity which was informed by the ideas about the world that those people held. In this view, the issue of human knowledge is inseparable from human practical affairs and human history (Kearney: 14).

Kearney is excessively narrow and doctrinaire in his embrace of the Marxist view of religion as purely and simply a ruling class ideology, as though peasants and urban semiliterates do not also get things done with textual symbols, and he does not address the problem of textuality directly. Nor has he explained satisfactorily the dialectic of religious symbols with concrete social realities. Nonetheless, his analysis of world view provides a useful counterpoint to those who argue that the attempt to make the world views of others a scholarly enterprise lacks sufficient academic rigor or that the worldly contexts of writing and reading, reciting and listening, are irrecoverable and thus irrelevant. On many counts, Kearney and Said represent the same trend in neo-Marxist criticism of the human sciences—one that differs as significantly from the Derridean view of textuality and writing shorn of context as it does from cultural idealism in the social sciences.

Said refers to an issue that the deconstructionist theologians do not address in this volume (although Derrida mentions it here and there in his writings), namely, that the differences between, say, the Judeo-Christian religious languages, scripture, and texts and those of other cultures (Islam) are real and worth considering. The affirmation of differences among cultures is routinely labeled "cultural relativism," a term of opprobrium. In the case of deconstructive criticism, the pointing to the problem of the "otherness" of texts which are not our own is reminiscent of the reply of Musaylima, the false prophet of Arabia, who, when accused of producing an inauthentic and imitable Qur'an, replied *lakum dinukum, wa liya din* 'you have your religion, and I have mine' (and in so doing cited the Qur'an, 109: 6). Are deconstructionists, like Musaylima, incurable textual relativists and thus unable to resolve such issues as, for example, what constitutes an authentic scripture *qua* textuality in the criticism of religions? Since the accusation of "relativism" has been levelled against poststructuralist critics (and cultural relativism against anthropologists and historians of religions), the problem needs clarification, however briefly, for the purposes of this paper.

The danger of relativism in its absolute forms (e.g., "the only meaning of a text is what it means to me," or "truth is exclusively defined by local cultural assumptions") is that comparative and critical studies become impossible—the apples versus oranges problem. This is what David Hoy, in addressing a familiar philosophical problem, refers to as the subjectivist or weaker form of relativism, which he distinguishes from a stronger form he calls "contextualism" (Hoy: 68-72; see Rorty, 1982). The fact that interpretations and thus uses of oral and written texts are relative to particular and different contexts is not an excuse for not offering arguments to justify one interpretation (or account of a native interpretation) over another (Hoy: 69). Ricoeur has also reasoned that establishing scholarly consensus for one interpretation over others is analogous to case-making arguments in jurisprudence, where it is precisely "facts" and "evidence" that are the focus of contentions that must be adjudicated (Ricoeur, 1971). In cross-cultural studies, as Kearney has maintained in his analysis of world views, the analyst needs to distinguish between what he calls external and internal categories. External categories are "*world-view universals* (Self, Other, Relationship, Classification, Causality, Space, Time)" which Kearney maintains are "necessary aspects of any human world view. Because they are world-view universals, they thus afford a means of comparing world views cross-culturally" (Kearney: 3). The internal or cultural-specific expressions of world view, of course, vary among societies as individuals and groups interact and, through myths, rituals, and other narratives, conduct their lives in the process of maintaining their particular world views. Both Hoy's contextualism and Kearney's world-view universals offer serious qualifications of subjectivist claims about the veridical relativism of texts and contexts.

We still want to know, however, what useful meaning "textuality" might have for religious studies. What does deconstructive criticism contribute to history of religions scholarship?

II. THE DECONSTRUCTIONIST THEOLOGIANS' VIEW OF TEXTUALITY

One issue on which some historians of religions (myself included) would agree with the deconstructionist theologians is the need to rethink essentialist predications, such as "sacred," of texts. In his paper in this volume, "Theological Text," Scharlemann argues, in agreement with the early writings of theologian Karl Barth, that "the categories of the sacred and of the written [do] not express the nature of the theological. To this we may add that they do not express the nature of "scripture" either. The problem the historian of religions has in predicating "sacredness" of texts considered as scriptures, however, is not Scharlemann's concern that "the nature of the theological" is not thereby expressed but rather that one is usually obliged to enter a circular discourse about sacred scripture; a text (Vedas, Qur'an, Bible) is considered scriptural because it serves sacred purposes, which we know to be sacred because a primal text (scripture) is involved. Phenomenologists have dealt with the category of the sacred, and hence sacred scripture, by circumambulating around it while claiming to be able to sense a noumenal core, which sacred symbols are said to express. William A. Graham has proposed dropping essentialist notions of scripture in favor of a functionalist or relational characterization. "A text is only scripture insofar as it exists in relation to a community of faith—persons who 'hear' it in the fullest sense of the word, who listen to its words, love and cherish them, and live by, with, and for them" (Graham, 1985b: 41; see Graham, 1985a). No particular literary or theological quality of a text, and certainly not necessarily such qualities as might be attributed to the biblical text, applies to all texts, written or oral, regarded by religious groups to be their scriptures.

In the absence of literary or textual criteria as such for identifying scriptures, Scharlemann, following Ricoeur, proposes a definition of "text" that points toward a working definition of scripture: "a text [for which we may simply read 'scripture'] is that written discourse upon which other texts can be written, as interpretations, and to which other texts are referred, but which, in turn, is not referred to any anterior texts" (also see Ricoeur, 1970). This definition may be grafted onto Graham's notion that scriptures are defined not by the literary (and hence, textual) qualities they may possess but rather by the purposes they serve for those who subscribe to them. (In the case of world religions generally, the term "written" is not, of course, always relevant.) It works in the case of the Qur'an, for which, in the Islamic view, there is no earthly anterior text (which is different from claiming that historical criticism cannot and should not investigate the possible linkages between formulae and narratives in the primary text and contemporary or prior texts). The Muslim assertion that the Torah and Gospel, though "historically" anterior to the Qur'an, are not its basis, incidentally, is compatible with Graham's and Scharlemann's views, which in theory can be applied to other traditions as well. This view of scripture has a weakness, however, insofar as it implies but does not account for the intertextual involvement of a dominent text such as the Qur'an throughout a given culture. More will be said about this below.

Robert Scharlemann believes the achievement of dialectical theology, the "theology of the Word," was "the manner in which the Word of God was distinguished from any written text, even the Old and New Testaments." Rather, it was that "No to our Yes and, in turn, that Yes within the No which could be *heard* as the voice speaking through the writing that becomes vocal in preaching." Moving from the early writings of Karl Barth, who presented this view in his commentary on the Epistle to the Romans in 1918, Scharlemann builds his notion of a text from the writings of Martin Heidegger and Paul Ricoeur. It is the text of preaching, the text related to the text of scripture, that Scharlemann wants to destruct (following Heidegger's notion of *Destruktion*, not of Derrida's Deconstruction).

> The text of preaching is like the score of a musical composition: it contains the notes of a performance, in which the performing instrument is the witnessing voice of the preacher and for which there is no guarantee that the Word of God will itself be heard when the performance is given. Not the category of 'sacred writing,' then, but that of 'authentic testimony' is the category of the theological: the witness, in speaking most on his or her own, with no other support than the power of the testimony itself, may happen to speak most apart from himself, and that happening is the living Word of God.

On the final page of his paper, Scharlemann ends where he began on page one, on a Barthian note, twisted into deconstructive obscurity: "'The writing of God' writes . . . similarly, a 'not' across any text, but then the text, which is a text, but not the text of God [for ('God is God,' written by God)], can be the text *as* which the Text of God is what it is." After Scharlemann has destructed scripture and its accompanying theological text, which is preaching as performance, and the writing is "destrued" and exposed for the "fractured" and rent document that it is, the Barthian divine No is still to be heard in counterpoint to the human Yes. This is the fideism to which I alluded above and which I find to be unconvincing as a way of explaining religious textuality. Nonetheless,

Scharlemann has defined Christian theological texts in terms of speech acts (preaching), and my contention is that speech acts are more or less corrigible fields of research for the historian of religions.

Carl A. Raschke, in "From Textuality to Scripture: the End of Theology as 'Writing,'" begins in a vein similar to that of Scharlemann, by referring to Martin Luther's distinction between the Word of God and the word of doctrines of men. Raschke's agenda is somewhat different than Scharlemann's, however. It is the words and doctrines of men, nineteenth-century theories of religion and twentieth-century secular theologies, that Raschke wants to deconstruct and take back to a bare bones assessment of what is in (or beyond) a religious text. The culprits who have misconstrued the textuality of the Word, in Raschke's view, are the purveyors of *Religionswissenschaft* (by whom he means historians of religion generally) and the tradition of religious hermeneutics since Schleiermacher, up to and including Paul Ricoeur. Indeed, Raschke wants theology, and if possible biblical studies, to absent themselves from what he states at the end of his paper is that "curious and littered archeological deposit we call 'religious studies.'" Raschke, too, ends up with Barth's notion of the divine No which shatters all religious reflection, all human attempts to articulate about God, all assessments of religion (theo-logy).

In *Church Dogmatics* (I, ii, 17), Karl Barth presented his view of religion as "the realm of man's attempts to justify himself and to sanctify himself before a capricious and arbitrary picture of God. The Church is the locus of the true religion, so far as through grace it lives by grace . . ." (Hick and Hebblethwaite: 32). Religion, then, is unbelief, to which Barth opposed the divine revelation known through the outpouring of the Holy Spirit. Barth had little patience for either the "Know-All" rationalist *Religionswissenschaftler*, such as Max Mueller, who maintained that "he who knows [only] one [religion], knows none" (Mueller: 8; Hick 34), or the Hegelian phenomenologist "who thinks he deals comfortably and in the end successfully with all religions in the light of a concept of perfect religion which is gradually evolving in history" (Hick and Hebblethwaite: 34). Barth also singled out the cultural relativism of ethnography and the skepticism of positivist approaches to religion, both of which appeared to promote objective tolerance of all religions but, in his view, amounted ironically to a form of intolerance toward the true religion, Christianity (which again is not the Christianity of European human sciences). Barth's analysis of the dangers of nineteenth-century academic concepts of religion was set forth brilliantly in *Protestant Thought from Rousseau to Ritschl* (Barth: 1959). One gathers that the deconstructionist theologians, especially Raschke, wish to enforce the Barthian cleavage between theology and religion (including religious studies). The Barthian mantle has curiously now been donned by those already clad in the Nietzschean Death of God style, which seems rather like parading around in the Emperor's new clothes. Derrideans demanding a voice in the intellectual tradition they wish to disinherit also have trouble with scholarly substance, or at least those of us who want to take their criticisms seriously experience difficulty in summing up their aphoristic points and drawing appropriate conclusions for field and textual study.

The cure for the ills of religious studies is not to reduce religion to a linear, one-dimensional, contextless set of manipulable textual strings, in which doing religious studies becomes like word processing—the most recent form of armchair scholarship. More importantly, when Derridean criticism is converted into a theological project it becomes a pernicious recrudescence of fideism in which the only salvation from the aporias of textuality is the divine Word or, as Raschke characterizes his salvific vision of deconstruction:

> The end of theology is the beginning of the movement of human language and existence into the millenium of dialogy, in which word as presence is no longer withdrawn from the alienating silence and clangor of history. The echoes of what has been said in the past fade into the stillness enshrouding the death of both gods and God, and from the boundless hush rises the "still, small voice" that passes between persons. The leaden idols are melted down by the fiery *logos* into the chaos of the *prima materia* before they are transformed through the alchemy of the word (Raschke, 1979: 91).

If I have read Raschke's text correctly it is a poem about intellectual self-immolation.

Derrida, as I read him, does not deny the reality of the worldly contexts in which humans write (utter, gesture, inscribe) the traces of their pleasures, failures, aspirations, experiences of power and repression, and what they mean. Rather, he denies along with many others that language mirrors what we commonly presume to be nature or reality. His retreat to textuality as the safest ground on which to attack the privileges of traditional epistemologies removes from his notion of text any way of knowing or even trying to know what roles texts play in textual communities. His relentless agnosticism about the knowability of the worldly context of *écriture* serves, however, to challenge the complacency of those humanists and social scientists who claim epistemological certainty for the schemata of their descriptions and interpretations of human life. Deconstruction, when it is cogently argued, can be a legitimate voice in the discussion of theory and criticism in the human sciences. An area of criticism which should be taken seriously is Derrida's deconstruction of speech act theory.

III. SPEECH ACTS IN POLYUNSATURATED CONTEXTS

In "Signature Event Context," Jacques Derrida (1977) undertook a critique of one of the more influential philosophical ways of analyzing language use in context, J. L. Austin's theory of speech acts (1962). A context, in Austin's view, delimits the ambiguity of human natural language by relating discourse to the circumstances in which it is uttered or written. As its name suggests, Traugott and Pratt remind us, "speech act theory treats an utterance as an act performed by a speaker in a context with respect to an addressee" (Traugott and Pratt, 1980: 229). Thus, in addition to the constative or propositional (true/false) functions of linguistic locutions, speech gets things done in the social world. As Austin put it, "we want to reconsider more generally the senses in which to say something may be to do something. . . ." (Austin: 91). The performative function may have two forces, *illocutionary* and *perlocutionary*. The illocutionary force of a speech act is the attempt on the part of a speaker (or writer) to accomplish some purpose, such as promising, warning, threatening, or commanding. The perlocutionary force of a speech act is the result it may get from the addressee (hearer or reader), such as to feel something (security or threat) or to take some action (open a window, pay a bill, join a cause). One of Austin's basic examples of a locution is the statement: "You can't do that." Its illocutionary force is the speaker's protest that someone cannot or should not do something. Its perlocutionary force is that someone is stopped, brought to his senses, or perhaps merely annoyed (Austin: 102). Speech act theory, therefore, proposes to examine the contextual conventions which determine the force of textual use in specific circumstances, not original or universal meanings.

Derrida raises the question: "are the conditions [*les réquisits*] of a context ever absolutely determinable? . . . Is there a rigorous and scientific concept of *context*? Or does the notion of context not conceal, behind a certain confusion, philosophical presuppositions of a very determinate nature?" He attempts to demonstrate why, in his words, "a context is never absolutely determinable, or rather, why its determination can never be entirely certain or saturated" (Derrida, 1977: 174). The replies to Derrida by speech act philosopher John R. Searle (Searle, 1977, and 1983) draw sharp lines between deconstructionist and pragmatist/semiotic linguistic views over the question of what role, if any, context should play in semantic investigations. Searle, following Austin, wants to establish the conventional rules which govern speech acts. As Stanley Fish has observed, however, "it is not surprising that a theory that substitutes for the principle of verification the notion of appropriateness [of] conditions would attempt to put those conditions in its place" (Fish, 1976: 1011–12). As I shall argue, at least in the case of religious speech acts, contexts are neither lawless (Derrida) nor law-abiding (Searle). Here, I follow Geertz's admonition about the semiotics of culture: "Believing, with Max Weber, that man is an animal suspended in webs of significance he himself has spun, I take those webs, and the analysis of it to be therefore not an experimental science in search of law but an interpretive one in search of meaning" (Geertz, 1973: 5).

Before proceeding further, two points about this debate are worth making. First, Derrida is not claiming that the world is void of non-linguistic entities, or that language contexts do not exist. His point is rather that it is in the very nature of texts (and indeed oral speech) that authorial intention is difficult, if not impossible, to apprehend and utilize as determinate of communicated meanings. I think Derrida is undoubtedly correct, especially when it comes to texts regarded as earthly manifestations of divine speech, as I have argued elsewhere (Martin, 1982: 361–64; 382-84). When one claims that (a) God said such and such, and (b) he or she knows what meaning God intended, matters of social siginificance generally follow for those addressed. Only theologians of a certain stripe seem interested in what God might have really meant when he said such and such, while historicists transfer the search for intended meanings to the *Sitz im Leben* of the text's historical production. It is the social-historical appropriation and interpretation of imputed authorial intention—divine or human—that forms the textual/contextual field of history of religions scholarship.

Second, most socio-linguists among speech act theorists do not claim that speech act contexts are in fact entirely saturable, that is, they do not claim that their theoretical analyses of speech act situations have the status of controlled lab experiments in the natural or life sciences. The analyses advanced by speech act theorists would seem to function more like the "ideal types" of the social sciences—an analytical devise for sorting out and classifying concrete examples found in field work. Thus, I am proposing that in the study of contexts it should be conceded to Derrida that contextual analysis can in principle never be completely saturated (see also Culler, 1982: 123–25). The question this concession poses is whether or not this "structural non-saturation" (Derrida, 1977: 174) or "boundless" quality of contexts (Culler) renders contextual studies as impossible or chimerical as Derrideans seem to think.

In the spirit of that semantic playfulness which characterizes the Derridean style, I would like to suggest a metaphor of sorts, that speech act contexts are "polyunsaturated." Speech-act contexts, like the atomic hydrocarbons of fatty acids and edible oils, are unstable and thus capable of multiple bonds. The rules that govern behavior in both cases are complex, changing, and not always known to the analyst. The complexity and even limited knowability of contextual processes no more warrants abandoning research on the oils we eat on our salads than it prohibits serious inquiry into Quranic recitation during the *salat*. What we need in such cases are theories to account for what seems to us to be going on. Admitting that we shall never know all of the psychological states, performative rules, and processes of symbolization in a given speech-act context is simply healthy scholarship, not an excuse to avoid it.

Characteristic of the analysis of religious speech-act contexts are the following considerations. First, religious contexts are multidimensional; cosmology and world view are among the cognitive elements of religious contexts (see Martin, 1982: 371–73; and 1984: 47–53). Second, as suggested above, when historians of religion describe the rules and formulas that seem to structure textual contexts, as in the case of Qur'an recitation and citation, they are treating cultural factors as ideal types, not as brute facts. And third, analyzing contextual configurations is a way of finding out not so much *what* texts (or their authors) mean as *how* people use texts in given contexts to get things done in the world.

> Let us be clear, with Fish, about what speech act theory cannot do: it can't tell us anything about what happens after an illocutionary act has been performed (it is not a rhetoric); it can't tell us anything about the inner life of the performer (it is not a psychology); it can't serve as the basis of a stylistics; it can't be elaborated into a poetics of narrative; it can't help us to tell the difference between literature and non-literature; it can't help us to distinguish between serious discourse and a work of fiction, and it cannot, without cheating, separate fiction from fact" (Fish, 1023).

Fish is responding to Searle, who wants to establish conventional rules for speech acts which hold up under the distinctions between brute and institutional facts, regulative and constitutive rules, serious and fictional discourse. Searle maintains that brute facts, regulative rules, and serious discourse refer to the real world whereas institutional facts, constitutive rules and fictional discourse do not. Rather, the latter set exists by virtue of what Searle calls "fictional references" based on socially "shared pretense," which are established and accepted between writer/speaker and reader/addressee under certain extraordinary conventions—extraordinary because they cannot be verified by reference to the real world (Searle, 1975). The issue Searle raises is important also for religious texts and their social use where, for example, historians of religions have presumed a logical difference between a landlord's directions for where to buy pork in Cairo and an Imam's *khutbah* (sermon) on Qur'an 2:173 "He hath forbidden you only carrion, and blood, and swineflesh." Is truth possible in only the first type of speech act (Searle) or in the second (implicit in a deconstructionist theology of the Word)? Are there different kinds of truth (cultural relativism) or no truths (Derrida)?

Stanley Fish, arguing in this case much closer to the textualism of Derrida—but also, curiously, in a way that is amenable to the "contextualism" of Hoy, Ricoeur and Rorty—holds that "these left hand terms [above] are merely disguised forms of terms on the right, that their content is not natural but made, that what we know is not the world but stories about the world, that no use of language matches reality but that all uses of languages are interpretations of reality" (Fish: 1023). In this view, which I share (cautiously), all language and textuality have "the power to make the world rather than mirror it, to bring about states of affairs rather than report them . . ." (Fish: 1024; see Rorty, 1982: 3–17). The consequence of following Fish rather than Searle is that speech act theory itself becomes an interpretation which operates on the unprovable premise that speech act situations are theoretically, if not always in fact, meaning-ful. The evidence that one may bring to bear upon this view is always circumstantial. Or, with Geertz, we may say that the historian of religions engages in "thick descriptions" when he or she deploys speech act theory to estimate what is happening when a Quran passage is recited to elicit a response in the world, or what world is created thereby in which to act. The analyst is looking at texts in context (the real world of birth and death, group conflict, political and sexual oppression, assent to power, etc.), and seek to offer a plausible interpretation of how meaning comes about and leads to social result.

In much of the foregoing, I have referred to the Islamic textual tradition. One may also view the Islamic case in reference to theories of text and context.

IV. ISLAM IN REFERENCE TO TEXT AND CONTEXTUALITY

Recalling Scharlemann's definition of a text as "that written (sic) discourse upon which other texts can be written (sic), as interpretations, and to which other texts are referred, but which, in turn, is not referred to anterior texts," we have in Islam a classic example, the Qur'an. The Qur'an does not exhaust the complexity of Islamic textuality either in modern times or in the classical past, but for the purposes of this essay the place occupied by the Qur'an in Islamic culture unquestionably predominates over all other texts. Indeed, as Said has noted, the Islamic case differs from that of Judeo-Christianity insofar as the Western humanities, which until recently prevailed in Euro-American liberal education, have treated the Bible as a text among texts. Quranic textuality, on the contrary, does not lend itself to *paideia;* it is *the* text *par excellence* (Said, 1974: 198–200).

The Quranic text occupies many kinds of cultural space in Islam, ranging from the cosmological to the legal, ritual, pedagogical, and general sociopolitical. The divine *Urtext* (*lawḥ maḥfūẓ*, 'preserved table'; *umm al-kitāb*, 'mother of the book'), of which all genuine scriptures—meaning especially the Torah, Psalms, and Gospel—are historical exemplars, establishes writing as the source of the will of Allah made humanly accessible. How this is so is indicated in the vivid cosmology portrayed in the Qur'an and in other classical genres of Islamic religious literature. The parallel but conjointly valued oral mode of divine communication is established in the cosmological drama of angelic transmission to prophets sent to historic communities (i.e., Muhammad, and before him Jesus, Moses and others) bidding them to maintain pious fear of Allah and to obey his prophets. Each pericope of text was "sent down" *(tanzīl)* to Muhammad on a specific occasion of his prophetic activity in the life of the nascent Muslim community *(umma)*.

Hence, one of the most distinctively Islamic genres of commentary *(tafsīr)* is formed by accounts of those auspicious moments which originally occasioned the divine acts of communication *(asbāb al-nuzūl)*. The other major form of commentary provides an *ad seriatim* phrase-by-phrase *explication de texte* based on the transmitted views of early Muslim authorities. Since the rise of Middle Arabic following the urban development of Islam in Mesopotamia in the eighth century, the textual manifestation of this unique symbiosis of eternal text (written and oral) with historic circumstance, as interpreted by attested authorities, was incorporated into the scribal manuscript tradition, and even today study editions of the Qur'an often print excerpts from the *asbāb al-nuzūl* and *tafsīr* literature on the same page, as adjunct texts, with each passage of the Qur'an. In this vein the *raison d'être* of each passage is understood not primarily by the passages which precede or follow it—for narrative and thematic thrust frequently change abruptly—but rather in the sheer miraculous elegance of each phrase (*āya*—'sign' from Allah) which may be said to have a significance *ab origine* with reference to the "occasion" on which it was "sent down." In most cases, contemporary significance is discerned cognitively, often through the aid of textual (written and oral) commentary. Typically, a Muslim preacher or religious essayist, when reciting or citing an *āya* of the Qur'an, will turn it to current social meaning by first locating its attested primal *raison d'être*. The cosmological and primal historic Arabian contexts properly situate the text, and serve as paradigms for the local liturgical and social circumstances of Muslims who read, recite, and hear the text.

The Quranic texture is woven into the moral/juridical fabric of Islamic society, where the Qur'an serves as the primary of the four fundamentals of moral and legal reasoning—the other three being citations of Muhammad's autoritative words and deeds *(ḥadīth)* which were transmitted from and by respected companions of the Prophet and the next two generations, the authority vested in the community through its interpretive consensus *(ijmāʿ)*, and the extension of these three to cover the whole of the Islamic experience in history by analogical reasoning *(qiyās)*. Although the last of these four, analogical reasoning, is the most disputed among Muslims because it implies a kind of separation between the text and the believers' social circumstances, it also maintains that revelation and reality form a similitude. Thus, the Islamic social ethos is influenced normatively by a world view which, like that of the Talmud, classifies all religious duties, social responsibilities, and transfers of property together in an elaborate system of interpretation of the divine will (i.e., fearing God and obeying his prophet), which in Islam is known by the term (*sharīʿa*.

The process of deciding disputed opinions or claims about the performance of religious duties, marriage and divorce, inheritance, and so on, often rests on securing a legal opinion or *fatwā* from an authorized scholar. Religious scholars or *ʿulamāʾ* render a legal opinion by bringing passages of the Qurʾanic text to bear on the issues at hand, woven together with citations from the canonical exempla of the Prophet and his esteemed companions, as well as trading on the acceptable precedents of concensus among the *ʿulamāa'*. In this way the norms of Islamic social ethos can be seen processually as an ongoing system of interpretation, but also as an "intertext" in which Qurʾan and *hadīth* are the warp of the normative design of the fabric of Islamic society. Modernists and reformists have crafted a different Islamic discourse, in large part against the traditional *ʿulamāʾ*, but nonetheless referring to the same Quranic text. The "Quranized" intertext of the contemporary Muslim concern with re-Islamizing their societies after colonial rule is a distinctive Islamic reworking of the Euro-American social science discourse about modernization.

Traditional Islamic pedagogy has always used the Quranic text as the first primer for memory and learning to write Arabic. Such schools, known as *kuttāb*, were regarded as purely practical incipits of education. The *kuttāb* inculcated in the many who would soon abandon schooling for gainful employment some possession of enough of the text to recite it in prayers and to recognize and use it in public discourse and some facility with arithmetic and measures to function fairly and self-protectively in the marketplace. Literacy in the classical commentaries on the Qurʾan and the Sunna (practice) of the Prophet, which required more advanced learning, available in the cathedral mosques and adjunct madrasas of most every Islamic city, led to socially perceived status among the *ʿulamāʾ* where one could earn a living as a teacher or even as a judge or other civil servant. Islamic discourse about matters of social, political and ethical import has been shaped by this traditional form of pedagogy whose incipit and referent is The Text.

The ritual dimension of Quranic textuality is located primarily in the oral-performative framework of Qurʾan recitation in its many contexts, such as at the congregational Friday prayer service, at funerals, etc., by specially trained reciters, and by individuals in solitary acts of reading (reciting) through the Qur'an at regular intervals, or simply select passages on given occasions. All such acts of reciting the Qur'an, whether for public performance or for private devotions, presume universal access to the text through memorization of the text itself (or part thereof) and of the rules that govern its proper enunciation. In liturgical contexts, meaning turns not so much on the semantics of *tafsīr* and other satellite texts as on the emotive power of the words themselves or the reciter who enunciates them. Reciters follow well-known rules of phraseology and melodic emphases which are flexible enough to permit a surprising degree of variation in creative effect upon audiences, among which have always been many who have not understood much or any of the classical Arabic of the Qur'an. Indeed, in the case of Qur'an recitation the text is often an object of social veneration quite apart from and independent of its semantic context. Popular veneration of auspiciously located copies of the text in the home or workplace, especially in nonliterate sectors of society, exemplify another aspect of the objectification of the text. This is a side of "text and contextuality" which deserves a study of its own.

Competence in reciting the Qur'an to good effect is not the sole extent to which scriptural utterance is framed by conventions which operate between speaker and addressee. Just how much Quranic citation and reference infuses everyday discourse has been studied both in Arabic-speaking (Piamenta—Middle Eastern) and in non-Arabic-speaking (Nakamura—Indonesian) regions of the contemporary Muslim world.

From these few examples just given, it should be clear that the proper understanding of textuality in Islam involves contextual considerations of many kinds. Much, of course, needs to be done in pursuit of this approach to understanding Islam as religion.

V. RETROSPECTIVE OVERVIEW

Historians of religions and deconstructionist theologians share a common concern with religious texts and textuality. Is there any common ground between these two approaches? I agree with Scharlemann that essentialist categories, such as "sacred," are loaded with Platonic and nineteenth-century metaphysical presuppositions; therefore, it is no longer useful, in my view, to predicate "sacred" of texts, including scriptures, when some sort of noumenal reality is implicated. For the time being, I prefer a functionalist definition of religious texts in which the primary problematic is for the historian of religions to determine how textual communities use texts to get things done in the world. Phenomenologists of religion, who assert essentialist ideas about "religion," such as noumenal realities which manifest themselves in hierophanies and the like, are obliged to resolve serious epistemological and ontological problems. This is an example of what Derrida has called onto-theology," and it is the onto-theological aspect of phenomenological analyses of religion that seriously compromises any claim to suspend judgment and establish pure descriptions of religious phenomena.

I also agree with deconstructionists that language, and thus texts, do not mirror reality, although we draw sharply different conclusions from this general trend in contemporary language theory. For Derrida and his followers, "writing"—the diffusion of any text within the large phenomenon of intertextuality—is by nature too fractured and slippery to say much at all about human thought and experience. Following Rorty and other poststructuralist critics, I maintain that reality is mediated to humans in social groups through culture, language in its variegated oral, written and gestural forms being the principal medium of culture. Humans use language to construct the realities with which they deal. In this sense, social and material realities are appropriated textually but they do not cease being social and material by being textualized into world views. Hence I arrive at the assertion in the title of this paper that texts are necessarily contextual (social), and vice versa that human contexts are textualized (culture). I have attempted to illustrate my argument with reference to the Islamic data, which resists any understanding of religious text which fails to take account of cosmological, pedagogical, ritual, and social contexts in Islamic civilization.

I part company with the deconstructionists most emphatically regarding their attempt to deal with the "Word of God" by desituating it from the intertextuality of scripture, liturgy, preaching, theology, moral discourse, etc. Although Scharlemann seems to imply a speech act notion of texts, preaching in particular (and in this regard there is some agreement between us), ultimately he wants to account for an extratextual "Word of God"—a hidden source, as it were—while I seek to explain and interpret how, in the social uses of texts, religious communities are creating a world and (much of the time) meaningfully acting in it. I have accused the deconstructionists of fideism, though I might also have argued, as I did in the case of phenomenologists of religion, that they have not escaped what Derrida calls onto-theology. In short, I think the deconstructionist theologians, like the phenomenologists of religion, argue for a destructible concept of text and textuality. I might also add that it is not always clear to me what they are trying to say.

WORKS CITED

Austin, J. L.
    1962   *How to Do things With Words*. The William James Lectures Delivered at Harvard University in 1955. Cambridge, Mass.: Harvard University Press.

Barth, Karl
 1959 *Protestant Thought from Rousseau to Ritschl.* Trans. Brian
 [1952] Cozens, revised by H. H. Hartwell. New York: Harper & Brothers.

Barthes, Roland
 1974 *The Pleasure of the Text.* New York: Hill and Wang.

Derrida, Jacques
 1976 *Of Grammatology.* Translated by G. C. Spivak. Baltimore and London: Johns Hopkins University Press.
 1977 "Signature Event Context." *Glyph* 1: 172–9.

Douglas, Mary
 1982 "The Effects of Modernization on Religious Change." *Daedalus* 111: 119.

Fish, Stanley E.
 1976 "How to Do Things with Austin and Searle: Speech Act Theory and Literary Criticism." *Modern Language Notes* 91: 983–1025.

Geertz, Clifford
 1973 "Thick Description: Toward an Interpretive Theory of Culture." In Clifford Geertz, *The Interpretation of Cultures* (New York: Basic Books, Inc.), pp. 3–30.

Goody, Jack
 —— *The Domestication of the Savage Mind.* Cambridge: Cambridge University Press.

Graham, William A.
 1985a "Qur'an As Spoken Word: An Islamic Contribution to the Understanding of Scripture," in Martin, 1985: 23–40.
 [1985b] "Beyond the Written Word of God: The Oral Dimensions of Scripture." Forthcoming article.

Hick, John and Hebbelthwaite, Brian, editors
 1980 *Christianity and Other Religions: Selected Readings.* Philadelphia: Fortress Press.

Hoy, David Cousins
 1978 *The Critical Circle: Literature, History, and Philosophical Hermeneutics.* Berkeley, Calif.: University of California Press.

Kearney, Michael
 1984 *World View.* Navato, Calif.: Chandler & Sharp Publications, Inc.

Martin, Richard C.
 1982 "Understanding the Qur'an in Text and Context." *History of Religions* 21/4 (1982): 361–84.
 1984 "Symbol, Ritual, and Community: An Approach to Islam." *Islam in the Modern World: 1983 Paine Lectures in Religion.* Edited by Jill Raitt. Columbia, Mo.: University of Missouri-Columbia.

1985 Editor, *Approaches to Islam in Religious Studies*. Tucson, Ariz.: University of Arizona Press.

Mueller, Fiederich Max
1873 *Introduction to the Science of Religion*. London: Longmans, Green, and Co.

Piamenta, Moshe
1979 *Islam in Everyday Arabic Speech*. Leiden: E. J. Brill.

Nakamura, Mitsuo
1982 "Noble Character and Social Harmony: Themes of the Muhammadiyah As a Javanese Movement." Paper presented at the University Seminar on Change and Continuity in South and Southeast Asia, Columbia University.

Raschke, Carl A.
1979 *The Alchemy of the Word: Language and the End of Theology*. Missoula, Mont.: Scholars Press.

Ricoeur, Paul
1970 "Qu'est ce qu'un texte?" *Hermeneutik und Dialektik, Aufsaetze II: Hans-George Gadamer zum 70. Geburtstag*, ed. R. Bubner, et al. Tuebingen: J. C. B. Mohr [Paul Siebeck]: 181–200.
1971 "Model of the Text: Meaningful Action Considered As a Text." *Social Research* 38: 529–62.

Rorty, Richard
1978 "Philosophy As a Kind of Writing: An Essay on Derrida." *New Literary History* 10: 141–60.
1982 *Consequences of Pragmatism (Essays: 1972–1980)*. Minneapolis: University of Minesota Press.

Said, Edward W.
1974 *Beginnings: Intention and Method*. New York: Basic Books, Inc.
1978a *Orientalism*. New York: Pantheon Books.
1978b "The Problem of Textuality: Two Exemplary Positions." *Critical Inquiry* 4:673–714.

Searle, John R.
1969 *Speech Acts: An Essay on the Philosophy of Language*. Cambridge: Cambridge University Press.
1975 "The Logical Status of Fictional Discourse." *New Literary History* 6:
1977 "Reiterating the Differences: A Reply to Derrida." *Glyph* 1.

ROMANCING THE TOME:
RABBINIC HERMENEUTICS AND THE
THEORY OF LITERATURE

William Scott Green
University of Rochester

ABSTRACT

It has become fashionable in some literary circles to depict rabbinic hermeneutics as allusive and indeterminate and to portray it as a harbinger of current dissenting theories of literature such as psychoanalysis and deconstruction. Consideration of rabbinic intepretive practices within the context of the religion that produced them calls that analogy into question. Rabbinic use of scripture was kaleidoscopic, and the determination of textual meaning required and assumed a sealed sphere of reference.

The Talmud has fallen on easy times. No longer a theological menace to be censored and defaced or an abstruse and trivial sophistry to be depricated and ignored, the Talmud and its interpretive discourse are now in vogue, suddenly legitimate and mainstream. The emergence of rabbinic interpretation is especially evident in recent literary studies, where talmudic terminology is the new banderole of the campaign to liberate criticism from its putative dulling preoccupation with "declarative, logical discourse," "the truth or falsity of logical propositions," and "the univocity of meaning" (Handelman:146).

Thus, in introducing their volume *Midrash and Literature*, Geoffrey Hartman and Sanford Budick suggest that *midrash*, the rabbinic term for exegesis, has come to signify

> a variety of "open" modes of interpretation, a life in literature or in scripture that is experienced in the shuttle space between the interpreter and the text. Abiding in the same intermediary space is a whole universe of allusive textuality . . . which lately goes by

the name *intertextuality*. In this spacious scene of writing the interpreter's associative knowledge is invested with remarkably broad powers, including even the hermeneutical privilege of allowing questions to stand as parts of answers. (xi)

They suggest that *midrash* connotes a kind of interpretation that in "confronting the undecidability of textual meaning . . . does not paralyze itself" but "is absorbed into the activity of the text, producing a continuum of intertextual supplements, often in the spirit of high-serious play" (xi). In their view, "its weaving together of prooftexts and commentary quickens our understanding of textual production and suggests a symbiosis of interpretive and creative writing" (xii). They mark *midrash* as "particularly interesting" because of its "unclassifiability and waywardness, . . . its ability to function without apparent boundaries" (xiii).

Among critics of traditional hermeneutics, it is now routine to invoke rabbinic interpretation as the root of reform:

> In the Jewish concept of interpretation, in contrast to the Greco-Christian tradition, interpretation is multivocal, indeterminate, rhetorical and poetic, as well as logical. . . . concerned with the affirmation of truth or falsehood in terms of uncovering deeper meanings. Instead of a logic of oppositions, the Talmud . . . uses a dialectial model of reasoning that presents and encourages opposing opinions. (Handelman:146)

Here the label "rabbinic" denotes a kind of exegesis that contrasts not only to the classical/Christian tradition of allegory, which effaces the literal meaning of the text, but also to the late nineteenth-century German Protestant hermeneutics, which affirms it:

> . . . the effects of Protestant literalism were to collapse and cancel the endless multiple meanings which the Rabbinic tradition ascribed to each word and letter of the Torah, and to make all the words subordinate to and embodied in the single word-become-flesh in a literal person; the consequence was a theology and hermeneutics of immanence, grace, and univocal meaning, and a finality to the free play of interpretation. The entire past history of interpretation was seen to only prefigure the final and complete interpretation, which abrogates all that came before and stands as the absolute signifier and signified together. The priority then is belief in (as opposed to continuous interpretation of) this singular figure for individual salvation. All of this was in direct conflict with the entire body of Jewish thought not only insofar as the identity of the messiah was concerned, but also the whole traditional method of interpretation of Scripture, which affirmed the principle of multiple meaning, the necessity of continuous inter-

pretation, historical understanding and adjustment, and the application of specific hermeneutic procedures, themselves considered to be of divine origin. The text was inseparable from its interpretation and commentary; interpretation is not a provisional prelude to a final understanding but part of the divine revelation itself[1]. (Handelman:131)

These assertions reflect a tendency in some areas of literary studies to construe rabbinic interpretation, especially of the Bible, as akin to, even a precursor of, influential movements in contemporary hermeneutics. Hartman and Budick call attention to "resemblances between midrash and highly similar critical phenomena which . . . have acquired central importance in contemporary literature, criticism, and theory" (x). Handelman is explicit. In her view, "There are striking and profound *structural* affinities between the work of some of our most influential (Jewish) thinkers like Freud, Derrida, and Bloom, and rabbinic models of interpretation" (xv).

"In Freud," Handelman observes, "the relation between dreamer and interpreter replaces the univocity of the author. The same is true of the colloquy of voices in the Midrash or Talmud; the interpretive process is collective. And the modern writer, like Freud and the Rabbis, yields up any notion of the finality or completeness of the text" (79). She further suggests that rabbinic interpretation and psychoanalysis engage in a nearly identical textual practice: "The assumption of a hidden all-pervasive unity of the text—not as ontological sameness but as simultaneous coexistence of various related and constantly proliferating meanings—accounts for some of the strangeness of Rabbinic and psychoanalytic technique, especially the use of plays on words and numbers" (149)[2]. Moreover, she deems fundamentally rabbinic the notions of Roland Barthes that a text is a "'production' and not a 'representation' of meaning," that "'to interpret a text is not to give it a meaning . . . but . . . to appreciate what *plural* constitutes it,'" that reading entails "cutting up the text into contiguous fragments, 'manhandling the text, interrupting it,'" and that the text "'practices the infinite deferment of the signified.'" "In all this," she writes, "we have a most apt description of midrash, even of the Rabbinic process in general; and . . . the Jew is the devotee of Scripture, the text, par excellence" (80)."

On this view, rabbinic literature embodies an exceptional interpretive practice with four distinctive traits. First, in rabbinic hermeneutics scripture is regarded as non-representational and self-referential. Interpretation operates within the language of the text; it moves from word to word and verse to verse. Second, rabbinic interpretation recognizes and exploits the polysemy and elasticity of language, so that the search for textual sense necessarily is an exercise of endlessly expansive playful association. The meaning of scripture can never be nailed down or locked up. Third, rabbinic exegesis is absorptive, adaptive, and continual. The various possible, even potential, meanings of biblical phrases, words, and even letters coexist metonymically and never annul either one another or the text's plain sense. Interpretation can never be definitive or complete. Finally—and uniquely in rabbinic exegesis—because textual meaning is indeterminate, interpretation is "absorbed into the activity of the text" (Hartman and Budick) and the "text is inseparable from its . . . commentary" (Handelman). All these declared traits mark rabbinic hermeneutics in kind, not merely in degree, as sharply divergent from, even antithetical to, conventional western strategies of reading. Against the "Greco-Christian" tradition of univocity, monologic reading, and metaphoric substitution (Handelman), or in contrast to unnamed "more objective and systematized modes of reading" (Hartman: 9), rabbinic interpretation is depicted as unsystematic, serpentine, and preoccupied with text and language. Its alleged salient and dominant characteristics are allusiveness, intertextuality, multiplexity, indeterminacy, and openness. These make it appear a harbinger of, or even coextensive with, current dissenting theories of literature.

The notion that rabbinic and contemporary hermeneutics—*midrash* and deconstruction, for example—are both similar to one another and diametrically opposed to mainstream western literary interpretation—often identified typologically with Christian Bible exegesis, especially of the Old Testament—has gained currency and popularity in recent years. To be credible, a defense of this claim must rest on an accurate description of rabbinic interpretive practice. But to succeed, the argument for similarity also must show how the purported "resemblances" and "affinities" between classical rabbinic interpretation and contemporary literary theory are more than mere operational likeness or superficial formal correspondence, how they point beyond themselves. The very claim of comparability requires an analogical model that classifies these two historically disparate hermeneutical enterprises in a single category and justifies their being examined together and in light of one another. Moreover, to be analytically useful, the case for similarity between the two must be grounded in a perception of their difference; it must show how the absence of identity makes the resemblance revealing. Otherwise, the assertion that rabbinic interpretation resembles current hermeneutics is trivial and can offer no insight; it is a terminological shell game, fun without profit.

The conception of rabbinic interpretation as congruent to trends in contemporary hermeneutics and literary criticism locates the resemblance between ancient rabbis and contemporary critics squarely in the realm of reading and envisages ancient rabbis primarily as interpreters of texts. It thus employs, yet again, the old model of rabbinic Judaism as a book-religion.

It is commonplace to classify rabbinic Judaism as a "'religion of the Book', religion in which practice and belief derive from the study and interpretation of Scripture" (Vermes: 60). The book-religion model depicts rabbinic Judaism as an interpretive supplement to a foundational text, an exegetical development out of scripture itself. It holds that "the Rabbis . . . founded . . . a religion of interpretation, a tradition of studying Scripture and putting it into practice that touched every member of the community and that elevated these activities to the very highest level" (Kugel:72). The model makes reading and interpreting the Bible the quintessential rabbinic activities.

By assimilating religion to reading, the book-religion model effectively reduces rabbinic Judaism to a process of exegesis and thereby marks other rabbinic activities as secondary and derivative. The model's analytical focus on how rabbis read makes biblical exegesis into rabbinism's driving force, and, more abstractly, the interpretation of literature becomes the decisive variable for our understanding of rabbinic religion. Rabbinic piety not only appears epiphenomenal and ancillary, but in principle and by definition it can be explained only as the consequence of rabbinic hermeneutical practice.

The book-religion model has dominated most of modern scholarship on ancient and rabbinic Judaism (Porton: 63–65), and its persistent appeal is understandable. The notion that for ancient rabbis "*midrash* . . . was an all-consuming activity" (Kugel:67), the claim that "Writing, the Holy Text, is the privileged term in Rabbinic thought" (Handelman:168), the conception of *midrash* as a "life in . . . scripture" (Hartman and Budick), and the idea that halakic observance was determined by Bible-study (Vermes, Kugel) all impute to rabbinic religion a strong biblical orientation. Rabbinic Judaism emerges as Bible-centered—the Bible read, the Bible studied, the Bible interpreted, the Bible put "into practice"—and thus as a kind of religion easily recognizable and comprehensible in the modern West. Indeed, the picture of ancient rabbis as Bible-readers expounding their religion out of scripture has a powerful intuitive plausibility in a culture where religion is conceived largely in Protestant terms. Moreover, because in our world "Bible" is merely a species of the genus "text," it takes hardly any imagination at all to place these Bible-reading talmudic sages into the more general category of literary exegetes and to suppose that for them—just as for us—the interpretation of texts was a principal passion and preoccupation. The authority of the book-religion model, therefore, lies in its self-evidence.

The book-religion model fails because it works too well. It makes ancient rabbis so familiar and so tractable, and takes us back to the beginning so fast, that we meet no one new on the way. The model's self-evidence, which is its power, blocks our perception of the particularities of rabbinic culture and thereby diminishes the likelihood of analytically useful comparison. The model's framework categorizes ancient rabbis so much in our image and after our likeness that it begs more questions than it answers. Its narrow focus distorts both the rabbinic textual and historical records.

There is no doubt that the documents now variously called the "Old Testament," the "Hebrew Bible," or *"Tanakh"* had a fundamental importance in the different Judaisms that surrounded the ancient Mediterranean. Interest in scripture is evident across a wide spectrum of literatures: Qumran, the New Testament, Philo, Josephus, and the church fathers. Varied sources suggest that, particularly from the late first century, scripture was read as part of the liturgy in both native Palestinian and diaspora communities, and archaeological remains suggest that synagogues often were constructed to make the scroll of scripture the center of the worshippers' visual attention.

The Hebrew Bible had a fundamental place in rabbinic Judaism and constituted an important component of its conceptual background. No rabbinic document could have been written without knowledge of scripture. Nevertheless, the rabbis' interest in scripture was hardly comprehensive, and vast segments of it, including much of prophecy and the deuteronomic history, escaped their interpretation. The Bible's role in rabbinic literature is more complex and fluid than the book-religion model suggests.

Rabbinic literature initially presents itself as formally autonomous of scripture. The Mishnah, a compendium of teaching that is rabbinism's first written product and its foundation document, rarely expounds scriptural passages or invokes them as proof of, and precedent for, its content. Although the Mishnah certainly presupposes and employs scriptural categories, especially those of the priestly portions of the pentateuch, it is unbiblical in language and structure. If the Mishnah can be said to have a major focus, it is the temple, not the Bible. The chain of tradition in the pseudo-Mishnaic tractate Avot 1:1–2:14—rabbinism's account of its own origins—identifies the teachers who inherit the Mosaic legacy by their possession of Torah, not scripture, and "the Torah that they teach does not consist in citations of verses of Scripture" (Neusner, 1986:46).

Explicit rabbinic interest in scripture appears in post-Mishnaic documents. Sifre to Numbers and Sifra, for example, structured as commentaries to Numbers and Leviticus respectively, attempt to correlate rabbinic teaching and scripture. They accomplish this task in large measure either by attaching passages from the Mishnah to scriptural words or verses or by devising exegetical discussions that confirm proper understandings of scripture. Sifra in fact is less an interpretation, a working out, of the implications of scripture than an *ex post facto* admixture of two already completed documents. Its very structure presupposes that rabbinic teaching and scripture are two distinct bodies of material.

The reversal of the Mishnah evident in Sifra is developed in the Palestinian Talmud, whose formulation and redaction—along with those of various *midrashim*—coincided with, and doubtless responded to, the rise of Christianity in the Roman empire (Neusner, 1983). "The second century masters [of the Mishnah] took commonplaces of Scripture . . . and stated them wholly in their *own* language and context. Fourth-century masters of the Yerushalmi phrased commonplaces of the Mishnah or banalities of worldly wisdom, so far as they could, in the language of *Scripture* and in its context" (Neusner, 1986:86). Later documents—the Babylonian Talmud and homiletical collections like Leviticus Rabbah—offer a still different picture. As Neusner shows, Leviticus Rabbah, for instance,

> is not an exegetical composition at all, nor even verses of Scripture read as a corpus of proof-texts. We have, rather, a statement that stands by itself, separate from Scripture, which makes its points only secondarily, along the way, by evoking verses of Scripture to express and exemplify those same points. We miss the main point if we posit that Scripture plays a definitive or even central role in providing the program and agenda for the framers of Leviticus Rabbah. (1986:128)

Finally, the Babylonian Talmud, which emerged in a cultural context not dominated by Christianity, treats scripture and the Mishnah as separate but virtually equal sources that are joined together (Neusner, 1986:130–132).

Thus, scripture neither determined the agenda nor provided the ubiquitous focus of rabbinic literary activity and imagination. Rather, it was the major—but certainly not the only—source rabbis used to produce their literature. They also drew extensively on their own materials. Indeed, M. Hagigah 1:8 baldly asserts that substantial protions of rabbinic teaching—for example, on matters as basic and important as Sabbath observance—have scant scriptural support. A well-known saying, attributed to the trannaitic master Simeon b. Yohai, compares the study of scripture to that of rabbinic teachings as follows:

A. "He who occupies himself with Scripture [gains] merit *(mdh)* that is no merit.
B. He who occupies himself with Mishnah [gains] merit for which they receive a reward *(śkr)*.

C. He who occupies himself with Talmud—you have no merit greater than this."

(y. Shabbat 16:1 [15c], b. Baba Meṣiʿa 33a)

To depict rabbinic Judaism as principally a religion of biblical exegesis, therefore, is to both oversimplify and overstate the evidence.

To account for the varied roles of scripture in rabbinic literature, it helps to remember that rabbinism's initial catalyst was neither the canonization of the Hebrew Bible nor readerly research of scripture but the demise of the second temple and its divinely-ordained cult, the rites of which guaranteed God's presence in Israel's midst. The loss of the Holy of Holies—the principal locus of Israel's invisible and silent God—meant the absence of a stable cultural center and generated an acute religious crisis, primarily in the realm of behavior.

The commanding influence of the book-religion model on the study of early Judaism and Christianity has tended to deflect scholarly interest away from the kind of religion manifested by the Temple and advocated by its priestly personnel. Levitical religion, as it might be called, conceived of the life of Israel as a comprehensive and integrated system of disciplined engagement with God. That engagement largely took the form of prescribed and repeated behaviors, directed by a caste of priests, that revolved around and focused attention on a sacred center, a stable reference point, where access to God was certain to occur. Levitical religion mapped out a system of categories—usually binary opposites such as clean/unclean, fit/unfit, holy/profane—in which everything that mattered had its place. Its preferred literary form was the list—for instance, the genealogies and series of rules of the pentateuch's P document—rather than narrative. In its ritual and its writing levitical religion promulgated a synchronic vision of a centered, structured, hierarchical, and orderly reality. Its practitioners celebrated precision, lineage, precedent, and concreteness, and had an exceedingly low tolerance for uncertainty, confusion, and ambiguity.

To underestimate the pervasiveness or persistence of levitical religion in Judaic and Christian antiquity is a mistake. The pre-70 Palestinian Jewish religious groups about whom we know the most—Sadducees, Pharisees, the Dead Sea Sect—all operated within its sphere. Levitical religion was a primary negative, and therefore defining, focus of early Christian writing, and it remained so well after the temple's destruction. Thus, Paul's early discarding of "the Law" sought to render levitical categories nugatory, and the evangelists could not tell of Jesus' death without recording that the curtain of the Holy of Holies "was torn in two, from top to bottom" (Mk. 15:38, Mt. 27:51; cf. Lk. 23:45). Other Christian writers, from the author of the Epistle to Barnabas, to Justin

Martyr and Irenaeus, made the rejection of routine levitical rituals a central theme of their compositions.

In contrast to their patristic counterparts, the post-70 founders of rabbinism aimed to perpetuate a levitical system. The dictates and concerns of rabbinic literature show that living rabbinically consisted in a host of behaviors—food, purity, and kinship taboos; observance of Sabbaths, holy days, and festivals; prayer—that depended on and promulgated levitical categories. The rabbinic use of scripture was thus embedded in a complex of rabbinically ordained practices, many of which—including most of the rules for the treatment of scripture itself—do not derive from scripture at all. Indeed, the shift from the Mishnah to Sifra described above suggests that rabbinism's initial concern was the elaboration and refinement of its own system. Attaching the system to scripture was secondary.

It therefore is misleading to depict rabbinic Judaism primarily as the consequence of an exegetical process or the organic unfolding of scripture. Rather, rabbinism began as the work of a small, ambitious, and homogeneous group of pseudo-priests who professed to know how to maintain Israel's ongoing engagement with God—its life of sanctification—in the absence of a cult, and who, on that basis, aspired to lead the Jews. By the third century, the rabbis expressed their self-conception in the ideology of the "oral Torah," which held that a comprehensive body of teachings and practices *(halakot)* not included in scripture had been given by God and through Moses only to the rabbinic establishment. Thus, ancient rabbis advanced the proposition that even without a temple Israel could still achieve holiness if the people's conduct conformed to rabbinic expertise and authority. Though rabbis articulated this claim in the language of the "oral Torah," they made it stick through their manipulation of the written one.

To achieve their goals, rabbis had to conquer a difficulty the pre-70 groups avoided: the absence of a sacred center. The community at Qumran at least had a real building in Jerusalem about whose recovery and control it could fantasize. But particularly after the Bar Kochba debacle in 132–35, rabbis must have known that the temple was gone for good. To compensate for that loss and to preserve the sacred center required by their piety, rabbinic Judaism developed a distinctive theory of the sanctity of scripture[3].

In rabbinic Judaism scripture had a sacred status, and human dealings with it were hedged about with behavioral restrictions. M. Yadayim 3:5 declares that "all the holy writings render the hands unclean" (also see M. Kelim 15:6, Yadayim 3:2, 4:6). A scroll's sanctity was not limited to its text, but extended to its blank margins (M. Yadayim 3:4, T. Yadayim 2:11) and its wrappings and containers (T. Yadayim 2:12). The sanctity of scripture outweighed even the Sabbath, and people were expected and permitted to violate Sabbath restrictions to save it and its wrappings from fire (M. Shabbat 16:1)—an exemption otherwise applied only to save a human life. Also, it was acceptable to make heave-offering unclean to rescue scripture from harm (T. Shabbat 13:2,6). A damaged, worn, or unfit scroll retained its sanctity and therefore was to be buried, by itself or in the coffin of a sage, but not burned or otherwise destroyed (b. Megillah 26b).

While the category "holy writings" apparently could include works in Hebrew and in translation (M. Shabbat 16:1), rabbis gave the scroll of the Hebrew Pentateuch, the *sefer Torah*, pride of place. It was the scriptural paradigm and prototype. Every Jew was obliged to write a *sefer Torah* (b. Sanhedrin 21b). According to M. Megillah 3:1, a Jewish community could do without a synagogue, an Ark, scripture wrappings, or other books of scripture, but not a Torah scroll. The talmuds' elaborate rules for the scroll's production and treatment decisively distinguish its content from ordinary writing. The *sefer Torah* was used in synagogue worship and was to be written without vocalization. It had to be transcribed on specially prepared parchment marked with lines (b. Megillah 19a)[4], in a particular script (b. Shabbat 104a, Sanhedrin 21b–22a; y. Megillah 1:11 [71b]), and with orthographic uniformity (b. ʿErubin 13a, Megillah 18b, Yebamot 79a, Ketubot 19b). In the scroll, seven Hebrew letters, each time they appeared, were to be drawn with *tagin*, three-stroke decorative crowns or tittles at the top of the letter (b. Menahot 29b). A sheet that contained four errors was to be buried, not corrected (b. Megillah 29b), but scrolls produced by Jews deemed heretics or sectarians were to be burned (b. Gittin 45b). Worshippers were expected to rise in the presence of the Torah scroll (y. Megillah 4:1 [2a]; b. Makkot 22b, Qiddushin 33b), and no other type of scroll could be placed on top of it (T. Megillah 3:20). To touch the parchment of a Torah scroll with bare hands was judged an outrage (b. Shabbat 14a, Megillah 32a).

Rabbis used the Torah-writing for purposes other than reading. They wore it in phylacteries and affixed it to dwellings in *mezuzot*. On account of the segments of Torah-writing they contained, these items too had sacred status. Along with the bags and straps of phylacteries, sacks for holding scripture, and the mantle of the Torah scroll, they were labelled "instruments of holiness" *(tšmyšy qdwšh)* and had to be buried, but neither burned nor discarded, when worn out (b. Megillah 26b). M. Taʿanit 2:12 requires that prayers for rain be recited in front of the ark containing the Torah scrolls, which was to be brought to the public square, and M. Sanhedrin 2:4 imagines that the scroll itself would accompany the Israelite king in battle, when he judged, and when he ate.

Other passages illustrate the special position of the Torah scroll in rabbinic culture. Sifra (Behuqotai, Pereq 8:10) asserts that the possession of the "*sefer Torah*" distinguished Israel from "the peoples of the world" and is the reason for God's persisting loyalty. Finally, rabbis were expected to perform the mourning rite of *qeri'ah*, the ritual tearing of one's garment, at the sight of a burned Torah scroll (b. Megillah 25b), and on seeing a torn scroll, they were to perform *qeri'ah* twice, "once on account of the parchment and once on account of the writing" (b. Mo'ed Qatan 26a; also y. Mo'ed Qatan 3:7[83b]).

These regulations suggest that rabbis regarded the Torah-writing itself as a sacred object. The idea that a missing or added letter in the Torah's transcription could "destroy the world" (b. 'Erubin 13a) and the notion that one grieves for damaged writing as one does for a deceased human being imply that rabbis construed the very letters of the Torah-writing not as mere signs of an immaterial discourse, but as sacred in themselves.

This possibility forces a reconsideration of the notion of the *sefer Torah* as text. Strictly speaking, the *sefer Torah* contains the two requisite components of text suggested by Robert Scharlemann. It is a "written work in contrast to an oral performance" and is "a writing upon which commentaries can be written but which itself is not a commentary on another text." But this definition can apply here only if we construe writing in a very minimal sense, to mean inscription or making rather than discourse. For although a scroll required writing in order to be sacred, there are reasons to suppose that the writing did not have to constitute a discourse. Consider, for example, M. Yadayim 3:5:

> A. A scroll *(spr)* that was erased and in which there remain eighty-five letters, like the section "And it came to pass when the ark set forward" (Num. 10:35–36), renders the hands unclean.
> B. A sheet *(mglh)* [of a scroll] on which was written eighty-five letters, like the section "And it came to pass when the ark set forward" (Num. 10:35–36), renders the hands unclean.

Tosefta Yadayim 2:10 (ed. Zuckermandel, p. 683, 1s. 2-5) adds:

> A scroll that wore out—if one can glean *(llqt)* from it eighty-five letters, like the section "And it came to pass when the ark set forward . . ." (Num. 10:35-36), it renders the hands unclean[5].

On this issue, the late third century Babylonian masters Rav Huna and Rav Hisda are said to have agreed that if the eighty-five letters appeared as words, the scroll would make hands unclean if the words were randomly scattered, and Hisda declared the scroll sacred even if it contained eighty-five scattered letters (b. Shabbat 115b). Moreover, rabbis supposed it possible to deduce "mounds and mounds" of behavioral practices *(halakot)* from the *tagin* attached to the top of certain letters (b. Menahot 29b). Since these tittles were strictly ornamental markings, their interpretation did not require discerning a discourse. They were deemed meaningful nevertheless, and the Babylonian Talmud certifies their significance by imagining that they were affixed to the Torah-writing by God himself. Finally and most important, the "official" Torah-writing, that used in worship, contained, and could contain, no vowels. It thus did not and could not "fix" a discourse in writing and is not a text in Ricoeur's sense. Constituted solely of unvocalized consonants—only half a language—the writing in the *sefer Torah* was mute. Like the scroll and the *tagin,* it was envisioned as a material object. In rabbinic Judaism, therefore, the sanctity of scripture appears to have depended neither on what the writing said nor even on its being read, but on how and by whom it was produced. A scroll of heretics or sectarians, after all, was not inspected for accuracy but was simply condemned to burning on the *a priori* grounds that its producers were untrustworthy.

Whatever else it may have been, the writing we would call "scripture" was conceived by rabbinic culture as a holy object, a thing to be venerated. The Torah scroll was rabbinism's most revered and sacred artifact, and its sanctity was socially demonstrated, objectified, and certified by a network of rabbinic behavioral injunctions. Thus, the *sefer Torah*—both as scroll and as writing—constituted the ubiquitous material reference point of rabbinic religion. As an artifact, the Torah scroll, with its holy and allegedly unchanged and changeless writing, formed the requisite stable center for rabbinism's system of piety. In the absence of the temple and its Holy of Holies, the scroll and its writing became for ancient rabbis primary repositories and conveyers of social legitimacy, cultural authenticity, and religious meaning.

Since, in rabbinic Judaism, properly inscribed Torah-writing was sometimes—perhaps often—not a text (as with phylacteries and *mezuzot*) but was always a sacred object, its artifactual status dominated and defined its use as a text. Because it was a holy artifact, the Torah-writing by definition was heavy with significance; it was meaning-full. But because it had no vowels, and hence contained no discourse, in another way the Torah-writing was also meaning-less—evocative but profoundly inarticulate[6].

The Torah scroll could not be read by itself because its writing was indeterminate script. To transform that script into a text, to make it readable, necessarily meant imposing a determinate discourse on it. For rabbis, in addition to supplying the absent vowels to make the letters into words, this transformation entailed the tradition of *qere'* ("what is read") and *ketiv* ("what is written"), in which some words were read differently from their written form, euphemisms were substituted for offensive written words (T. Megillah 3(4):39–40; b. Megillah 25b), and some written words and passages were not read at all. It also involved knowing how to divide lines of script into verses, when to introduce accents, stresses, and pauses (M. Megillah 4:4; b. Megillah 3a, Nedarim 37b; y. Megillah 4:1 [7d]; Genesis Rabbah 36), and the customary melody in which the scroll was chanted (b. Berakhot 62a, Megillah 32a). Since none of these, including the essential vowels, could ever be the property of the script, in rabbinic Judaism reading the *sefer Torah* was less a matter of deciphering an inscription than of reciting a previously known discourse and applying it to the writing[7].

For rabbis, reading the *sefer Torah* could not be the consequence of ordinary literacy, though that surely was a prerequisite. Because the Torah-writing was both sacred and illegible, making it intelligible was a highly disciplined activity that demanded specialized knowledge. Since rabbis could neither recite what they wrote nor write what they recited, the determination of scripture's discourse had to reside almost entirely with them. Some sources suggest rabbinic awareness of this implication. For instance, b. Sanhedrin 3b-4b reports a lengthy dispute about whether authority is given to the vowels (*yš 'm lmqr'*) or to the consonants (*yš 'm lmsrt*) in delineating scripture's discourse. Although the discussion favors the authority of vowels—and thereby confirms that scripture's discourse was not fixed by writing—the disagreement itself shows that rabbis appealed to both principles and outlawed neither. It thus depicts the sages, not the rules, as the final arbiters of discourse. More explicitly, an important saying, attributed to R. Isaac, a third century Palestinian master, holds that:

A. The vocalization (*mqr'*) of the scribes, the [orthographic] omissions (*'ytwr*) of the scribes, and the [scripture words that are] read but not written and the [scripture passages that are] written but not read
B. [are] practice[s] (*hlkh*) [revealed] to Moses from Sinai.

(b. Nedarim 37b-38a)

The phrase that concludes the saying at B is a standard rabbinic expression that refers to the "oral Torah." The passage thus claims that not only *qere'* and *ketiv*, but also the orthography and vocalization of scripture—its writing and its discourse—are not in scripture; rather they are the possession solely of rabbinic tradition. For rabbis, the credibility of scripture's discourse was guaranteed only by proper acculturation and training, in short, by rabbinic discipleship.

The rabbinic theory of scripture thus contained three complementary components that aimed to justify both the sages' vision of themselves and their claim to leadership over Israel. First, by declaring scripture sacred, rabbis endowed it with a unique and unassailable status. As a holy object, scripture possessed a givenness, a fixity, and a substantiality that made it seem independent of rabbis or their traditions. Second, rabbis reinforced the impression of scripture's autonomy and centrality by making ownership of a *sefer Torah* a religious obligation for every Jew. From a rabbinic perspective, scripture was not only the distinctive possession of all Israel; more important, it was the personal property of each individual Israelite. Finally, while they affirmed scripture as the heritage of all Jews, rabbis simultaneously claimed that its writing and its discourse were part of "oral Torah." They thereby asserted their singular mastery over—indeed, their exclusive right to manipulate—the sacred artifact they deemed the emblem of Israel's identity. In effect, rabbis proclaimed themselves coextensive with scripture and sought to acquire for themselves and their own discourse the same objectivity they attributed to it. The Palestinian Talmud (y. Mo'ed Qatan 3:7 [87b]) makes the identification explicit:

> He who sees a disciple of a sage who has died is like one who sees a Torah scroll that has been burned.

In their theory and use of scripture, rabbis had it both ways. As much as scripture was the general legacy of all Israel, it also was intimately and inextricably bound to rabbinism's particular tradition. In the rabbinic view, in order to be "Israel," Jews had to invest themselves in scripture; but to do so, they had equally to invest themselves in the sages' authority. When we recall that all these components were realized in concrete and prescribed behaviors, the effect of the theory becomes clear. With their use of scripture, rabbis sought to develop and sustain a sociology of knowledge that made them indispensible.

The sanctity of scripture gave its writing an intrinsic efficacy, an almost totemic quality. The discourse attached to it had an unimpeachable authenticity and the power of authentication; it could make other discourse legitimate. Thus, in rabbinic Judaism the writing and discourse of scripture had to be inherently separable from, and could be neither merged nor confused with, the commentary upon them. To mix the two would have deprived rabbis of an artifact to control and violated the basic levitical distinction between the sacred and the profane. In rabbinic writing, therefore, passages and words of scripture are almost always identified as such by an introductory formula, such as "thus scripture says," "as it is written," "as it is said," or "a [scriptural] teaching says."

The routine and nearly ubiquitous marking of scriptural passages undermines the claim that rabbinic interpretation of scripture is "intertextual"—at least in any revealing or distinctive sense—or that it is "allusive" in any sense at all. Indeed, in obvious contrast to the "inner biblical exegesis" described by Michael Fishbane, in which later expansions and modifications are intricately embedded in earlier texts, and contrary to early Christian materials such as Luke's infancy narrative or the Book of Revelation, which subtley appropriate various Old Testament images, the rabbis' use of scripture is explicitly referential.

The rabbinic tendency to identify antecedent materials is not limited to scripture. The talmuds usually mark citations from tannaitic teachings with expressions such as "we have learned" (for the Mishnah) and "it was taught" or "our rabbis taught" (for *beraitot*, extra-Mishnaic teachings). The attributive formula "Said Rabbi X" and the little chains of tradition ("Said Rabbi X, said Rabbi Y"), typical of all rabbinic documents, served the same purpose. Rabbinic writing displays its sources.

But if the adjectives "allusive" and "intertextual" are analytically useless for a critical description of rabbinic hermeneutics, what about the correlative claim for "the endless multiple meanings which the Rabbinic tradition *ascribed* to each word and letter of the Torah" (Handelman, italics supplied)? The following brief but representative passage helps to assess that judgment. It is from the Mekilta of Rabbi Ishmael, Tractate Shirta, Chapter 8 (ed. Horowitz-Rabin, p. 144, ls. 14–22) and comments on the last two words of Ex. 15:11, "Who among the gods is like you, Lord? Who is like you, majestic in holiness, awesome in praises, *doing wonders*."

A. "Doing wonders"—
B. "Did *('śh)* wonders" is not written here, but "doing *('wśh)* wonders"—in the Age to Come.
C. As it is said, "Therefore, says the Lord, the time is coming when men shall no longer swear, 'By the life of the Lord who brought the Israelites up from Egypt,' but, 'By the life of the Lord who brought the Israelites back from a northern land and from all the lands to which he had dispersed them'; and I will bring them back to the soil which I gave their forefathers" (Jer. 16:14–15).
D. Another interpretation: "Doing wonders"—
E. He did wonders for us and he does wonders for us in each and every generation.
F. As it is said, "I will praise you, for I am filled with awe; you are wonderful and your works are wonderful; and you know my soul very well" (Ps. 139:14).
G. And it says, "You have done many things, Lord my God, your wonders and your thoughts towards us" (Ps. 40:6).
H. Another interpretation: "Doing wonders"—
I. He does wonders for the fathers, and in the future [he will] do [them] for the sons.
J. As it is said, "As in the days of his going forth from the land of Egypt, I will show him wonders" (Micah 7:15).

K. "I will show him"—what I did not show to the fathers.
L. For, look, the miracles and mighty acts that in the future [I will] do for the sons, they [will be] more than what I did for the fathers.
M. For thus scripture says, "To him who alone does great wonders, for his mercy endures forever" (Ps. 136:4).
N. And it says, "Blessed is the Lord God, God of Israel, who alone does wonders, and blessed be his glorious name forever, and may the whole earth be filled with his glory. Amen and Amen" (Ps. 72:18–19).

The passage begins at B by noting a difference between the orthography and vocalization of scripture—its writing and its discourse. The word ʿśh can be vocalized—and these are not the only alternatives—as a verb in the *qal*, third person masculine singular perfect ("did", "has done"), or as a *qal* masculine singular present participle ("doing", "does"). Its defective spelling favors the former, but the discourse-tradition, for good reason, affirms the latter. The passage exploits the discrepancy and, by the mere gloss with the rabbinic term "Age to Come," imputes an eschatological intention to the participle. The verses from Jeremiah, appended without comment at C, make "the Age to Come" refer to the return from exile.

The second interpretation (D–G), which focuses on the noun "wonders," consists of an assertion (E) the God's wonders for Israel are constant, which is then bolstered by two verses from Psalms. Considered apart from the statement at E, however, the verses discuss only God's wonderful qualities and actions, but neither Israel nor her generations. The third interpretation (H–N), also on the theme of God's wonders, asserts at I, with support from the verse from Micah at J, that Israel's past will be replicated in her future ("*As* in the days of his going forth. . . ."). K–L makes this mean that God's acts for Israel's "sons" will be greater than those for the "fathers." The identifying formula at M ("For *thus* scripture says") suggests that the psalm citations at M–N support this idea, but, as above, the verses simply praise God as the sole worker of wonders and make no reference to the future.

Although the interpretations in this passage are formally distinguished from one another at D and H by the disjunctive device *davar 'aḥer* ('another interpretation'), they operate within a limited conceptual sphere and a narrow thematic range. As is typical of most lists of *davar 'aḥer* comments in rabbinic literature, the three segments not only do not conflict but are mutually reinforcing. Taken together, B–C, D–G, and H–N claim that God's past wondrous acts in Israel's behalf will continue, and be even greater, in the future. Thus, rather than "endless multiple meanings," they in fact ascribe to the words "doing wonders" multiple variations on a single meaning.

The literary technique for presenting that meaning is worth noting. Instead of providing an actual exegesis of the words from Ex. 15:11, the passage strategically juxtaposes verses from prophecy and Psalms and preinterprets them with brief comments and glosses that are in no way integral to the verses themselves. The verses at C, F, G, M, and N stand alone, without elaboration. By gathering discrete verses from scripture's three divisions—the pentateuch, the prophets, and the writings—the list form makes scripture itself seem naturally and ubiquitously to articulate a single message about God's persistent devotion to Israel. By providing multiple warrant for that message, the form effectively restricts the inerrpretive options. In this case, it excludes the possibility that God's miraculous acts for Israel have ceased.

If it is doubtful that rabbis ascribed "endless multiple meanings" to scripture, it is no less so that rabbinic hermeneutics encouraged and routinely tolerated the metonymical coexistence of different meanings of scripture that did not, and could not, annul one another. The evidence examined above calls into question two proposals in particular: that rabbinic reading of scripture could entail the Heideggerian practice of "crossing out", and that in rabbinic bible interpretation "the literal is never cancelled" (Handelman: 55)[8]. As to the first, since scripture's writing was only a facsimile of language, there was no written discourse to cross out. When rabbis recited "adonai" at the sight of the tetragrammaton they probably did not encounter the text of God's proper name, which, by all accounts, they did not, and perhaps could not, pronounce anyway (Schiffman: 133–136).

The following passage suggests that the second proposal also will not do. Sifre to Numbers, Pisqa' 117 (ed. Horowitz, p. 134, ls. 11–13), reads as follows:

- A. "And the Lord spoke to Aaron" (Num. 18:8)—
- B. I understand (*šmʿ*) [from this] that the speech was to Aaron.
- C. A [scriptural] teaching says (*tlmwd lwmr*),
- D. "It is a reminder to the children of Israel, so that an unqualified man [, not from Aaron's seed, should not approach to burn incense before the Lord, and should not be like Qorah and his company; [this was done] as the Lord instructed (*dbr*) him through (*byd*) Moses)" (Num. 17:5).
- E. This teaches us that the speech to Moses, who told [it] to Aaron.

C–E use Num. 17:5 to counter the obvious meaning of the discourse of Num. 18:8. The words recited there as "The Lord spoke to Aaron," are to be understood to mean that God did so "through Moses." Thus, the clear sense of the verse—as Loewe shows, the concept of "literal" meaning is an anachronism in a rabbinic context—is effaced, and a single contrary meaning, suggested by Num. 17:5, is assigned to replace it. The form of the passage presents that judgment not as an interpretation but as a fact of scripture.

The rhetorical pattern of this brief passage is typical of much rabbinic scriptural interpretation, especially of Sifra, Sifre to Numbers, and Sifre to Deuteronomy, and its effect should not be overlooked. The structure provided by B, C, and E ("I might think . . . But scripture teaches . . . Therefore . . .") limits rather than multiplies the possibilities of scripture's meaning and clearly is designed to reject what rabbis regarded as erroneous understandings. In this case, since rabbinic ideology held that God spoke directly only to Moses, Num. 18:8 had to mean something other than what its discourse plainly said. A different but very representative and forceful demonstration of the rabbinic limitation of scripture's meaning occurs in a famous passage at b. Baba' Qama' 83b-84a. There, rigorous talmudic argument that skillfully manipulates verses from Leviticus and Numbers shows that the famous *lex talionis* of Ex. 21:24 ("An eye for an eye, and a tooth for a tooth") does not mean what it says but refers instead to pecuniary compensation.

By juxtaposing discrete biblical verses in the form of a list, and by strategically placing them in established rhetorical patterns and propositional frameworks, rabbinic interpretation made scripture appear to speak by itself and for itself and also to restrict its own reference. Much rabbinic use of scripture was kaleidoscopic. Unlike Ireneaus' Rule of Faith, in which the theological value of the "Old Testament" requires the reader's acceptance of a fixed narrative line, rabbinic rules of interpretation *(middot)* provide instruction on how fragments of the holy writing can be mixed and matched to reveal patterns of signification. But the patterns can be meaningful only if they are constructed within a sealed sphere of reference. If the sphere is broken or corrupted, the pieces scatter randomly or fall into a heap. For rabbinism, scripture's sphere of reference was constituted of rabbinic practice, ideology, and discourse, but, most important, of the community of sages themselves.

Nothing in the materials considered above supports the judgments that, in their use of scripture, rabbis confronted the "undecidability of textual meaning" or that their mode of interpretation celebrated "endless multiple meanings." This result ought not to surprise us. As heirs and practitioners of a levitical piety, rabbis could afford little tolerance of ambiguity, uncertainty, or unclarity. The holy writing on the sacred scroll that was the stable center of their system could not appear to speak, as it were, with a forked or twisted tongue.

By controlling the scripture both as sacred artifact and as intelligible text, sages guaranteed that it would always refer to their concerns and interests, that it would always validate and justify—but never contradict—their *halakah* and the religious ideology that undergirded it. In their various literary compositions rabbis did not so much write about or within scripture as they wrote with it, making it speak with their voice, in their idiom, and in their behalf. The rabbinic interpretation of scripture, therefore, was anything but indeterminate or equivocal. Rather, it was an exercise—and a remarkably successful one—in the dictation, limitation, and closure of what became a commanding Judaic discourse[9].

NOTES

[1] The larger argument of Handelman's book is more extreme than these quotations suggest. The book envisions western history as a struggle between two mutually exclusive "structures of thought and patterns of organizing reality" (xvi), or "concepts of meaning" (xvii), one identified with rabbinc Judaism, the other with Greece and Christianity. It holds that the severity of the conflict and the ultimate defeat and displacement of rabbinic interpretation by Greco-Christian hermeneutics account for the isolation of the Jews from western culture, society, and polity up to, and including, modern times.

> The neglect, displacement, or censorship of the Jewish hermeneutic tradition by the philosophers of interpretation is not accidental. Of course, the continental philosophies of hermeneutics arose in a milieu that had excluded Jews from participating in its intellectual, mercantile, and general cultural life since the Middle Ages. And yet, this exclusion of the Jews ultimately goes back to the great debate precisely over the issue of interpretation—interpretation of the Bible. This original conflict of interpretation, we may say, led to the rejection of the Jewish interpretive science of psychoanalysis two thousand years later. As we have seen, when the Christians' claims were rejected by the Jews, they in turn rejected the validity of the Jewish tradition of interpetation—the oral law which had been handed down side by side with the written Scriptrues—and tried, through the Christian claim of a new covenant, to make obsolete and unnecessary all the commentary, explanation, and interpetation of the Rabbis. (130)

Handelman's schematic treatment severely ovestates the differences between rabbinic and patristic hermeneutics and fails to acknowledge that "built into the patristic understanding of exegesis is the conviction that the Christian's theological vision continues to grow and change . . ." (Greer: 198). Moreover, to match rabbinic and Christian uses of the Hebrew Bible produces a skewed contrast. In some ways, it would be more accurate to examine rabbinic use of the Old Testament with Christian use of the New. For the latter, see Preus, who is elegantly summarized in Kermode.

[2] Although Handelman claims to examine only structural similarities between them and to prescind from tracing "historical influence" (xv), her book posits a direct historical continuity from talmudic interpretation to some contemporary hermeneutical schools, particularly psychoanalysis and deconstruction. Although rabbinic interpretation was denied significance in western culture, in Handelman's judgment "the Talmudic mode of thought became the ingrained model of the Jewish psyche" (147). Rabbinic heremeutics reemerged into western culture during the post-Enlightenment "search for an alternate metaphysics" (126).

> But an alternate metaphysics and anti-Christian tradition had existed all along in Rabbinic thought. As the Jews were emancipated from their ghettoes beginning with the Enlightenment, became secularized, and attempted to assimilate into modern culture, Rabbinic modes of thinking commingled with,

altered, and became altered by an abrupt confrontation with the disintegrating Greco-Christian culture. Many strange hybrids were produced. (126)

She applies this general thesis to psychoanalysis, for instance, as follows:

> It is my thesis . . . that psychoanalysis was the Jewish science in a far deeper way than has been recognized. Its founder, who affirmed a "common psychic structure" with the Jews, created what might be called a secular version of the Talmud, and an interpretive science whose methodology was in its finest details deeply Rabbinic. (132)

For the record, there is no evidence that Freud ever studied or knew any rabbinic literature. Though he may have learned some Hebrew—which he rapidly forgot—his Jewish education, which may have ended when he went to gymnasium at age nine, was carried out largely in German and centered on Ludwig Philipson's German translation of, and rationalistic commentary on, the Hebrew Bible (McGrath). On this basis, it is hard to understand how he can have produced a method "in its finest details deeply Rabbinic"—except by sheer accident.

This kind of evidence, however, has no place in Handelman's thesis, which justifies itself with a different—and, frankly, troubling—sort of appeal. Since, in Handelman's view, talmudic thinking was the "ingrained model of the Jewish psyche," and since Freud shared a "'common psychic structure' with the Jews," simply being a Jew made him a necessary recipient and purveyor of rabbinic hermeneutics. The same presumably could be said of Derrida or, for that matter, each and every modern Jew. The disturbing implications of the very notion of "the Jewish psyche," and of the "us/them" dualism and Jewish triumphalism necessary to the book's argument, require no elaboration.

[3] This is not to claim that only rabbinic Judaism conceived the scroll of scripture as sacred but rather that the complex of restrictions discussed here is not present in other ancient Jewish writings. The Community Rule and Damascus Document, for instance, are silent on the question of the production and handling of scripture, and the common storage of what we regard as scripture together with writings produced by the sectaries themselves suggests that they may have given equal treatment to all writings they deemed valuable. Though the "Law of Moses" has authority in the Damascus Document, for instance, it is not clear that the sectarians' own writings did not have for them what we would identify as a scriptural authority.

[4] Faur's claim (106) that lines on the parchment "symbolize the invisible trace of the Holy Spirit," depends on his particular reading of y. Megillah 1:1 (70a) as a "folded pericope" (105). The passage itself offers no explicit warrant for the idea. Moreover, the drawing of lines, whose purpose is to keep the writing straight, was also practiced at Qumran. For a fuller account of the particularities of orthography and vocalization in the production and recitation of scripture, see Dotan.

[5] See Neusner (1977:142–143) and Lieberman (155) for Tosefta's ruling that a scroll, and not just a sheet, with eighty-five letters renders the hands unclean.

[6] The traits of the Torah scroll underscore the importance of Ricoeur's insistence, also shared by Scharlemann, that the minimum component of a text is the sentence, "the first and simplest unit of discourse" (Ricoeur: 148). By thus requiring that we distinguish discourse from writing, the *sefer Torah* challenges the deconstructionist use of "writing" as a dominant metaphor for complexity in communication. The Torah scroll was surely writing, certainly scripture, but it had neither textuality nor complexity until a discourse not in it was recited over it and attached to it. Moreover, the muteness of the Torah scroll explains why, despite its sanctity, it cannot satisfy Scharlemann's definition of text as "as writing in which there is a convergence between the meaning and the reality."

[7] Faur (118–138) discusses this issue in terms of semiotics and semantics but bypasses both the question of the definition of text and Ricoeur's analysis of discourse as constitutive of text. Regrettably, the book's synchronic approach blurs all distinction between the classical rabbinic and the medieval (principally Sephardic) Jewish writings it examines, and ignores nearly all

modern scholarship—European, American, and Israeli—on rabbinic Judaism and literature. The lack of literary focus and historical precision weakens the force of its analyses.

[8] Handelman writes: "Say the rabbis, 'No text ever loses its plain meaning' (*Shab.* 63a; *Yev.* 24a), even though every word of Scripture has many interpretations on many levels" (55). But as Raphael Loewe demonstrated nearly a quarter-century ago, in a classic article not listed in Handelman's bibliography, the phrase *'yn mqr' ywṣ' mydy pšwṭw* means that a biblical passage "cannot be distorted from the meaning of its *'peshat,'*" and was used to circumscribe the interpretation of a verse of scripture (164–167).

[9] My thanks go to Professors Jacob Neusner, Gary G. Porton, Jonathan Z. Smith, Abraham J. Karp, Beverly R. Gaventa, Ernest Frerichs, Fitz John Porter Poole, S. Dean McBride, Eugene D. Genovese, Howard Eilberg-Schwartz, and Mary Gerhart for invaluable corrections, essential clarifications, and stimulating criticism. Earlier versions were read at Arizona State University and the Pittsburgh Theological Seminary and were much improved by the responses of participants in both colloquia.

WORKS CONSULTED

Dotan, Aaron
    1971   "Masorah." In *Encyclopaedia Judaica*, 16:1403–1414. Jerusalem: Keter.

Fishbane, Michael
    1986   "Inner Biblical Exegesis: Types and Strategies of Interpretation in Ancient Israel." In Hartman and Budick, pp. 19–37.

Faur, Jose
    1986   *Golden Doves with Silver Dots: Semiotics and Textuality in Rabbinic Tradition*. Bloomington: Indiana University Press.

Greer, Rowan A.
    1986   "The Christian Bible and Its Interpretation." In *Early Biblical Interpretation*, pp. 107–203. By James L. Kugel and Rowan A. Greer. Philadelphia: The Westminster Press.

Handelman, Susan
    1982   *The Slayers of Moses: The Emergence of Rabbinic Interpretation in Modern Literary Theory*. Albany: State University of New York Press.

Hartman, Geoffrey
    1986   "The Struggle for the Text." In Hartman and Budick, pp. 3–18.

Hartman, Geoffrey and Sanford Budick, Eds.
    1986   *Midrash and Literature*. New Haven and London: Yale University Press.

Kermode, Frank
    1986   "The Plain Sense of Things." In Hartman and Budick, pp. 179–194.

Kugel, James
    1986   "Early Interpretation: The Common Background of Late Forms

of Biblical Exegesis." In *Early Biblical Interpretation*, pp. 9–106. By James L. Kugel and Rowan A. Greer. Philadelphia: The Westminster Press.

Lieberman, Saul
    1939   *Tosepheth Rishonim*, Part IV. Jerusalem: Mossad Rabbi Kook.

Loewe, Raphael
    1964   "The 'Plain' Meaning of Scripture in Early Jewish Exegesis." In *Papers of the Institute of Jewish Studies, London*, Vol. I, pp. 141–185. Ed. by J. G. Weiss. Jerusalem: Magnes Press.

McGrath, William
    1986   *Freud's Discovery of Psychoanalysis: The Politics of Hysteria*. Ithaca: Cornell University Press.

Neusner, Jacob
    1971   *A History of the Mishnaic Law of Purities*, Vol. XIX. Leiden: E. J. Brill
    1983   *Midrash in Context: Exegesis in Formative Judaism*. Philadelphia: Fortress Press.
    1986   *The Oral Torah: The Sacred Books of Judaism*. San Francisco: Harper & Row.

Porton, Gary
    1981   "Defining Midrash." In *The Study of Ancient Judaism*, Vol. I, pp. 55–92. Ed. by Jacob Neusner. New York: Ktav.

Preus, James Samuel
    1969   *From Shadow to Promise*. Cambridge: The Belknap Press of Harvard University Press.

Ricoeur, Paul
    1981   "What is a text? Explanation and understanding." In *Paul Ricoeur, Hermeneutics and the Human Sciences*, pp. 145–164. Ed. and trans. by John B. Thompson. Cambridge: Cambridge University Press.

Scharlemann, Robert P.
    1987   "Theological Text." In *Semeia* 40. Ed. by Charles Winquist.

Schiffman, Lawrence H.
    1983   *Sectarian Law in the Dead Sea Scrolls*. Chico: Scholars Press.

Vermes, Geza
    1975   "Bible and Midrash: Early Old Testament Exegesis." In *Post-Biblical Jewish Studies*, pp. 59–91. By Geza Vermes. Leiden: E. J. Brill.

www.ingramcontent.com/pod-product-compliance
Lightning Source LLC
Chambersburg PA
CBHW032258150426
43195CB00008BA/496